THE DEATH AND
RESURRECTION OF
ELVIS PRESLEY

THE DEATH AND RESURRECTION OF ELVIS PRESLEY

Ted Harrison

REAKTION BOOKS

Published by Reaktion Books Ltd
Unit 32, Waterside
44–48 Wharf Road
London N1 7UX, UK

www.reaktionbooks.co.uk

First published 2016
Copyright © Ted Harrison 2016

Printed and bound in Great Britain by
TJ International, Padstow, Cornwall

A catalogue record for this book is available from the British Library

ISBN 978 1 78023 637 7

Contents

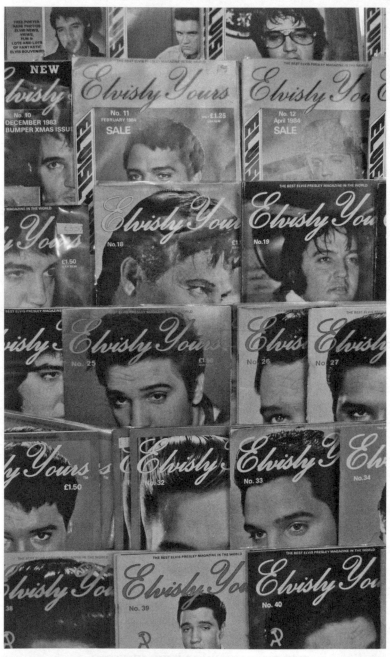

Collectors' items: original 1980s *Elvisly Yours* magazine, one of the most successful of the many print and online magazines about Elvis Presley.

Introduction

Elvis Presley is not dead.

Although his mortal remains rest in the Meditation Garden at Graceland, the King of Rock 'n' Roll lives on – in the hearts and minds of many thousands of his fans around the world. He is much more than a cherished memory; he remains a living presence. To some devotees he is a constant companion. He is a physically absent but ever-present friend. His music plays constantly in their ears. His image is all around them. In the homes of true fans there are pictures of the King in every room: posters, souvenirs of Graceland, prints of Elvis on duvets and pillows, even looking up from plates at mealtimes. There are truly dedicated fans who have his picture permanently tattooed on their bodies.

Elvis fans are united by their love for and devotion to their hero, yet there is no such person as a typical Elvis fan. They defy categorization by gender, age or class. It cannot be said that Elvis today is only idolized by a generation of grandmothers who developed an adolescent crush on the American singer back in the 1950s and whose lives have never moved on. Every year new fans discover him. There are young people whose parents were not born when the physical Elvis was laid to rest at Graceland but who have found the King and developed an overwhelming passion for him. They have discovered his music as it has been reissued and remixed, perhaps to be used on the soundtracks of films or to promote products or enhance commercial brands. Elvis no longer has to be bought from record shops or listened to on forbidden radio shows. He can be downloaded at any time. Elvis is now available 24 hours a day. There are even online radio stations entirely devoted to his music.

This book tells the story of Elvis, but not in the traditional way that starts with his birth in a Tupelo shack and ends with his ignominious death in his bathroom at his Graceland mansion. It harks back, where relevant, to his life story, but in reality it is about his life after death. The book looks at why Elvis has, as it were, risen from the grave to take on a new life as an heroic myth. It looks ahead to the future and suggests, to adapt the famous words of President Ronald Reagan, 'We ain't seen nothing yet.' New, young fans are especially fortunate: they can look forward in their lifetime to many astonishing things to come, things that people of Elvis's day would have considered miraculous. Already his recordings are being digitally reworked to create amazing new sounds. The potential for his music to be presented in creative, innovative ways is almost limitless. More and more new inter-pretations of his music will come along, creating a Presley sound that not even Elvis himself could have imagined. Shows are being produced that create much of the magic of an original Elvis con-cert by blending old film and live music. But that is only the start. Thanks to modern technology and capitalist enterprise, it will not be long before Elvis walks again. It will indeed be as if he has been raised from the dead. Fans will be able to attend concerts and see and hear their idol as if he is truly there in the flesh.

The Presley family no longer owns Elvis. In 2013, the legal rights to license his likeness and image, along with the income from Graceland, were put up for sale by the media rights man-agement consortium that was then the owner, and found a buyer. While he is in one sense public property, the legal rights to exploit his image and likeness, in other words the marketable brand, has been sold. Even the management of Graceland has been forfeited in exchange for dollars. Few fans know the names Authentic Brands Group, Leonard Green and Partners, Joel Weinshanker and the National Entertainment Collectibles Association, but they are the people who profit or have profited when the fans spend their money in the name of Elvis. Elvis today rises phoenix-like from the flames of the old family business, fanned and fuelled by international capitalism.

This is a book about a myth: the powerful myth that is Elvis Presley and its enduring reach and influence. It is also a book about how the myth is fast becoming a new reality as previous restrictions on the exploitation of the singer's legacy are lifted and investors see there are huge sums of money to be made from it. The Elvis myth lives on with renewed vigour. But what is a myth? It is not an untruth. It might be a tradition or a legend from long ago, or it could be a story of recent origin. It might be based on fact; a myth can also have the quality of fiction. Frequently fact and fiction are interwoven into a fable, or a set of stories, that is both larger than life and greater than literal truth. It is frequently the case that myths are told about heroes and heroic events.

And so it is with Elvis.

Of course Elvis was a real man, as his recordings, films, biographies, surviving friends and family all attest. He was born in Tupelo, Mississippi, on 8 January 1935. He had a meteoric rise to fame, became a recording superstar and was hailed as the King of Rock 'n' Roll – yet died prematurely on 16 August 1977. At the end he was alone, obese and addicted to prescription drugs. It looked as if his dazzling career had nowhere to go but down.

Yet his death triggered an extraordinary wave of grief and started a new Elvis movement that has continued to grow and expand. Since Elvis's death, not only has he continued to sell records, but he has possibly gained more fans than he ever had in his lifetime as a new wave of children and young adults discover him. Many of the greatest stars of rock and pop, both his contemporaries and those who followed him, have made a point of paying homage to Elvis as their first and greatest influence. 'Before Elvis there was nothing,' said John Lennon.

The face and name of Elvis Presley are among the most widely recognized icons of modern times. Of all modern brands perhaps only Coca-Cola is better known. Hundreds of millions of people around the world, with no special interest in his life or music, recognize Elvis. His is one of the few names that need no surname. Say Elvis in Beijing, Patagonia, Soweto or Vladivostok, and there will be nods of recognition across the language barrier. Elvis is a touchstone, says one lifelong American fan. 'People are charmed when they know that I'm an Elvis fan and immediately start talking about their own experiences.'[1]

There have been other celebrities who have died before their time – John Lennon himself, Marilyn Monroe, James Dean, Jimi Hendrix – but none of them approach Elvis in their posthumous fame. The only rivals perhaps are Michael Jackson and Princess Diana, but even they fall short. There have been other artists who have died, when their fortunes were at a low ebb, and whose reputations have grown faster and higher in death than in life. Several of the great classical composers died young, in poverty and obscurity, and it was only many years later that their music came to be recognized as great. Uniquely, with Elvis, it is not just his music that has survived death to be discovered via recordings by new generations. He himself has been raised, like a medieval saint, to a figure of cultic status. It is as if he has been canonized by acclamation. Hundreds of his fans around the world have 'shrines' in their homes dedicated to Elvis and spend time there on a regular basis, engrossed in their memories and offering him their thoughts and prayers. Fans go on pilgrimages to places associated with him, however obscure the connection. Scotland's Prestwick Airport celebrates the fact that Elvis touched down there once as a GI in transit in 1960. Fans head to the Elvis Presley Bar that commemorates the King's one and only visit to Britain.

His face, 'his extreme handsomeness', said one fan, 'is worth worshipping all on its own'. Elvis however goes deeper than outward appearance and instant appeal. There is a strange, profound and otherworldly resonance to be discovered within the messianic and mythological elements of his legendary story. There are reports of ordinary people undergoing dramatic conversion experiences and dedicating their lives to the King. He appears to fans in dreams. Healing miracles have been attributed to him. Most intriguingly, in story and iconography, his name and image are juxtaposed with those of Jesus, whom Christians believe was the Son of God. 'If a carpenter can be a messiah,' one fan writes, 'why can't a singer?'[2]

But why Elvis? Other stars have had good looks. Other singers have been famed for their divine voices. Some have even had both, yet no one is, or has ever been, quite like Elvis. He has come to represent so much to so many people. He is a unique force within contemporary culture and mythology. At the same time Elvis has become a worldwide commercial brand that is traded as a commodity.

Today Elvis's body lies in a small family memorial garden in the grounds of his former home in Memphis, Tennessee. He lies beside his mother Gladys, his father Vernon and his grandmother Minnie Mae. There is also a memorial to Elvis's stillborn twin Jesse Garon. The graves are overlooked by a statue of Jesus standing, arms outstretched, attended by two angels, on a plinth on which the family name 'Presley' is carved. The mansion and estate of Graceland are now a museum and visitor attraction. It is one of America's most popular destinations, visited by over half a million people every year. In 2013 it was voted America's number one iconic attraction by readers of *USA Today*. It is the focus of the annual Elvis Week in August, when tens of thousands of fans from around the world come to Memphis to celebrate the King. Through the night, on the anniversary of his death, they process silently through the grounds and around his grave carrying candles.

There have been numerous books about Elvis. Many are written for fans by fans; others are the memoirs of his friends, family and associates. There have also been some books written to rubbish and demean the King. Libraries of books have dissected every nuance of his films, records, character and life story. But Elvis has come to represent something far stronger and deeper than his fans realize. This book takes a new approach and focuses not so much on the life of Elvis as on his posthumous legacy. It will explore how Elvis has become an iconic figure who both typifies and defies the whole notion of celebrity. It will explore the origins of the mythical Elvis; not the Elvis who died, but the Elvis that has risen again.

Elvis may have been dead since 1977, but in many ways he remains a living influence. His is truly a story of death and resurrection in a modern age. And it is, arguably, a story that is still in its early stages.

'The End is Where We Start From'

Every true Elvis fan knows the story of how the young unknown singer auditioned at the Sun Studio in Memphis in the summer of 1954. It has gone down in history as the moment rock 'n' roll was born – late in the evening of 5 July. In those days, when a disc was being cut, musicianship and raw talent were more important than technological wizardry. The studio boss, Sam Phillips, had the latest tape-recording equipment, but compared to today it was rudimentary. What mattered was that present in the studio were two professional musicians and one genuine raw talent.

Not that Elvis Presley had that evening made much of an impression, or at least to begin with. He was nervous and the few numbers he had sung were restrained and stilted. Then, so the story goes, during a break in recording he relaxed and started singing a song by the African American blues songwriter Arthur 'Big Boy' Crudup. Scotty Moore, one of the two musicians accompanying Elvis, described what happened.

> All of a sudden, Elvis just started clowning. I joined in as soon as I found out what key we were in. Then, the control room door opened. Sam came out and said, 'what you all doing?' Elvis said, 'just goofing.' Sam said, 'well that sounds pretty good. Back up and let's put it on tape.'[1]

Where it all began – Elvis made his first recording at the Sun Studio in Memphis. Today it is on the itinerary of every serious Elvis fan making a pilgrimage to the city.

What Sam Phillips recognized was that in the Elvis version of 'That's All Right, Mama', and its spontaneous and instinctive fusion of black and white culture, he had heard something special. He enhanced the sound with a subtle aura of quavering echo, one of the few add-ons at his disposal in those basic days of studio recording. It was the first time he had used the effect in recording a white singer. 'It was a stroke of genius,' Albert Goldman was to note in his epic and controversial biography of Elvis,

> perhaps the most brilliant inspiration of this famous producer's career . . . He added to this new star's raw and untrained voice the electronic prosthesis that masked his vocal faults while it transformed – or should we say transfigured? – his vocal quality into the now legendary Presley sound.[2]

The moment Sam Phillips captured the sound on tape he knew he had found the elusive sound he had long hoped to find. 'A white man with the negro sound and the negro feel', he used to say, would make him a billion dollars. It was radical, almost dangerous thinking for its time and place. In the Southern states of the USA in the mid-1950s, segregation and racial prejudice were a way of life. African Americans, or 'Negroes' in the dated and unreformed language of the era, seldom mixed with white Americans of European descent and certainly not on equal terms. It was not until the year after Elvis's recording debut that Rosa Parks famously refused to move from a 'whites-only' seat on a segregated bus in Montgomery, Alabama. And it was nine years before Martin Luther King Jr delivered his celebrated 'I have a dream' speech. Over the course of his career, however, Sam Phillips worked with musicians across the racial divide. He recorded Roy Orbison and Johnny Cash as well as B. B. King and Ike Turner. He was right; there was a billion dollars to be made, and much more, if only he could meld together the music of the two traditions, although few of those dollars were to come his way.

The story of Elvis over the following 23 years is one of a meteoric rise, a downward slide, a second wind and a sad end. Dozens of versions of this story have been told. Some have been more popular with fans than others. A fan might favour the Elvis story packed out with statistics, dates and details. Another might prefer his life story told in mystical, religious tones. 'He was born in a house little bigger than a stable,' begins one of the Elvis sagas from a popular oral tradition, finishing with the words 'and he died in ignominy betrayed by his friends'.

When Elvis burst on to the music scene he was both a breath of fresh air and a culture shock. Initially he was viewed as a threat by staid Middle America; respectable, God-fearing, straight-laced, traditional, white society which held the power and controlled the wealth of the country. His physical movements when performing,

from the grinding, gyrating hips, to his caressing of the microphone, were thought so sexually explicit that he was denounced
as a malign influence on young Americans' morals. His promotion
of African American music alarmed white Middle America even
more. Elvis's appeal was apolitical, but as potent as, or perhaps
more potent than, any overt political challenge to the status quo,
especially in that he appealed to a new, younger generation of
Americans. He was challenging the assumptions that underpinned
the racial segregation of the time. Not only did Elvis appreciate
and adopt music rooted in African and slave culture, but he went
further. He used his body as an instrument and the instinctive
movements, gestures and thrusts that became identified with the
early Elvis were his unique interpretation of what he had seen as
well as heard on Beale Street and elsewhere, where he had watched
the black musicians of his youth. 'The body itself', one American
musicologist noted, 'was the primary instrument through which
African rhythm was publicly choreographed.'³ Thus Elvis's movements were a public exhibition, not only of sexuality, but 'black
sexuality'. And furthermore, and especially disturbing to Middle
America, these allegedly depraved movements were seductive.
'This sexual seduction of whites into blackness was unstoppable.'⁴

With hindsight fans have come to realize that when American
establishment figures, with the backing of the American mainstream media, accused Elvis of being vulgar and deliberately
sexual,

> This was the cover for what was really meant, what was
> really feared, and that was that Elvis would lead to equal
> rights and racial integration. Following his appearance on
> the Milton Berle television show [on 5 June 1956], when his
> sensual performance of 'Hound Dog' sent the audience wild,
> Elvis was savaged by critics who described his leg-shaking,
> hip-swiveling performance as 'noxious' and his singing as
> 'caterwauling'. Often the criticism had a racist edge, since

Elvis was singing what was considered 'black music'. One critic summed up his performance as 'the kind of animalism that should be confined to dives and bordellos'.[5]

Frank Sinatra, the top crooner of the day, whose music was soon to be overshadowed by rock 'n' roll, described the new sound as

the most brutal, ugly, degenerate, vicious form of expression it has been my displeasure to hear. It fosters almost totally negative and destructive reactions in young people. It smells phoney and false. It is sung, played and written for the most part by cretinous goons and by means of its almost imbecilic reiterations and sly, lewd, in plain fact, dirty, lyrics, it manages to be the martial music of every sideburned delinquent on the face of the earth . . . This rancid-smelling aphrodisiac I deplore.[6]

Although not directed at Elvis by name, it is thought by many fans to be a direct shot aimed at the up-and-coming King.

'Elvis Aron Presley didn't start life as a particularly unique or notable individual, except for his outstanding singing voice,' says Louie Ludwig, author of *The Gospel of Elvis: The Testament and Apocrypha of the Greater Themes of 'The King'*. He was however in the right place at the right time, just as teenage culture came into being, when a post-war generation of young people, with money in their pockets, began to make their own choices as consumers. Young Americans were beginning, as Ludwig notes, to

chafe at the cultural yoke of their society, funding a revolution by jamming nickels into juke boxes and sneaking under bed sheets to tune into Alan Freed and the few others who dared play 'race' music on high-powered radio stations. But media moguls of all stripes were beginning to face the reality that listeners weren't going for the standard wartime formula of a crooner backed by dance orchestra. Those nutty kids seemed to prefer gulping hillbillies like Buddy Holly and mad shamans like Little Richard. What was missing was a personality who could bring this wild, new energy into the mainstream.[7]

Their parents were baffled that their offspring preferred the raucous sounds of rock 'n' roll to the smooth, polished, tuneful sounds they had danced to and which they recognized as popular music. The new music was also the product of emerging technology. The electric guitar had been invented in the 1930s, but in the 1950s it started to be mass-produced and became affordable. It emerged as the instrument of choice for the new rock 'n' rollers and was used to create the distinctive new style.

Elvis arrived not only in the right place at the right time, but in possession of exactly the right talent and image. It was a chance arrival, rather than anything planned. And he also had the right background in music, having absorbed African American culture from an early age. There was nothing manufactured about Elvis. Unlike the boy bands of later years, brought together by manipulative managers to surf a tide of musical fashion, Elvis was the genuine article. His family background had given him access to the music of the impoverished South, both black and white, and his indulgent mother gave him space and encouragement to daydream.

Elvis was raised as an only child and developed a close relationship with his mother, Gladys, a relationship that has attracted the subsequent interest of psychologists who have seen Oedipal undertones in it. It is not surprising from his background that Elvis became a strange and rather lonely teenager. His musical interests and tastes extended beyond those of his peers and community. His dress sense was quirky and individualistic. He stood out from the local crowd as a bit of an oddball, although in his final years at Humes High School he gathered supporters and protectors, including Red West and George Klein, who were to remain in his inner circle for many years. The style he had developed was not the result of a marketing or business plan, it was just Elvis pleasing himself and expressing his individuality. As an obscure teenager he had his dreams. Many of them were drawn from the comic books he read. He may well have imagined himself as a superhero in the making, but no one who knew him at the time had any way of foretelling that the look and sound he nurtured would become so celebrated and iconic. It was very much later that curious apocryphal stories emerged of the child Elvis being shown his destiny by angels.

When Elvis started making waves within the musical world, the record industry moguls quickly realized that there was no point in complaining about his style and music; if money was to be made from this new musical fashion, they had to come to terms with it. Sam Phillips had sold his interest in Elvis's recording career to RCA in 1955, a deal he much regretted later, but at the time he needed the cash. RCA, a major recording company, had a direct stake in ensuring Elvis was a money-spinner. 'Perhaps all of us, including the man we have declared King, would be better off today if the good Sam hadn't sold Elvis' contract to RCA,' notes Louie Ludwig. 'If Elvis had been given time and freedom to get comfortable being a rhythm and blues success, part of an exciting, regional sound, he might be alive today. Instead, he was tossed to the publicity mill, nutted and homogenized, turned from prodigy to product, and eventually to parody, sold before his time.'[8]

The conservative interests in American society, who had been horrified by the emergence of this lewd and challenging entertainer, quickly accepted that Elvis was not a flash in the pan. They began to explore how the forces he had unleashed could be tamed. At the height of Elvis's early career, the U.S. military public relations department grabbed an opportunity. It realized what a publicity coup could be had if it were to get involved in the process of repackaging and manipulating Elvis. It was a time of military conscription and, when Elvis dutifully joined the army in 1958 and his thick, black, slicked-back hair was cut, his reputation started to change. That was the day he really died, said John Lennon, expressing the disappointment of many of the younger generation.

Elvis could probably have avoided the draft; many wealthy Americans found ways of avoiding military service. It was even

Teenage girls sign their names and send messages to Elvis on an Elvis movie poster, 1956.

suspected that his manager, Colonel Tom Parker, saw the public relations advantages of having his boy join up and volunteered him. Most likely the initiative came from the army and Parker did not want to make a fuss by having Elvis oppose the draft, for reasons that were to emerge later. Fans protested vehemently when the call-up was announced. Paramount Studios, who had started work on the film *King Creole* with Elvis as the irreplaceable star, asked for the draft to be delayed. The draft board agreed a sixty-day deferment, allowing the film to be completed, much to the relief of studio accountants.

Joining the army was the career move that took Elvis from cultural rebel to America's favourite son. When his manager later locked him into contracts requiring him to make a succession of popular but unchallenging formulaic, eye-candy films, Elvis was forever established as the all-American icon. The fact that he was making money also helped to make him respectable in his home country. *Life* magazine had initially described Elvis as a 'howling hillbilly'. By the time *Life* reported that Elvis had struck a massively generous deal to appear at a Las Vegas hotel, its attitude was very different. In an essay first published in 1979, Stephen R. Tucker asked if a pattern of response to Elvis was in the process of being established. On the one hand there was revulsion at his strangeness and on the other, admiration of his commercial success. Two presumably antithetical values were confusingly joined in one personality. Was wild non-conformity to be rewarded?, Tucker wondered. Did getting rich quickly make Elvis more palatable?[9]

After his military service, Elvis continued to perform his earlier work, yet the sound of the music and the accompanying movements had lost their edge. It was not that Elvis had noticeably mellowed, but that society had moved on. The sexual revolution of the 1960s took matters that had once been hidden and unspoken and made them open and mainstream. Elvis was no longer so shocking. By the time he had added old-style gospel music to his repertoire, any vestige of threat to the morals of youth had vanished.

All youthful stars, even Elvis, grow up. Elvis matured into the jumpsuit Vegas King. Although he was known and loved around the world, he never travelled away from North America, except during his army days, when he was based in Germany. While his mind took him into strange territory through the exploration of esoteric religions, under the tutelage of his hairdresser Larry Geller, his ever-expanding body stayed rooted in his homeland, sustained by the cocktails of drugs prescribed by his personal physician George C. Nichopoulos, or 'Dr Nick'. His world became smaller and smaller. He was often confined to sleazy, plush hotel suites in Las Vegas, alone or gambolling with his cronies, while his manager was downstairs in the casino gambling away Elvis's earnings.

In his final months Elvis was a sad shadow of his former self. He toured from venue to venue, little knowing where he was. 'His eyes were lidded during most performances, his speech slurred. In one city he forgot the words to a song. Everywhere he looked tired.'[10] In December 1976 the Dutch fan Ger Rijff went to an Elvis performance and noted that the singer looked bad. His face was pale and bloated. His voice was slurred and he appeared not to be in control of his body movements. Some fans thought he was drunk and were embarrassed to watch him. Even members of his backing band 'didn't enjoy watching Elvis slide. There was backstage talk not just about Elvis's moods, but about his ability to function.'[11]

Even without his problems, the latter-day Elvis was considered by many fans to be a travesty of his former self. Gone was the sexy idol, to be replaced by a bejewelled glamour star who had more in common with the effete and bespangled Liberace than his previous raunchy self. He had become an androgynous figure employing make-up and extraordinary clothes for theatrical effect. Right at the end, say some of his most savage critics, he was more eunuch than male sex symbol.

Many devoted Elvis fans were angered by the publication in 1982 of a biography by Albert Goldman simply called *Elvis*. It was a study of the singer that dared to describe in lurid detail the pathetic finale to a declining career, 'when his once-remarkable memory fails him and his voice is very uneven. So often does he crack on the high notes that measures have to be taken to disguise his failures. The back-up singers are miked so that when Elvis reaches for a high note and misses', one of the men behind covered for him.[12]

His last concert was given on 26 June 1977 in the Market Square Arena, Indianapolis. The audience cheered and screamed with wild enthusiasm, but the surviving recordings and images of Elvis show him moon-faced from medication and sweating profusely. After singing his final scheduled number, 'Can't Help Falling in Love', and handing out his last scarf, Elvis returned to Graceland. His home was unusually quiet, since several of his trusted friends, known as the Memphis Mafia, were no longer welcome there. Elvis had felt a deep sense of betrayal that two of his former bodyguards, Sonny and Red West, had decided to write a candid book about their years with Elvis, exposing many of his character flaws and weaknesses. In his heart Elvis knew his life could not carry on the way it was. He talked of making major changes to his life, of quitting the drugs and firing his manager. But it was not to be. He was found dead in his bathroom. Paramedics and an ambulance were called and he was rushed to hospital, but it was too late. His last words, according to his girlfriend Ginger Alden, were: 'I'm going to the bathroom to read.'

Fans around the world tell of the moment they heard the news of the singer's death. It is recalled as one of those rare moments in a lifetime, known as a flashbulb memory, when a news event etches itself immovably into the individual memory. Where were you when President John F. Kennedy was assassinated, when the Twin Towers were attacked, when Elvis died? Most people of a certain age, who forget where they were last week, can answer those questions with pinpoint accuracy and recall exactly how they felt.

The moment was so imprinted in the memory of one truck driver that he could recall every detail, as he wrote on a blog 36 years later. He had just ordered a meal at a truck stop in Illinois when the music on the radio was interrupted by a newsflash.

The young waitress turned to me and ask if I heard the radio bulletin? She turned quickly to the telephone mounted on the back wall behind the counter, anxiously dialing some one, frantically asking them if they were listening to the radio? She was talking very fast and excited. She came back to me and began to ask what else the news had stated. She said she just couldn't believe that Elvis was dead. She kept holding her face in her hands covering her mouth. It wasn't very long another young lady entered the Truck Stop running and hollering at the waitress as they held on to each other, each asking if the other heard from their friends about the news. Before I finished my cheeseburger and fries there was a crowd of people, mostly girls and young ladies, however the boys who came with the girls were quiet and trying to be polite and helpful also. The place was a regular wake. It was like they all lost a close friend as they comforted each other with the news and asking each other, what would happen now? They were crying, calling on the telephone, talking about Elvis like he was family and they were oblivious to anything else or anyone in the Truck Stop.[13]

Over the ensuing days thousands of fans gathered at Graceland and piles of flowers and messages built up at the gate and along the wall outside. The world's media converged on Memphis, and Elvis's funeral two days later became a media circus. There was a public viewing of Elvis's body. Over a three-and-a-half-hour period he was seen by hundreds of fans who filed through the mansion to see him in his open casket. The crowd standing outside the gates under the August sun was said to number 100,000, despite the stifling heat. On 18 August, after a service at Graceland, Elvis's body was carried by eight pallbearers to the hearse for its journey to Forest Hill Cemetery. As the bearers and mourners emerged from the house, 'there was a loud cracking overhead and a dead limb fell from one of the oak trees.'[14] It took over an hour for Elvis and a motorcade of white Cadillacs to cover the three miles to the cemetery. It was briefly to be his first resting place, alongside his mother, before they were both reinterred at Graceland.

Other celebrity figures have been widely mourned, but arguably the only other time since Elvis that the death of a public figure has made such an impact was almost exactly twenty years later, when Princess Diana died. Public shock and grief was felt all round the world and was expressed through flowers and messages being left in huge quantities in public places. Not even the death of John Lennon, which horrified the world, made the same emotional impact. When President Jimmy Carter said, 'with Elvis Presley a part of our country died as well,' he was expressing the mood of the time. His summation of the singer's career and influence was highly pertinent.

He burst upon the scene with an impact that was unprecedented and will probably never be equalled. His music and his personality, fusing the styles of white country and black rhythm and blues, permanently changed the face of American popular culture.[15]

Even Frank Sinatra had changed his tune. 'There have been many accolades uttered about Elvis' talent and performances through the years, all of which I agree with wholeheartedly. I shall miss him dearly as a friend.'[16]

The death of Elvis was the end of one era and the beginning of a new one. For some people it was a life-changing event. It was as a direct result of hearing the news that Kiki Apostolakos left her home in Greece to go and live in Memphis. Previously she had had no special interest in Elvis, but after her Damascene moment she dedicated her life to his memory. For years she visited his grave every day. She would go early in the morning, before the visitors arrived, to clear away any leaves or debris that had fallen in the night and place fresh flowers on the gravestone. In Greece she had been a teacher. In Memphis she supported herself by working as a waitress in order to devote her life to Elvis. She talked of her visits to the grave as like going to church. She would pray for Elvis and his family as well as for the world more generally. Every morning, she would say, was a fresh experience: 'I feel like a child going to meet someone exciting for the first time.'[17]

From the very first days after Elvis's death something of profound cultural significance happened. There was grief, of course, as there is after any death. There was also a sense of shock and horror that a celebrity, who only a few years earlier had been at the peak of his success, should die in tragic circumstances. But there was something else. Some of the commentators in Memphis at the time of his funeral sensed a strange mood. 'Already the myths are being manufactured,' reported the BBC's Michael Cole. 'I've met fans who say they are convinced he is still alive and articles attacking the man have been written saying that he believed he had supernatural powers and that he would be reincarnated.'[18]

Many fans heard the news of Elvis's death, but refused to believe it. Not even the public display of his corpse satisfied those who were in denial. They refused to accept that he had died in any real sense. Elvis, they convinced themselves, lived on. The death of anyone young is a reminder to members of every generation of their own mortality. Many of the most loyal fans were deeply in love with Elvis and felt that through his music he reciprocated that love. For many fans, their responses to his death were similar in intensity and kind to those that might be experienced following the death of a lover, spouse or child. In normal circumstances, coming to terms with the death of a family member involves accepting what has happened and then, over time, discovering a way to cope with the physical absence of the one who has gone. Yet the death of Elvis did not bring a similar physical void into the lives of his fans. It was not as if a husband was no longer in the bed or a child in the house. While Elvis had been a constant presence, this presence had not been physical; and strangely, as fans absorbed the news of Elvis's death, he continued to be all around them. The radio played Elvis music even more than usual. Fans turned to their record collections for comfort. The newspapers and magazines of the time were full of pictures of the King. For many fans, the normal processes they might have gone through to enable them to cope with grief were subverted by the very ubiquity of the man. They had none of the practical and sometimes cathartic tasks to perform that accompany a family death. There was no funeral to arrange, no will to execute, no personal possessions to dispose of. Instead, after death, not only was there nothing they could do, Elvis was still everywhere they turned, just as he had been when he was alive. And it was not the bloated Elvis of his final sad days. That Elvis was no longer living in Graceland. Fans were liberated by Elvis's physical death to reinvent him for themselves. They could forget the floundering, rhinestone Vegas Elvis and recreate an ideal Elvis in their memories. Perhaps it was the only avenue of grieving available to them.

Forty years on and Elvis the superstar has become Elvis the super-legend. He is remembered and celebrated in many different ways. His records are still played and are continually repackaged, remixed and resold. Elvis art thrives, as do Elvis jokes and Elvis books. More academic works have been written on Elvis than on any other popular entertainer. Despite dying at a low point in a waning career – overweight, in a parlous physical and mental state and dependent on an irresponsible level of potent medication – today Elvis has risen again, perhaps to greater heights than ever.

'He Has Sounded Forth the Trumpet that Shall Never Call Retreat'

The most unexpected of all the developments since his death is the way Elvis has acquired, to some devotees, an aura of the semi-divine, or at least a sacred status akin to that granted saints in medieval times. Many religions have saints, who have been described as 'charismatic, mediating agents between our everyday world and remote and powerful spiritual forces'.[1] The dead Elvis, the mythical Elvis, has become such a saint. In an increasingly secular world it is strange that saints can still emerge by popular acclaim, but even stranger that the 'saint' most widely recognized should be Elvis Presley.

So, why Elvis? Is it the voice? Yes, that must be part of the explanation. It is rich, sonorous, intimate and can still, after sixty years, send shivers down the spine of the lifelong fan. The quality of his voice is such that many women talk of having fallen in love with the man through the medium of the voice. They feel, as they listen, that he is singing to them alone. In 'Love Me Tender' he assures the fan that it is she who has made his life complete and fulfilled all his dreams. He vows to love her until the end of time. His repertoire of music is wide and fits all moods. Early Elvis is testosterone-fuelled and dangerous. Latter-day Elvis is smooth, comforting, understanding, empathetic. Gospel Elvis is inspirational and spiritually uplifting. Whether on tape, vinyl or in digital format, somehow the recorded sounds from so many years ago stay fresh and immediate. Furthermore that sound is capable of being remixed, rearranged and rebranded for modern and future generations.

Is it the look? Yes, there is something about the image that haunts the memory. Whether he stares from a poster, young and Adonis-like, or struts the stage in waist-stretching jumpsuit, sweat pouring from his brow, he projects a unique charisma and charm that the camera is able to capture and preserve.

Of course it can be argued that it is not the real Elvis who is so universally known. It is not the fallible, flesh-and-blood son of Vernon and Gladys, the poor boy from Tupelo who made good. It is an Elvis of myth and legend reconstructed afresh after his death and continually reinterpreted by every generation and culture.

It might be argued that Elvis is a contemporary represen-tation of a timeless archetype, a universal and collectively but unconsciously inherited idea, pattern of thought or image. Archetypes are often found in folk stories and fairy-tales to rep-resent common emotions, fears or aspirations. Professor Patsy Hammontree from the University of Tennessee conducted a study of Elvis's fan base. Having examined his wide and univer-sal appeal, she concluded: 'he somehow provided a transcendent figure for millions of people . . . an archetypal appeal to the col-lective unconscious. Fans cannot say specifically what drew them to him. They simply know that they were powerfully attracted, and knowing it is adequate for most of them. The result is both a worldwide community and a worldwide communion.'[2]

So what archetype, or archetypes, might Elvis represent? First, he represents the American Dream. This is the most immediately recognized archetype. He is the poor boy who by his own talent and effort becomes rich and famous. This aspirational element of his story resonates with many people and is a theme found in several thriving Christian ministries. There are a number of popular preachers, especially in the USA, whose message suggests that if followers believe hard enough, work hard enough and obey the instructions of their church, they will be rewarded with wealth and success. Most Christian churches suggest that these rewards are deferred and may be anticipated in the afterlife; perhaps the Elvis story resonates because it promises the potential for greatness in this life.

The image Americans have of themselves is that their nation is the land of equal opportunity, where it is possible for anyone of talent and perseverance to move through life from log cabin to White House. This ideal may be far from reality, but it is nevertheless a constituent part of the national self-image of the USA. But more than that, might Elvis also embody the new ideals as expressed by Martin Luther King Jr in his famous speech of 1963 addressing the Washington Civil Rights March?

> I have a dream that one day on the red hills of Georgia sons of former slaves and the sons of former slave-owners will be able to sit down together at the table of brotherhood. I have a dream that one day even the state of Mississippi, a state sweltering with the heat of injustice, sweltering with the heat of oppression, will be transformed into an oasis of freedom and justice.

Elvis, by crossing the musical Rubicon, represented a new social order that was not to be delineated by race. Arguably he enabled a shift of attitude to take place, a shift that today is so well established that blatant expressions of racism are socially unacceptable and outlawed where they were once entrenched. Viewing Elvis's social legacy from this perspective, however, produces complications. It sits uncomfortably with the fact that to some groups within Western society Elvis has been adopted as an icon of the old ways. Elvis symbolism is widely seen in the trailer parks of the Southern states where white poverty is endemic and racial resentment simmers on. To some within the poorer strata of white society, sometimes derogatorily referred to today as 'white trash', Elvis represents a different set of values. He is one of them, a poor white boy who did them proud.

It also has to be acknowledged that from the perspective of some African Americans, Elvis himself is a suspect figure. There was a degree of subdued resentment that it was a white boy who had taken the glory when black music was 'discovered', commercialized, reshaped and adopted by the post-war generation. Elvis was accused of stealing not only the music, but the body movements as well. The teenage Elvis used to hang out in Memphis bars watching African American musicians in action. He was much inspired by the style of musicians like Bo Diddley and there are huge similarities between the mannerisms of the young Bo and the young Elvis. The effervescent performer Little Richard pointed out the financial disparities between what Elvis earned and what the black singers from whom he had learned his craft received. In one film, Little Richard claimed, Elvis was paid $25,000 for performing three songs, while he only received $5,000. 'If it wasn't for me, Elvis would starve,' Little Richard was reported as saying.

It was hard for many black Americans in the South to overlook the fact that Elvis was born in Tupelo, Mississippi, home town of the foremost Dixie race-baiter and former Congressman Jon Rankin. Elvis also had to live down and deny this quote attributed to him: 'The only thing Negroes can do for me is shine my shoes and buy my records.'

Did Elvis really say that? Attempts made by several writers to substantiate the quote have failed and it is now believed to be a fabrication that turned into a damaging slur that has never quite gone away. In determining the truth it should not be forgotten that at one time the impoverished Presley family lived in the black area of Tupelo and Elvis ran errands for a local African

The Tupelo hut. Elvis was born in a house little bigger than a stable and at the moment of his birth a strange blue light hovered overhead – so goes one version of the Elvis birth narrative.

American grocery store in exchange for food. While it was an experience that taught Elvis tolerance, at the time it stigmatized the Presley family in the eyes of many of Tupelo's white residents. Later in Memphis, Elvis and his cousin Gene Smith were happy to date two black girls, but when they were spotted in Vernon's car by two white police officers they were threatened with being beaten up for infringing the unwritten race code of the era. They only escaped a beating by telling the officers that they were members of a gospel choir doing some extra practice.

In later years, Elvis was to be endorsed by many celebrated African Americans. 'He was an integrator, Elvis was a blessing. They wouldn't let black music through. He opened the door for black music,' Little Richard once said, despite his views on what Elvis was paid.[3] Indeed in 1990 Little Richard collaborated with the band Living Colour to record an angry number about Elvis and his legacy: *Elvis Is Dead*. 'Elvis was a hero to most, But that's beside the point. A Black man taught him how to sing. And then he was crowned king . . . I've got a reason to believe, We all won't be received at Graceland.'[4] Yet the resentment and suspicion never entirely went away. When in 2004 Jack Soden, the CEO of Elvis Presley Enterprises, was asked what the biggest challenge in maintaining Elvis's image is, he talked of the

> frustration we feel when we hear someone repeat the old, and wrong, statement that Elvis was prejudiced and that he ripped off black music. Right from the beginning, Elvis continually explained that all of his early influences and heroes were black musicians and artists. He never took credit for creating rock and roll. He said it was r&b with a new name, and he was just doing it his way. As for being prejudiced, his friends, including many black friends, would tell you that just wasn't true. If Elvis were alive, he would want to set that straight most of all.[5]

The issue resurfaced when Paul Simon decided to record his *Graceland* album, with its direct reference to Elvis and American history, in South Africa. He wanted to record with black South African musicians, but at the time the world was still boycotting the country over apartheid. Elvis was of course not involved, except by implication, but for a while old memories and rumours of Elvis were revived.

Muddying the racial waters further has been the song which many fans, black and white, identify as Elvis's own theme tune:

> Glory, glory hallelujah
> His truth is marching on.

No modern tribute show is complete without a performance, in authentic Elvis style, of 'An American Trilogy'. Indeed the three-song medley is the climax of the show and is ideally performed with live band, backing singers and flute solo. As closely as fans associate this work with Elvis, he only started singing the arrangement in 1972, five years before his death. The singer-song-writer Mickey Newbury did not compose the trilogy until 1971 and 'with Richard Nixon in the Oval Office and the Vietnam War ending ignominiously, most assumed it was meant ironically' rather than written in a spirit of patriotism.[6]

Elvis, in all probability, did not appreciate the irony. In 1970 he had travelled to Washington with the intention of meeting President Nixon. It was one of the most bizarre episodes in the singer's life when he turned up at the White House uninvited but was granted an audience, to the astonishment of both his entourage and the presidential staff. Within two years of the meeting 'An American Trilogy' had entered his Vegas repertoire and he gave the song a 'slow, reflective, melancholy' mood.[7]

The words Elvis made his own consist of quotes from three songs that date back to the tragic years of the American Civil War when, between 1861 and 1865, the forces of the North of the

Elvis and Nixon. Some conspiracy theorists say that Elvis never died but was spirited away by the authorities either to work as an undercover agent in the war against drugs or to protect him from the wrath of drug barons. Elvis made an unscheduled visit to the White House to offer his services to the government's anti-drugs campaign, 21 December 1970.

United States faced the army of the South in a series of brutal military campaigns. The issue at the heart of the conflict was the abolition of slavery. Slavery, argued abolitionists, contradicted the ideals of America's founding fathers who, to quote Abraham Lincoln, 'brought forth on this continent a new nation, conceived in liberty, and dedicated to the proposition that all men are created equal.' Politicians from that swathe of Southern states known during the Civil War by the nickname of Dixie argued that ownership of enslaved African labourers to work the cotton fields and provide domestic servants was an economic essential. When Elvis sang of Dixie he was not making a political statement, but identifying with his roots in Mississippi and Tennessee and his origins as the son of an itinerant and landless white family.

> ... Dixieland, that's where I was born,
> Early Lord one frosty morning
> Look away, look away, look away Dixieland.

Many Elvis fans today fly the Confederate flag. The blue cross with thirteen white stars on a red background is most often seen in the Elvis home states, where the flag signifies political conservatism. Yet the flag is also seen on car bumpers and on the bedroom walls of Elvis fans around the world. What was once a potent, partisan emblem has taken on another meaning. It is one of the recognizable Elvis symbols. That the flag of the supporters of slavery should be combined with an image of a man who brought black music into the mainstream of Western culture is another unappreciated irony, an irony deepened by the fact that a snatch of a ballad with direct roots in the music of the slaves is also included in Elvis's signature song.

> So hush little baby
> Don't you cry,
> You know your daddy's bound to die ...

If Elvis bridged the divide between black and white cultures, it was not solely through his music. His family had lived alongside the descendants of the Southern slaves and had shared the same economic hard times, the same powerlessness, poverty and hopeless destiny. And they found comfort through the same faith and its promise of glory to come.

The third part of Elvis's signature trilogy is the rousing chorus of hope and triumph taken from the marching song of the Civil War's Northern, Federal Army: 'Glory, glory hallelujah!'

Few Elvis fans living outside the United States now appreciate the historical and political meaning of 'An American Trilogy'. In the same way that the original purpose of the pounding timpani and ethereal brass of Elvis's introductory theme music, taken from Richard Strauss's *Also sprach Zarathustra*, is forgotten by his fans – it was originally intended to create a musical picture of a sunrise – so the music and the words of 'An American Trilogy' have been appropriated and reinterpreted by Elvis's followers. To them it is no longer a song of reconciliation dating from the divisive years of the Civil War, albeit one with ironic overtones; it is now about the King himself. He was born in the South of the USA. His roots were in the land of cotton; he came from the dirt and soil of a real place. Later, it was his destiny to suffer and die. Yet ultimately he was to triumph and the truth of Elvis was to go marching on.

The archetype of Elvis, the poor boy who made good who through his fusion of black and white music heralded an era of greater racial tolerance, is more complex than at first it might appear. The undercurrents whipped up by years of segregation and exploitation have yet to settle. However, Elvis's relevance and appeal go far beyond his native land to places where the cultural history of the USA has far less relevance.

Might Elvis therefore be better understood if he is seen as a far more ancient archetype, one of universal rather than simply American relevance? Was he the classic hero who undertakes the

heroic journey? 'He suffers various trials and ordeals. By over-
coming them he transcends the human condition, after which
he belongs to a class of semi-divine beings,' Susan MacDougall
told the Australian National Elvis Presley Convention in 2004.
Siegfried, King Arthur and Robin Hood were other examples she
gave of such heroes. 'The physical journey through life is a metaphor for inner development. Trials and quests are obstacles to be
overcome, and are the means by which the hero achieves self-in-
tegration, balance, wisdom and spiritual health.'[8]

She might have added the archetype with which Elvis himself
had been most familiar since the days of his boyhood obsession
with comic books – the superhero. Elvis's favourite had been
Captain Marvel Jr, who was the alter ego of Freddy Freeman, an
ordinary and inconspicuous teenager. On saying some special
words, Freddy could transform himself into Captain Marvel.
Elvis's 1950s hairstyle could well have been based on that of
the captain. The lightning bolt on Captain Marvel's jumpsuit
may also have been the inspiration for Elvis's TCB logo. Captain
Marvel Jr represents a modern version of the ancient archetype
of magical transformation.

Or perhaps Elvis is best understood as the archetypical
wounded or flawed king. This figure, found in medieval legends
such as the tales of King Arthur, shows how it is through his pain
and his weaknesses that the king derives his strength and authority. One group of Elvis fans has interpreted a birthmark that they
believe Elvis had on his thigh as the stigma of the wounded king.
They believe that from birth he was destined for this spiritual
role. A wounded king, says Maia Nartoomid, who writes on Elvis
and mysticism, is 'someone appointed for a spiritual service'
whose body is wounded or maimed. This 'correlates with Elvis's
illnesses'. The wound

> release[s] illumination to the people. The concept here
> is that in order for the world karma to be resolved there

must be someone who is willing to 'pay the price' of suffering, to balance the energy deeds that have been tallied in imbalance within the world over time. This is a similar function to that which Christ served at a much higher level of experience.[9]

Elvis's story, concludes Susan MacDougall, 'resonates strongly within us because he taps into unconscious "cultural memories". Whether as a secular or religious hero, pagan or Christian, Elvis is becoming elevated to a higher plane.'[10]

Another Elvis comparison is made with the legendary ancient Greek musician and prophet Orpheus, who had, it is said, similar qualities to those later associated with Elvis. It was said of him that he could charm all living things with his music. He descended to the underworld to rescue the one he loved. At one stage in his life story it is said that he spurned the love of women, 'although many burned with desire for him'. He was murdered, as he was singing, by attackers whose burning love for him was unrequited. He has become the archetype of the inspired singer and was revered within a religious cult known as the Orphic Mysteries.

Visually the young Elvis represents the classic archetype of beauty. 'If we compare Elvis's face with those of ancient heroes, kings and gods, there are some striking similarities,' observed Susan MacDougall. 'The shapes of the noses and lips are particularly striking. The setting of the eyes and the shape of the face fit to varying degrees. Whether or not heroes and kings actually looked like their representations, they display the ideal of beautiful features of their era. Elvis certainly seems to have conformed to the ideal of Greek beauty.'[11] His features are a timeless representation of eternal youth, of vigour, of power and self-awareness. The face of Elvis can be seen in ancient statues of Apollo, Hermes and Dionysus. He is there in idealized representations of Alexander the Great. He is Michelangelo's David and the face of the Statue of Liberty. According to one source, Elvis's photographs were used as studies when rebuilding Old World statues damaged during the bombings of the Second World War.[12] Elvis can be seen in the paintings of the Pre-Raphaelites and others influenced by the nineteenth-century aesthetic movement. His face takes both male and female form; for all Elvis's masculinity, he also represents an androgynous notion of perfection.

Yet Elvis is more than a collection of archetypes, an Elvis fan might argue. He is more than a modern icon, God or saint. He is much more than a subject for academic debate and sociological investigation. Elvis is also fun! What he created in his lifetime, his music, his performance and his unique style, have all survived his death for the enjoyment of subsequent generations. They are constantly rediscovered on DVD, CD and through tribute artists in both their original and numerous updated forms.

The joy, hilarity and rejuvenating effect of being a fan of the King should not be underestimated. Being an Elvis fan is not a dour, humourless pursuit. It is the opportunity to be creative, gregarious, childish, relaxed, playful and absurd. To go to a concert by an Elvis tribute artist or impersonator, whether a large-scale event in a huge auditorium or a small intimate gathering, is to enter a world of make-believe. Of course it is not the real Elvis performing and many tribute artists ham up the parody element of their act. It is a genre of entertainment that enables the singer and audience to enjoy a familiar and popular repertoire of music within a tried and tested formula of presentation. The 1950s, '60s and '70s produced some of the greatest popular tunes of all time. Elvis made many of them his own, but he also covered material made famous by other artists and so a stage Elvis may not only sing the usual Elvis numbers but is permitted to dip into the catalogues of other great artists of the era. Elvis recorded The Beatles' 'Yesterday', Dusty Springfield's 'You Don't Have to Say You Love Me' and Frank Sinatra's 'My Way', as well as the works of lesser-known blues singers. Of course, he also made a name for himself with his take on gospel music.

A modern Elvis evening is a chance for the older generation to wallow in nostalgia and for the younger members of the audience to discover some irresistible tunes and ever-memorable lyrics. There is audience participation too. The experienced Elvis-goers know when to lift their hands and sway in time to the music, when to clap, when to shout 'Viva Las Vegas', when to 'Pray Together'. A good tribute artist is not performing for the audience, but with the audience. He must be seriously professional to give value for money, but always light-hearted and self-deprecating. When one impersonator, in the course of singing 'Suspicious Minds', struggled to recover from an athletic Elvis pose, he made a last-minute change to the words. 'I'm caught in a trap, I can't get up . . .'

On another occasion that same evening, there was a delay to the start of the second act of the show. The house lights in the theatre had dimmed, but the curtains remained firmly shut. Suddenly there came a shout from the back, 'Elvis has left the building!' The temporary technical glitch was immediately forgiven. Elvis fans usually know when and how to laugh at themselves. Over-the-top and kitsch souvenirs may be taken seriously by some, but most fans buy them to delight in their sheer, surreal daftness. If the kitchen needs a clock, why not get one where the pendulum doubles as Elvis's swinging hips and legs? If a middle-aged man is going to be seen out in shorts, match them with an outrageous Elvis-print Hawaiian shirt!

At an Elvis-themed wedding, a couple choosing to make or renew wedding vows in the presence of their friends and in front of an Elvis lookalike are genuinely declaring their love and loyalty, but they also know that the words they use are not themselves to be taken too seriously. References to 'hound dogs' and 'teddy bears' in the ceremony are part of the fun of the occasion.

When outsiders ridicule the world of Elvis fans, many fans laugh along with them in full realization that what they do is ridiculous – but no more so than many other leisure pursuits. Being an Elvis fan, and keeping it in perspective, is probably a healthy antidote to the stresses of modern living. It is a letting-the-hair-down hobby with the added advantage that Elvisdom is a safe and friendly world in which fans can allow their latent eccentricities to flourish. When Elvis fans gather they do so both as enthusiasts and friends enjoying the fellowship of the moment.

Fans are however not a uniform body. Some take themselves far more seriously than others. It would not be an exaggeration to say that some fans are obsessed with Elvis, or some specific aspect of his memory. In some cases the obsession is with the idea that Elvis was in some way a supernatural being. Others obsess that he is not dead and that he will return. Whatever form this obsession takes, the absent Elvis has taken over their lives. And behind both the fun and the obsession is the same figure – the mythological Elvis.

3

Down to His Last Million Dollars

The Elvis story might have been very different if his family had been left the fortune they might have expected when he died. The ongoing interest in Elvis can, to a significant extent, be explained in terms of the slick and profitable marketing of the Elvis brand. The family would have had no incentive to set up the Elvis business if the singer's finances had not been at such a low ebb at the time of his death. Had Elvis left a substantial portfolio of rock-solid investments, Graceland would probably have remained a private home and the family would have had no need to turn the Elvis image into an income stream. But thanks to the ineptitude and dishonesty of Elvis's manager, despite his substantial lifetime's earnings, Elvis left his family with financial worries, not security.

Elvis Presley's will was filed at Tennessee's Shelby County Probate Court five days after the singer's death. It was a twelve-page document written in tight legalese and had been drawn up on 3 March 1977 by a Memphis attorney, Drayton Beecher Smith, and witnessed by the attorney's wife Ann Dewey Smith, Elvis's fiancée Ginger Alden and his old friend and fellow musician Charlie Hodge. It covered every future scenario the attorney could imagine, however remote. When boiled down to its essentials, however, the message was simple. Lisa Marie, as Elvis Presley's one legitimate child, was the sole heir. Her grandfather Vernon would look after her interests until she reached the age of 25 and both he and Lisa's great-grandmother Minnie Mae would be provided for from the revenues of the estate for the rest of their lives. No provision was made for Priscilla, nor any of Elvis's entourage or girlfriends, not even Ginger Alden, his fiancée at the time of his death. Once Lisa Marie came of age, everything would be hers. The probate judge Joseph Evans observed on receiving the will that when Elvis's assets had been valued it would probably be the largest estate the state had ever recorded.

Evans knew that despite the superstar's later decline, over his lifetime Elvis's income had been huge. Some years his personal income was more than $5 million; allowing for inflation, that equates to $30 million at present values. The media consensus was that he should have been the richest entertainer of all time. Uniquely for a performer of his era, he should have 'generated more than a billion dollars in earnings from his concerts, tours, films, recordings, promotions and franchises'.[1] The judge guessed, as did the public at the time, that with past and continuing sales and royalties, Elvis would have died a multimillionaire. It was widely rumoured that Lisa Marie was worth $150 million.

When the official valuation of the estate was made, however, it surprised the judge and shocked Elvis's fans, his family and the media. Elvis was down to his last million dollars in the bank. Including property, jewellery, automobiles and other personal possessions, the King's kingdom was worth a mere $7 million. The inventory itemizing the King's possessions was 76 pages long. Everything was included, even his twenty pairs of pyjamas. Much on the list had cost him a fortune to buy yet would be of little value on the open market, but for the Elvis connection.

By the standards of most of his fans, that was still a fortune, but Elvis in life had committed himself to considerable ongoing expenses. The upkeep of Graceland cost $500,000 a year. He had an expensive and lengthy private payroll. His extravagant lifestyle and impulsive generosity kept pace with, and in the final years frequently overstretched, his income. At the time of his death, the superstar had been teetering on the brink of insolvency.

Now that Elvis was dead, things looked very bleak for his father, Vernon, who had been entrusted to manage the estate for the benefit of Elvis's sole legitimate heir, the nine-year-old Lisa Marie. Vernon himself was not in good health, but had he been fully fit he would still have been ill-equipped to take over responsibility. He had in his youth served a jail sentence for issuing a worthless cheque and money was not his forte. While he enjoyed the wealth his son had brought him, he had no business acumen. So he did what his son had done and handed the responsibilities over to Elvis's manager of 22 years, Colonel Tom Parker. Parker had been away from Memphis at the time of Elvis's death, but returned immediately; not to mourn, but with a contract in hand for Vernon to sign.

From a business point of view death doesn't change anything, the Colonel told Vernon. Only if you show signs of weakness will things fall apart. The Colonel was being disingenuous, however. He quickly realized from the worldwide reaction to the King's death that everything had changed. A week earlier he had, with some embarrassment, been booking the next Elvis tour around venues where the star's growing obesity and failing ability to deliver as a performer would not be too conspicuous. Now he knew that a dead Elvis was a goldmine waiting to be exploited. Vernon signed the contract without protest, even though its terms were stacked massively in the Colonel's favour. 'Vernon had always been something of a pushover as far as The Colonel was concerned.'[2] In his distraught state, Vernon was especially vulnerable and the Colonel took full advantage of the situation.

As well as being one of the few people to have given a thought to Elvis's posthumous earning power, the Colonel had another good reason to keep close control of the Elvis business. He was perhaps the only person who knew the reason behind the parlous state of Elvis's affairs. It was not only the star's irresponsible spending habits, although they contributed to the problem. It was greed, the rapacious greed of the Colonel himself. For twenty years Parker had been milking Elvis's income stream for his own benefit. He was a high-rolling gambling addict and needed a continuous stream of money to meet his casino debts. From the moment he signed Elvis as a raw talent and captured the trust of his naive and financially inexperienced family, every deal he fixed was directed at benefiting himself. In the early days he struck some lucrative deals which propelled his client's income into the stratosphere, but they were always structured to his own advantage. Initially his 10 per cent cut seemed modest and well deserved. By Elvis's death that 10 per cent had been manipulated up to 50 per cent. That was the deal Vernon accepted when he signed the contract shortly after his son's death. As the Colonel was often heard to say, 'I owned 50 percent of Elvis when he was alive, and I own 50 percent of him now he's dead.'[3]

When Vernon himself died within two years of his son's death, Elvis's affairs had to be returned to the probate court so that suitable trustees could be approved who would manage Lisa Marie's inheritance. The young girl's mother, Elvis's former wife Priscilla, his accountant and his bank were the three trustees proposed. Up until then Priscilla had not been aware of the true state of the Presley finances. 'Everyone was publicly saying how much money Elvis had made,' she told the *Orange County Register* in 1988. 'But the estate was in bad shape and how it got that way is amazing because when you look at it you say, Oh my God, why didn't somebody do something? Why weren't there any investments? Why wasn't there money put away?'

Initially, like Vernon, Priscilla and the trustees believed in the integrity, honesty and efficiency of the Colonel. In 1979 they confirmed to him in writing that they appreciated the work he had done and wanted him to continue to manage the late singer's affairs on the same terms. It was expected that the agreement would be rubber-stamped by the probate court. However, Judge Evans had other ideas. He was shocked to realize the full extent of the Colonel's hold on the Presleys and the percentage he was charging for his services. Before approving any future arrangements, he decided to investigate further. His decision was a turning point in the Elvis story. But for the concerns of a Shelby County probate judge the future of Elvis Presley Enterprises would have been very different.

A Memphis attorney, Blanchard Tual, was appointed Lisa Marie's temporary financial guardian and began a thorough examination of Elvis's business arrangements. He was a specialist in entertainment law and practice and his 300-page report was unstinting in its criticism. Since Elvis's death Parker had 'violated his duty both to Elvis and to the estate' by charging commissions that were 'excessive, imprudent . . . and beyond all reasonable bounds of industry standards'. The attorney concluded that Parker's cut was indefensible. 'A 50 percent fee was exorbitant . . . It raises the question of whether Parker has been guilty of self-dealing, of a breach of the fiduciary relationship owed to Elvis.'[4]

Tual uncovered numerous instances in which Parker had hatched deals that were primarily in his interest and not that of the client he was contractually obliged to serve. For instance, in 1973 Parker sold all future royalties that would be due to Elvis from the record company RCA for his master recordings for $5.4 million, a fraction of their worth. Today, when an Elvis recording hits the number one spot in the charts, Lisa Marie gets nothing directly from the sales. The only royalties the estate sees are those due on recordings made after 1973. Essentially Parker sold his client's pension pot for a knockdown price so that he, Parker, could enjoy his cut immediately. When tax was paid and Parker had taken his substantial cut, Elvis was left with $1.35 million, most of which was used to finance his divorce settlement with Priscilla. Furthermore, as Tual discovered, Parker himself continued to receive money from RCA behind Elvis's back in consultancy and other service fees.

Parker ensured that merchandising rights were channelled through a company called Boxcar Enterprises. By 1977 Parker's share in Boxcar had increased to 56 per cent, with 22 per cent going to the Presley estate. Tual's report noted: 'It has not been explained why, since Elvis was the star and totally responsible for the merchandising rights, he had such an incredibly small percentage of Boxcar.' The suggestion offered by the report was simply that 'Elvis was naive, shy and unassertive. Parker was aggressive, shrewd and tough. His strong personality dominated Elvis, his father and all others in Elvis' entourage.'[5]

Over and above the cut Parker received from Elvis's earnings, the Colonel expected regular gifts from record companies, hotels and promoters, either in cash or kind, which were never split with Elvis. The Colonel's self-serving side deals were numerous. He undersold his client in a concert deal with a Vegas hotel and casino in exchange for gambling credit. Parker's biographer Alanna Nash saw the relationship between star and manager as analogous to a marriage that starts well and then degenerates. She compared Elvis to a battered wife who does not want to leave the marriage because it is the only life she knows and who eventually begins to believe she is not worth anything. Certainly, Parker kept Elvis in the dark about what a huge star he was, and that other managers didn't take such a huge percentage and make side deals for themselves left and right. For that reason Parker preferred Elvis not to fraternize with other stars. He might start talking business.[6]

The report presented to the probate court was a devastating analysis of Parker's business empire. Not only was the Colonel siphoning off a huge amount of Elvis's income, he was also failing to maximize that income. He failed to organize the singer's tax affairs with any degree of proficiency and over the years Elvis paid far more to the Internal Revenue Service than he had to. Indeed the IRS was simply allowed to make its own calculation as to how much was owed and the family meekly paid up. Vernon's insecurities over financial matters and his distrust and fear of authority were partly the reason for this. Also, as it transpired later, the Colonel had his own reason for wanting to avoid investigation by any government department.

The attorney had no hesitation in advising that Lisa Marie's interests were not best served by Colonel Parker and that he should no longer have a hand in her affairs. Furthermore, he should be required to repay everything he had earned from the Presley business since Elvis's death.

Parker had been actively exploiting Elvis's death from the first opportunity. On 18 August, when Elvis had been dead less than 48 hours, he had signed a deal through Boxcar granting a merchandising company, Factors Inc., the exclusive licence to exploit the name and likeness of Elvis Presley. Factors paid Boxcar, and thus the Colonel, $100,000 up-front and guaranteed him an annual income of $150,000. Once Tual's report went public, the Colonel's credibility was badly damaged. He was accused of

> knowingly violating the artist/manager trust and continuing to abuse it after Elvis's death. There is evidence that both Colonel Parker and RCA are guilty of collusion, conspiracy, fraud, misrepresentation, bad faith, and overreaching. Agreements were unethical, fraudulently obtained and against industry standard. Those actions against the most popular American folk hero of the century are outrageous.[7]

The Colonel realized that his days as a main financial beneficiary of the Elvis legend were numbered. Judge Evans ordered that all payments by the estate to the Colonel cease and that the estate sue him for improper management of their affairs. The Colonel did not cave in meekly, however, even when RCA took legal steps to distance itself from him. He filed a counterclaim

against the estate claiming that he had been Elvis's business part-
ner and was entitled to half of Elvis's assets. 'No one seriously
believed that he and Elvis had been partners over the years,' noted
Sean O'Neal. 'Those close to Parker at the time say the suit was
just part of his overall strategy to push the Presley estate to the
edge of bankruptcy.'[8]

Parker knew that he was in a better financial position than
the estate to fund a long-running legal battle. His plan was to
string it out for as long as he could so that in the end the estate
would, at best, relent and re-employ him, or, at worst, offer him a
substantial sum of money to go away. The Colonel's most effective delaying tactic was to switch the case between states and
venues. The estate was forced to respond by employing parallel teams of attorneys in each location. Ultimately Parker threw
the whole legal process into chaos by revealing that he was not
the man they thought they were dealing with. He admitted the
secret he had been trying to hide from officialdom all those years:
Colonel Thomas Parker was in fact an illegal immigrant from the
Netherlands called Andreas Cornelius van Kuijk. This was the
true reason he did not want the IRS or any government department looking into his affairs too closely. As the legal process
became increasingly complex, the Presley estate was fast running
out of money.

'By the start of 1983, Parker's bleed-'em-white strategy was
paying off.'[9] The case had already cost the estate $2 million, an
amount it could barely afford. Obviously Elvis's income from
touring had dried up and now there was precious little money
coming in from any other source. Radio stations around the world
continued to play his music and fans bought records, but thanks
to the Colonel's past dealings, this did not translate into income
for Elvis's family. By 1981 the estate was running at an annual
deficit of $160,000. On top of that the IRS had valued the estate
for inheritance tax and estimated the estate's royalties since 1977.
A tax bill of $10 million was issued.

An out-of-court settlement had to be reached and so in 1983 it was agreed that Colonel Parker would surrender his claims to any Elvis assets in exchange for a cash payment of over $2 million from RCA Records. At the same time RCA paid the estate $1.1 million in royalties owed on recordings sold since 1973. All parties claimed the agreement had been arrived at amicably. Priscilla made no public criticism of Parker, even though she must have realized that he was responsible for losing the estate millions of dollars in revenue and leaving it in a parlous state.

With no Colonel or Vernon to hinder her, Priscilla now took control of Elvis's affairs on behalf of their daughter. She had no background in business, but she did have an untutored flair and an innate toughness. She made a grim assessment of the situation. Not only had a large proportion of royalties that might have been expected from record sales been forfeited, she discovered, but even the rights to payment for Elvis's part in arranging the songs he performed had been lost through the incompetence or neglect of his manager. The Colonel had failed to register Elvis's involvement with the revenue-collecting authorities. It was looking increasingly likely that the mansion house and grounds at Graceland would have to be auctioned. It was the main tangible asset the estate owned and with the Elvis connection it could be expected to fetch more than its plain market value.

It was the last thing Priscilla wished to do and a sale would have raised several difficulties. What would happen to the family graves? Although Elvis had initially been buried in Memphis's Forest Hill Cemetery, he had been reburied, with a special civic dispensation, in the grounds of Graceland. This followed an attempt made within two weeks of the funeral to steal the body and ransom the corpse for $10 million. The plot was foiled when one of the thieves, Ronnie Lee Adkins, tipped off the police and a television journalist. No charges were brought but, 25 years later, Adkins confessed that the body-snatching plot was all a hoax designed to convince local officials that Elvis would be safer at Graceland. This was a canny commercial move, as it turned out, as Elvis's grave, placed in the Meditation Gardens at Graceland that Elvis had built in his lifetime, became the main focus for every fan visiting the mansion.

When contemplating the sale of Graceland, the future of Elvis's remains and those of the family members buried alongside him became a serious issue. Would they have to be exhumed and reburied? The fans, especially those who had been allowed unofficial access to the grounds to visit the graves, were fearful of the future. Opening Graceland as a museum to Elvis was the only other viable option. Initially Priscilla wondered if the visitors could be limited to just the trophy room and racquetball court. This would keep the mansion feeling like a family home. Priscilla's advisers doubted that such limited access would draw sufficient people to make the venture worthwhile. Sentiment had to give way to commerce.

With hindsight it can be argued that but for the financial weakness of the Elvis estate the Elvis phenomenon might never have taken off. Or, if it had, it might not have been so long-lasting. Suppose Elvis had left a portfolio of sound investments. There would have been no need for the trustees of Lisa Marie's inheritance to consider opening Graceland to the public. There would have been no commercial imperative to reissue Elvis music or agree to other artists remixing his tracks. If fans had not had access to a place of pilgrimage, to Elvis music in the new formats, if there had been no Elvis Week, would the Elvis phenomenon of today been anything like as strong? It is an unanswerable question, but a fascinating one for social historians.

As it was, Priscilla had to take control and in 1982 she recruited Jack Soden to help her. He had been an associate of her friend and adviser Morgan Maxfield, a Kansas City-based financier who had died in a plane crash. She was, reported Sean O'Neal,

Elvis's grave at Graceland. He is buried alongside other members of the family. It is where a constant stream of fans leaves votive offerings of flowers, cards and toys.

impressed with Soden because his vision of the potential of Graceland was similar to hers. She was also impressed that he was completely detached from the adoration of Elvis. In fact Soden wasn't even a casual fan. Priscilla believed that a fan would not be able to make tough decisions about what was best for Graceland from a business standpoint. Questions about how Elvis would have liked things done would not become an issue. In Soden, Priscilla found someone whose only concern would be the consolidation of profits.[10]

Soden has been at the centre of the Elvis business ever since and has become the public face of Elvis Presley's ongoing world-wide enterprises.

Opening Graceland took a year of planning, during which Priscilla and her team toured other attractions and homes in America that were open to the public. They researched both the Disney method and how the National Park Service managed visitors. They went on tours of Mount Vernon, Monticello and Biltmore. However, it was the media magnate Randolph Hearst's extravagant faux castle at San Simeon, California, kept exactly as it had been when the Hearst family had lived there, that provided the model for Graceland. Even though the Graceland mansion was within easy walking distance of the proposed ticket offices, visitors would be bussed across the road in small groups and returned in the same way to the souvenir shops to spend their dollars. Guides, it was decided, would be based on the Disneyland staff. They would have a clean-cut all-American look and be trained to deliver a tightly vetted script and deflect any contentious questions.

It is estimated that it cost $500,000 to convert Graceland from a family home to a tourist attraction. Not only did visitor facilities have to be provided, but the interior of the house needed some revamping. The decor had to be returned to its 'original' state. 'According to Priscilla, in the years after she divorced Elvis, Graceland had been turned into a house full of crimes against good taste.'[11] Out went the red velvet curtains and furniture and in came white carpets, blue curtains and gold furnishings. Priscilla spent all the ready cash the estate had left. She could not even raise a loan, as the house had been mortgaged in 1977 when Elvis needed money. She even had to pre-sell tickets to raise money to buy uniforms for the tour guides and other key items. Graceland opened for tours on 7 June 1982. The upper storey, where Elvis died, remained out of bounds to visitors, but the grounds and the main living and recreation rooms were included in the tour.

'With no easy comparisons, we didn't really know what kind of response there would be to Graceland,' Jack Soden told students at his alma mater, Regis University in Colorado, in 2005. It was an anxious time for Priscilla and Soden, but they need not have worried. On the first day 3,024 visitors paid $5 each to see Elvis's home. 'What Graceland has become exceeded all of our expectations,' Soden reflected. They recouped their $500,000 investment in under forty days. Graceland quickly became not only profitable, but the cornerstone of the Memphis tourist industry.

The only other asset Priscilla owned was potentially as valuable but far less tangible. It was the memory and surviving star quality of Elvis himself. Priscilla's business challenge was unusual, if not unique. Normally, in order to grow a profit, an entrepreneur has to identify a product, source that product, oversee manufacture and sell it to an initially indifferent public. In the case of Elvis the normal marketing model was turned on its head. Priscilla had a universally recognized brand. She had ownership of many of the assets connected with that brand. She had entrepreneurs clamouring for a 'piece of the action'. Her task was not to increase awareness of the brand. Elvis was so universally recognized that that would have been a next to impossible challenge. She did not even have to increase the revenue generated by the brand. What she had to do was seize control of it. She had to ensure that the money Elvis could generate in death went to the estate for her daughter and, now that the Colonel could no longer siphon off his cut, was not instead shared with the thousands of opportunists around the world.

In the short term she had a cash crisis, but in the long term she had to ensure that Elvis did not enter the public domain so thoroughly that any claim she had to rights to his image

and likeness would become unenforceable and thus worthless.
Very quickly after Elvis's death, several enterprising but unofficial traders recognized the potential earning power of the late
singer. The massive demand for commemorative merchandise led
to the rapid and uncontrolled growth of a post-mortem souvenir
merchandising industry. A wide range of inventive products of
varying quality, over which the estate had little control, flooded
the market. As the Elvis fan and academic lawyer Professor David
Wall has observed,

> Elvis culture had effectively entered the public domain.
> Mainly intended for sale in the strip-malls across the road
> from Graceland and the many memorabilia fairs. Some of
> the more unforgettable products were: 'Love Me Tender
> Dog Chunks'; 'Always Elvis Wine'; the much sought after

There's no bigger star lighting up the Rock and Roll Hall of Fame than Elvis,
the King.

'Elvis Sweat', that carried the profound message 'Elvis poured out his soul to you, so let his perspiration be your inspiration'. The souvenirs were successful, but few royalties found their way back to the estate.[12]

Despite the Colonel's appreciation of future profits to be made, he had, as had often been the case, signed the deal with Factors Inc. hoping to pocket some instant cash rather than to establish a long-term project. Up until the point Factors Inc. was told by Judge Evans to stop trading in Elvis memorabilia, their control of the Elvis image and likeness had been inconsistent, veering between the slack and the authoritarian.

The British businessman Sid Shaw, founder of the company Elvisly Yours, has said that in his opinion 'Factors Inc. was very poor at policing the Elvis market and Elvis products were sold everywhere in the USA.' Nevertheless in 1978, when a line in Elvis busts he was selling in the UK proved popular with fans, 'I received a letter from a law firm representing Factors threatening to sue me unless I immediately stopped selling my busts of Elvis. I ignored them and soon after Factors went bankrupt in Britain.'[13]

Jack Soden, who was now taking care of the Elvis business, recognized the huge potential Sid and the other independents were tapping into. It confirmed his and Priscilla's fears that if nothing was done to take complete control of the situation, future profits from marketing Elvis would slip through their fingers.

In most circumstances, controlling the exploitation of a celebrity image is a tricky balancing act. Wall refers to it as a paradox.

The 'paradox' arises from the observation that, on the one hand, too much open circulation of a celebrity culture can lead to the development of secondary or even generic meaning that not only threatens the holder's exclusive rights over the property, but also has the potential to demean, debase or even destroy the overall integrity of the culture. On the other hand, too much restriction through over-zealous control could effectively strangle the celebrity culture by killing off sensibilities of personal ownership and affiliation.[14]

In other words, fail to police the exploitation of the image and ownership is lost to the fans; police it too tightly and the fans drift away. In the case of Elvis getting the right balance was especially problematic. Priscilla and Jack Soden guessed rightly that however fiercely they protected their legal rights to Elvis, the fans would stay loyal. They could therefore afford to take a tough line. They said it was to protect the memory of Elvis. They wished him to be remembered in his prime. What they did not state so explicitly was that they wanted the estate to take the lion's share of the profit generated by that memory.

All aspects of Elvis's memory that could in any way be claimed to be an intellectual property came to be so jealously guarded that his name is almost synonymous with litigation. 'In fact Elvis Presley Enterprises, widely regarded as one of the most effective organisations of its genre, has been referred to as the "Darth Vader of the merchandising-licensing business".'[15] The irony of the situation that completely escaped Elvis Presley Enterprises was that the image they so jealously guarded was itself pirated. 'Elvis of course didn't "own" the songs he sang, all of which were written by other people,' Erika Doss points out in her book *Elvis Culture: Fans, Faith and Image.*

> And he didn't 'own' the various images, from rockabilly rebel to Las Vegas showman, that he lifted from bits and pieces of other images and shaped into his personae. He understood the fabricated nature of his image . . . Yet despite his history of musical and visual hybridity, Elvis is today claimed by his estate as a legally held, legally enforceable and essentially monolithic entity.[16]

Is this what Elvis would have wanted to happen? He was very laid-back about the whole issue of identity and 'he never had any real problems with how he was imitated and appropriated, either. His own calculated creation of a multiformed image, of an identity derived from diverse sources, was central to the way he thought about himself and acted around others.'[17] The dead Elvis, as represented by the estate's lawyers, has not always had his own way and Sid Shaw was no pushover. Years of legal conflict started when the estate told Shaw he could only sell souvenirs in the USA if he paid royalties of $50,000 per item. At that time Shaw was offering a range of 300 products and faced paying a sum of $15 million. It was an offer Shaw had no option but to reject. He told the publication *Managing Intellectual Property* that he had always been prepared to pay a reasonable royalty to the Elvis estate, but such an offer was never available: 'I've never said I would never deal with these people. But their idea of a deal was getting lots of money and I was getting fed up.'[18]

So Shaw decided to take the battle to them and he was summoned to a showdown meeting in New York on 26 March 1985. He was faced with a panel of three lawyers who interrogated him. 'It was like the Spanish Inquisition,' he recalled.[19] The meeting was going nowhere when a fourth lawyer was called in and presented Shaw with a writ. As far as he was concerned, it was an ambush. When Shaw refused to cave in, the estate took him to court to curtail his sales in the U.S. At the hearing, he was called to the stand as a hostile witness, and even asked about his associations with a joke British political movement called the Monster Raving Loony Party.

The crunch came, *Managing Intellectual Property* reported, when lawyers produced a pair of knickers (panties) and showed them to the court. The suggestion was that by marketing Elvis underwear, Shaw was demeaning the image of the King. But Shaw retorted that the idea came from The Beatles, who had marketed underwear very successfully. He told the lawyers not to get their 'knickers in a twist'. The clerk then asked him how to spell 'knickers'. The joke was lost on the judge, and did Shaw's case no favours.

Shaw is convinced he was treated badly by the American court system. He was forbidden from trading in Elvis souvenirs in the USA, a prohibition that made him even more determined to succeed in the international market. He effectively presented his battles with the estate as a dogged defence of the little man against a giant corporation. He retained his sense of humour throughout and in many ways he has had the last laugh. When he was pursued in the British courts, the Elvis lawyers were far less successful.

Other entrepreneurs were less combative and gave way in the face of the Elvis legal juggernaut. Jack Soden, as Graceland's chief executive, made no secret of his intentions and was open about his methods, saying that all they wanted was 'to run our own business and not have every little schlocky guy around ripping off Elvis and putting his face on edible underwear and all kinds of things that demean the long-term value of what we've got'.[20] He further described the mission of the company as 'clearing the swamp' of what it saw as a vast collection of tacky and unauthorized souvenirs and products that had appeared following Elvis's death. The formal Elvis Presley Enterprises position is couched in slightly less colourful language, but expresses the same sentiments. EPE's Licensing Division is charged with the responsibility of 'protecting and preserving the integrity of Elvis Presley, Graceland and other related properties. We accomplish this through the pursuit of the right commercial opportunities that fit with our financial strategies while maintaining desired branding and positioning for Elvis and our other properties.'[21]

It is not just business people who have found themselves in conflict with EPE. In 1999, the prestigious Danish choreographer and dancer Peter Schaufuss devised a ballet called *The King*, chronicling Elvis's life. In Denmark it played to full houses and standing ovations, but just ten days before the company was due to bring the ballet to Edinburgh and London, EPE announced that the persona of Elvis should not be depicted on stage without permission from the estate. Schaufuss reluctantly cancelled the Scottish engagement and reworked the production in time for the London opening. He had to change twenty numbers and ditch such Elvis essentials as 'Heartbreak Hotel' and 'Are You Lonesome Tonight?' After a meeting with representatives of EPE in Los Angeles, Schaufuss decided to change the ballet's storyline completely and turn it into the story of an aspiring Presley impersonator.

The principal mission of EPE, notes Wall, 'is to preserve its own economic interests, which is no surprise and it would be considered negligent not to do so'. But the use of legal powers and threats of court action, 'the naked use of law' as Wall puts it, 'can be both brutal and expensive, even destructive. It is brutal, because it rarely achieves its stated goal and it rarely attracts public sympathy or support, often achieving the opposite. Although costs are usually awarded in a successful action, the whole exercise is rarely cost effective.'[22]

Over the years, despite a stack of court judgments in its favour, Graceland's business arm has arguably lost control of the mythical Elvis. It has retained sufficient legal control over the image to be able to generate an income and, consequently, for Elvis to be a tradable commodity, but has not made itself popular in the process. Sid Shaw says of his own dealings with the corporation that he became their guinea pig in their relentless pursuit of power and control and their greed. This is not an unbiased perspective, but even if it is only partly true, was all this alleged power, control and greed an effective strategy? Arguably not, since at the grass roots of fandom, the long-term objective of total financial control of the memory of Elvis has long been forfeited. At the artistic, creative, cultural and generic level, Elvis can now be said to be public property. EPE, recognizing this, now embraces the diversity of popular Elvis and attempts to channel it. Thus Elvis Week is an EPE event even though it started out as an unofficial and spontaneous gathering of fans. Today, on the anniversary of his death, thousands of fans bring a huge range of homemade, unlicensed tributes to offer at his grave. They are untroubled and unpoliced by the EPE legal department. But it no longer matters to the estate, for the fans also buy licensed souvenirs, stay at Graceland-owned hotels and pay for tickets for the ancillary Elvis entertainments.

More than thirty years after Elvis's death, his estate still resorts to the law to protect Elvis's memory and the value of his legacy. Yet lessons appear to have been absorbed and the legal approach is now arguably less heavy-handed. Nevertheless the lawyers are still kept busy. There is, says Wall, a very strong case to favour more free circulation and less restriction. 'The most effective form of governance of a celebrity culture is not simply that owners of popular cultures should talk tough, but cut a bit of slack every now and then.'[23]

Wall emphasizes, however, that without the authority gained from the earlier legal interventions and the strategies of governance 'under the shadow of law', EPE would not have been as effective in protecting its commercial interests and the estate may not have survived as a financial success. Had it not been for EPE's 'legal actions during the 1980s to establish its rights in the Elvis celebrity culture, then its core symbols (Graceland and contemporary Elvis knowledge) would probably have been lost and "Elvis" would have become generic, possibly losing its specific meaning and cultural value in the process.'[24]

From a business perspective, the Jack Soden–Priscilla Presley strategy turned out to be highly successful. They policed those aspects of the Elvis image that could be legally defined and simultaneously allowed fans to evolve their own versions of Elvis. The King has now been reshaped and reinterpreted by the fans in a multitude of ways through impersonation and simulation, the growth in Elvis art, an increasing spiritual following and the Internet. Elvis is now embedded in his own global subculture over which the official Elvis estate has relinquished control. As long as it does not detract from the profitability of EPE, it can be safely left to go its own way.

Brand Elvis

The Elvis business empire, with its core visitor attraction, evolved stage by stage. In 1984 two of Elvis's most extravagant toys were brought back to Graceland. His private jets had been sold by Vernon in a panic to raise cash for the troubled Presley estate, but an arrangement was made with the new owners to put *Hound Dog II* and *Lisa Marie* on long-term display. Since then they have stood incongruously, as if boarding passengers, on a special plot alongside Elvis Presley Boulevard in Memphis, looking as if they are still capable of flying, but with no runway and nowhere to go.

The Elvis Presley Automobile Museum was opened in June 1989 at Graceland Plaza, across the street from the mansion. It had twenty automobiles on show, including the world's most famous pink car, the 1955 Cadillac Fleetwood.

November 1991 was a significant month which saw a seal of public approval being given to all that the estate's business arm had done to rescue Graceland. The property was listed in the National Register of Historic Places; later, in March 2006, the property was designated a National Historic Landmark. Another important year in terms of national recognition was 1993, when the u.s. Postal Service released an Elvis Presley 29-cent postage stamp. In under a year a $36 million profit was made on sales, outstripping any previous stamp release. Five hundred million

A total of 500 million American 29-cent Elvis stamps were printed and released on the King's 58th birthday. In under a year, a $36 million profit was made on sales, outstripping any previous stamp release.

stamps were printed and they were first issued on 8 January, Elvis's 58th birthday. The launch was accompanied by a major television advertising campaign and Elvis lookalikes were engaged to promote the stamps in post offices around the country. The picture on the stamp, by artist Mark Stutzman, was of a yellow-jacketed Elvis caressing a chunky metallic retro microphone. The image had been chosen by ballot: in April the year before, nearly 1.2 million votes had been cast, with 75 per cent of voters preferring the option of a young Elvis to a portrait of a more mature Elvis. The stamp became the most recognizable item of philatelia in American history. Complete sheets of the stamps are now collector's items, as are first-day covers and especially any stamp and envelope cancelled with the words 'Return to Sender'.

The American stamp was not the first. Grenada issued stamps in the King's honour on the first anniversary of his death in 1978.

Elvis has since been featured on international stamps around the world from Antigua to Zaire, and during Elvis Week 2015 a new American Elvis 49-cent stamp was issued featuring a 1955 black-and-white picture of the King.

On 1 February 1993 Lisa Marie celebrated her 25th birthday and inherited her father's estate in her own right. As the day approached, rumours spread about her intentions. Fans feared she might initiate far-reaching changes. In the event, 1 February came and went with little change. Lisa Marie was advised to form a new trust, the Elvis Presley Trust, to continue the management of the business, with exactly the same top management team in charge. Her mother, Priscilla Presley, and the National Bank of Commerce continued to serve as co-trustees. Priscilla was especially relieved. She had foreseen that if Lisa Marie had assumed direct control, her new husband Danny Keough might become involved. She feared, correctly as it turned out, that the marriage would not last, and a divorce settlement with the Presley estate as the prize to be divided up would have been a nightmare.

After the divorce, Lisa Marie's next marriage was to prove even more interesting. In 1994 she married Michael Jackson at a private and secret ceremony in the Dominican Republic. Despite the joining together of two of the greatest names in the history of popular music, Elvis fans were vociferously opposed to the marriage. It was the strangeness of Michael's character that alarmed them, as well as the persistent rumours that he had inappropriate relations with children. Some fans genuinely feared for the safety of Elvis's grandchildren. Fans were also concerned that Graceland would revert to being a private home, since Jackson had no need for the tourist-generated income. Had they wished, he and Lisa Marie could have shut the gates, hired extra security guards to keep fans out and lived behind Graceland's walls. Jack Soden had to issue a press release scotching the rumours. 'Lisa Marie is very intent on leaving all of Elvis Presley's assets independent and intact.'[1] In the event Lisa Marie's second attempt at matrimony also ended in failure. Some fans believe she quickly tired of living in her husband's bizarre and childish world. In the end the only matter that interested the press and public was the divorce settlement. Fortunately there had been a legally binding prenuptial agreement signed and both parties returned to their former status and fortunes.

The commercial development of the Graceland portfolio continued incrementally and unhindered, as did the ever-vigilant legal policing of the brand. Even businesses that started up with the full support and cooperation of the Graceland lawyers were not guaranteed success if they did not get the balance right between appealing to both fans and the wider public. Several entrepreneurs have opened Elvis clubs and restaurants in downtown Memphis over the years. They have tended to do well during Elvis Week, but have often struggled the rest of the year. In 1999 the Graceland-owned Heartbreak Hotel welcomed its first guests and, thanks to its name and its close proximity to Graceland, has proved popular with fans, although fifteen years later visitors were reporting that it was in need of upgrading and renovating.

Ten years after coming into her inheritance, Lisa Marie had a rock-steady business producing a regular income. It was managed cautiously and although some of the ideas for spin-offs, such as a clothes label and a restaurant chain, did not succeed, the central business was well secured. The Elvis officially presented to the world was a rather bland representation. The fans on the Graceland tour were given a story that emphasized Elvis's rags-to-riches life story. The pill-popping, obese and occasionally crazy Elvis of latter years was airbrushed out of the picture. As Professor Erika Doss puts it,

> Within the world of Elvis Presley Enterprises there is only an 'official' image of a clean and generous Elvis who seems to burst forth from his Tupelo/Memphis womb a fully developed, heroic and autonomous Rock and Roll King. His real

history, his transgressive cross-race, cross-gender history, ignored and denied, his dirtier and more decadent parts swept away, his putrefaction corrected, the 'official' Elvis presented at Graceland is like some exotic stuffed animal on display in a natural history museum. Taxidermy, after all, is about gutting and mounting the lifeless in ostensibly life-like, and hence real (or 'official'), poses and settings.[2]

Doss goes further and hints at an implicit political agenda. 'He's conservative and controlled, seamless and uncomplicated, fixed – even paralyzed – as not much more than a symbol of monopoly capital.'[3]

The Graceland portrayal of Elvis inevitably conflicts with that of many fans who see it as too simple, too sanitized and too commercial. For some it is the very weakness and vulnerability of their flawed hero with which they identify. 'Elvis has always been . . . something more ethereal,' noted Doss in 1999, 'a feeling, a soulmate. Many contemporary fans recognise that Elvis Inc. has shifted the balance of Elvis's identity to a more completely commercialized representation that essentially excludes his deeper and more emotive meaning in their everyday lives.'[4] The guardians of Lisa Marie's assets were not interested in any image of Elvis that conflicted with their own money-spinning version.

By 2004 Elvis Presley Enterprises was valued at over $100 million and taking care of a business worth $40 million a year. Income came from two main streams – royalties and licensing on the one hand, and the visitor revenue from Graceland on the other – in roughly equal proportions. In the winter the estate ran at a loss, which was more than compensated for by the summer peak. It was a good, steady earner with huge potential for expansion for any entrepreneur with ideas and capital to invest. And like all valuable assets it attracted the interest of potential buyers.

Enter Robert F. X. Sillerman, who in 2004 was listed by the Forbes organization as the 375th richest man in the USA, valued at almost $1 billion. Under the banner of a new company, CKX Inc., Sillerman bought the rights to control Graceland's tourism, the Presley trademark rights, all intellectual property owned by the estate and control of all the music rights held by the estate. While Lisa Marie and her mother continued to exert a strong influence on the Elvis image, they were persuaded to relinquish 85 per cent of their legal ownership of the Elvis brand, receiving $53 million of the payment due in cash. Lisa Marie kept the deeds to Graceland and ownership of family and personal items. She said in a statement that her greatest responsibility to her father was to preserve and protect his legacy, and 'this is an exciting new structure that opens up an incredible array of opportunities with a major infusion of new investment capital to do just that.'

The sale took almost everyone not involved by surprise. The veteran Memphis journalist Bill Burk, who normally had an excellent nose for an inside story, admitted, 'the sale shocked Hell out of me, as it did everyone. I checked with many, many Elvis insiders after the fact and no one, no one had any inkling this was coming down the line. So, kudos to EPE and Sillerman for keeping this so extremely secretive because, heretofore, EPE has had more leaks than a screen door trying to hold water.'[5] Some fans said that Lisa Marie had been badly advised. The Elvis Information Network explained that 'Lisa Marie has $25 million in debts (of which she will be absolved under this deal)' but still concluded that 'on the face of it, the sale doesn't seem like a bright move.'[6] When fans were polled by CNN, 55 per cent disagreed with her decision. She might have done better to have issued shares in EPE, which fans would have bought to claim a financial as well as emotional stake in the King's legacy. One group of fans started an online petition, resentful of Lisa Marie's decision to sell the majority control of the company that managed her father's estate. Many fans feel as if they, as much as Lisa Marie, are the beneficiaries of the Elvis legacy, not financially but emotionally. Some were alarmed when they heard that the company was now a subsidiary of Sillerman's media empire, although some were reassured on learning that the existing management team would remain in charge. Indeed Priscilla was offered a lucrative ten-year contract to continue in her post. CKX announced ambitious plans. A three-mile strip of Elvis Presley Boulevard would be transformed into an entertainment district. A hundred and twenty acres of land was bought in the vicinity. Sillerman, together with investors and developers, talked of spending between $250 million and $500 million on redeveloping the area surrounding Graceland. There would be a new hotel, theatre and convention centre. CKX talked of setting up Elvis-related attractions in other parts of the USA and around the world. Europe, Asia and the Middle East were in their sights. 'Elvis sells all over the world, and that's where the real opportunity for growth lies for us, to take more of Elvis and Graceland out to the world,' said Jack Soden, still in post as chief executive of the Graceland company, but now an employee of a much larger organization.

Slowly, the marketing of Elvis began to change. In 2005 Elvis Presley Enterprises decided for the first time to advertise Graceland and its attractions on American television. The creative team was briefed to produce two commercials designed 'to remind viewers that Elvis was a genuine, fun-loving person, not merely an icon and to invite people to visit his home in Memphis to see where and how he lived.'[7] The advertisements were designed to coordinate with two prime-time CBS programmes about Elvis that were scheduled and targeted towards viewers on a range of women's lifestyle channels including HGTV, Lifetime, Food Network, Style, Discover Home, WE, Lifetime Movie Network and SoapNET. 'They will create a significant buzz around Elvis Presley and we hope to capitalize on this increased focus,' said Jennifer Burgess, Graceland's director of marketing. 'Spring is also the time of the year when families plan summer vacations and we want to put Graceland on their radar screens as the perfect family destination.'[8]

Over the years, and with the Graceland business team growing the asset, many fans have noticed changes at Graceland – not to the core attraction, the mansion house and garden, but to the way they are being presented. The ethos of the place is subtly different. A New Zealand fan, Susan Brennan-Hodgson, recalls her first visit to Memphis in 1988 and compares it to her current impression of the way the business is managed. On the first occasion she had what she describes as the trip of a lifetime. At the mansion house she had the feeling that Elvis had just stepped outside but would be back any minute. 'His presence was strong. Nowadays, all this has changed, and the greedy money-makers have taken over. Everything and anything Elvis is highly commercialised, the true spirit of Elvis has been lost along the way.'[9]

Many fans have felt taken for granted. In 2004 mutiny was in the air. There was talk of the fans boycotting all official Elvis Week events, with the exception of the vigil. An open letter was sent to fan clubs by two Illinois fans, Randall and Kelley Bart, claiming that it was time 'for the Fans to stop being taken advantage of'. There were numerous topics of concern, they said, from unsound management decisions to the care of Elvis's artefacts. Elvis Week, Randall and Kelley claimed, had become stale, with many events being repeated and run into the ground. The fans' concerns, they claimed, had been discussed on fan message boards, at round-table discussions hosted by Graceland, at the Presidents' Forum online, and

> at all times they have fallen on deaf ears with the upper management at EPE. It apparently seems EPE only cares about the bottom line, dollar wise . . . Enough is enough and now is the time for Elvis Fans worldwide to unite! Elvis once said, 'Without my Fans I'd be nothing.' If only the company that bears his good name felt the same way.[10]

Jack Soden responded for the estate. His letter began by suggesting he was the injured party.

I have been surprised, disappointed and hurt by many of the things I have read . . . I am disappointed that there are people who are so quick to embrace ugly rumor and innuendo and we have all been hurt by the implication that the dedicated hard work of scores and scores of devoted Graceland employees has gone, at least amongst some fans, apparently unrecognized and unappreciated.

Later in a long letter his tone changed to one of conciliation and flattery. 'Elvis Fan Clubs have been an active and dynamic tribute to his lasting Legacy of music, love and generosity. The Fan Clubs were, are, and always will be the backbone of the Elvis Phenomenon.' Further on he promised change. 'We will listen a lot and we will be there with all the support and help that is asked of us . . . We will provide all the help and support possible to the Fan Clubs and, most importantly, with the help and support of the Fan Clubs the world will be reminded just why there is only one Elvis Presley!'[11]

The advantage of being part of an extended business empire was that the Elvis business could hope to have access to a larger pot of investment money. The drawback, as EPE soon discovered, was that Graceland's fortunes could rise and fall in line with the success and failure of the wider business. Shortly after the Elvis deal, Sillerman acquired 19 Entertainment, the British company behind *American Idol* and the UK's *Pop Idol*. All looked good for a while. EPE bought several apartment complexes west of the Graceland plaza and north of the mansion and building work, or at least work on demolishing old buildings, started.

Elvis Presley Enterprises remained a hard outfit with which to do business and with Sillerman's dollars could plan its dream of creating a massive Elvis centre around Graceland which it would control. It was tough on independent businesses that stood in the way, as the owners of the store Memories of Elvis discovered. The shop, across the road from Graceland, had survived for 27 years.

It had hundreds of regular customers, but at the end of May 2005 the owners were told their lease would expire after six months and they would have to cease trading. 'Among many emotions that we are experiencing are those of deep sadness, disappointment, sense of loss, and even denial,' Memories of Elvis wrote in a letter to their customers.

> We were here in the days shortly after the death of Elvis when the house was still a residence and the public could only visit the gravesite. This store has been my child, of sorts, with many struggles, yet many victories . . . My loyal friends and customers, you are the best group of people in the world; many of you remembering our beginning in the small shop directly across from the gates. Those were wonderful times and we have continued those friendships until the present.[12]

When, in 2008, the banking crash and the recession hit the American and world economies, the Elvis business was not immune from the effects. Visitor numbers at Graceland dropped as the fans, despite continuing to grow in number, were forced to tighten their belts. Profits fell back and CKX announced a strong likelihood that 'the original preliminary design plans' for the redevelopment of Graceland 'may require significant modifications or abandonment for a redesign'. In 2009 Lisa Marie herself sold 100,000 of her shares in CKX over a two-month period. In 2011 the major development at Graceland was put on hold. 'Although we continue to consider the exact scope, cost, financing plan and timing of such a project, we expect that the redevelopment of Graceland, if and when pursued, would take several years and could require a substantial financial investment by the company,' said a CKX statement.

A Bloomberg profile of Sillerman's empire asked if the tycoon's inexperience as a real-estate developer was the cause of his business problems following a long run of success. 'I'm not very knowledgeable about real estate,' he admitted in an interview. 'I think I've demonstrated that to the world.' Priscilla however blamed the economy in general and not Sillerman personally. 'I have a lot of confidence in Bob. When the timing is right, I'm sure all this will come back on the boards.'[13]

Despite the setbacks to the building programme, the CKX plans to develop Elvis-related attractions away from Graceland were slowly taking shape. Through its Elvis business subsidiary it was fixing a deal to stage an Elvis-themed show in Las Vegas in partnership with Cirque du Soleil, the company famed for spectacular circus shows. *Viva Elvis* was billed as a tribute to the life and music of the King and included dance, acrobatics and live music. When it opened at the Aria Resort and Casino, Priscilla was there and the show attracted good reviews. Robert Sillerman said *Viva Elvis* would be loved by devoted Elvis fans, fans of Cirque du Soleil and anyone who loved the music of the era.

It was a huge investment and one that in the long term turned out to be less successful than Priscilla and Sillerman had hoped. All in all, the high hopes Sillerman had brought with him were being dashed. In May 2010 the Elvis company found itself under a new ownership structure when Sillerman resigned as chairman and CEO of CKX, although he remained the company's biggest shareholder. Less than two years later CKX, along with the Elvis subsidiary, was sold to a New York private equity firm. Apollo Global Management bought the company for just over $500 million in a deal that required approval by both Sillerman, as chief shareholder, and Lisa Marie Presley on behalf of the trust created by her father's estate. Lisa Marie again kept hold of legal ownership of Graceland and her father's artefacts.

Apollo acquired Elvis at a bargain price, opined the blogger Alan Hanson.[14] When the deal was reported in the financial press, subeditors could not resist the obvious puns. 'Apollo Decides It's Now or Never for Graceland Offer' was the *Financial*

Times headline. The new owner was a private equity group that had been founded by another American entrepreneur, Leon Black, known outside the business world for having bought one of the four versions of *The Scream*, the celebrated picture by Munch. It was reported that Apollo had no plans to change the CKX management team. The deal brought to an end a period of uncertainty.

Apollo bought far more than Elvis for their dollars; the deal included the name and image of Muhammad Ali and the rights to several prime-time TV formats. Apollo added them to an existing entertainment portfolio that included a cinema chain, casinos and a cruise line. Looking at the books of its newly acquired Elvis business, Apollo's first priority was to explore how best to increase visitor numbers at Graceland, which appeared to have flattened out year-on-year. Would they be able to double the numbers, perhaps even to an annual figure of one million? What investment would have to be made to reach that figure? Would improved marketing be the answer or a development of the site into an attraction with broader appeal?

Viva Elvis produced by Cirque du Soleil at the Aria Resort and Casino, owned and operated by MGM Resorts. Las Vegas, Nevada, 17 July 2011.

It also had to explore new ways of extending the earning power of the brand off-site. There were hard lessons to learn about how this might be achieved and the feedback from the Cirque du Soleil project was not hopeful. On 31 August 2012 the show was pulled, with poor ticket sales blamed. It had run for 900 performances and had been seen by a million people, a smash hit by most standards, but revenues were not enough to keep the high-cost show in business. Elvis fans had generally enjoyed the show, but some lamented that they had never managed to see it; with the cheapest ticket $69, it was far too expensive.

Meanwhile at Graceland, despite problems in Vegas, regular visitors found new attractions on which to spend their dollars. In 2013 two new exhibitions were staged and another that had opened the year before was extended. 'Elvis' Hawaii: Concerts, Movies and More!' opened to the fans in January to coincide with the Elvis 2013 Birthday Celebrations and the fortieth anniversary of 'Aloha from Hawaii', his groundbreaking video concert. The exhibition let visitors fantasize about Elvis's Hawaii. One special feature was never-before-seen footage of Elvis on the boat heading to Hawaii in 1957 and colour footage of his first Hawaiian concert. On display together for the first time were all of the jumpsuits worn by Elvis during his Hawaiian concerts, souvenirs Colonel Parker had had made to promote *Blue Hawaii*, the crown and pendant given to Elvis during the 'Aloha from Hawaii' concert and many other unique items linked to the islands and the King. A second exhibition, which focused on Elvis in Las Vegas, opened two months later. The 'Elvis: Live from Vegas' collection included the first jumpsuit worn onstage by Elvis in 1970, his leather and chains suit and his three-piece Spanish flower suit worn in 1972, plus such diverse Presleyana as his hotel receipts. When it comes to Elvis, nothing is considered too trivial.

By popular demand, 2013 also saw the extension of 'Elvis . . . Through His Daughter's Eyes', the exhibition that had been opened by Lisa Marie the year before, initially for just one year.

The relationship between Elvis and his only child was explored through family photos, home movies and even Lisa Marie's baby footprints, childhood tricycle and crib.

As they enjoyed these new opportunities to celebrate the King, interested fans, while also scanning the financial news pages, would have spotted some potentially more significant Elvis news – another commercial restructuring. The section of the Apollo Global Management holding that managed the Elvis brand would, it was announced, from henceforth be repackaged as Core Media. As seasoned observers of the business world know, rebranding and restructuring are seldom good omens. They are often devices used to mask underlying problems or to prepare a business for sale.

In typical modern management style, the new brand created a new website and drew up its mission statement. 'CORE Media Group', it declared,

is a new kind of entertainment company that creates, manages, and cultivates compelling, original content and iconic entertainment brands. From timeless icons like Elvis Presley and Muhammad Ali to enduring properties of the future like *American Idol* and *So You Think You Can Dance*, CORE Media Group is the driving force behind many great entertainment brands. Our expertise, vision, insight, and creativity propel their expansion: into new markets; across all media channels; to reach more fans; and deliver greater value. Talent and creators of original and iconic properties alike trust us to get the most out of these great brands . . . As we move forward, we will always be discovering, creating, and developing the next great properties and the next great ways to propel them even further.[15]

Despite such confident statements, many fans began to worry that the more Elvis was in the hands of the moneymen and corporate strategists, the less secure the future of Graceland and the Elvis legacy would be. The Elvis blogger Alan Hanson even wondered aloud if the Elvis management company might go out of business.

> That's a possible consequence of how Apollo financed its purchase of CKX. It used what's called a 'leveraged buyout,' which means that Apollo borrowed the $509 million to buy CKX, specifically from Goldman Sachs Bank. While Apollo's worker bees pore over CKX's financial statements looking for ways to make the company more profitable for future sale, CKX's ongoing profits will be used to pay the interest on the bank loan. The danger, then, is that should CKX not make sufficient profits over time to make the interest payments, Apollo could default on the loan and send CKX, and EPE along with it, into bankruptcy and foreclosure.[16]

He admitted the scenario, while alarming, was unlikely, but the fact that he aired his concerns was significant. Fans were getting anxious. 'EPE is now in the belly of a behemoth company that values the Presley image solely as a way to make money,' Hanson said. 'As things stand at the start of 2013, EPE has the potential to thrive or it could be driven out of business entirely. And there's nothing Presley fans can do about it.'[17] Hanson thought that in reality,

> at some time during the next five years or so, Apollo will most likely sell EPE, along with the other CKX companies, for more than its original $509 million investment. Apollo will then pay off the bank loan it took out to buy CKX, pocket the profit, and move on to find other companies to purchase and flip in the same way. EPE will probably end up in the portfolio of another private equity conglomerate, unless a small investor group surfaces to purchase the Presley brand and run it themselves.[18]

Indeed, less than a year after it was set up, CORE Media had bundled together their Elvis and Ali interests into a business package and started looking for buyers. The sale was entrusted to a merchant bank, the Raine Group, which focuses, as it says of itself, 'exclusively on the digital, media & entertainment and sports & lifestyle sectors'. Again, when reporting on the move, the press could not resist the puns. 'The sale of marketing rights to the Elvis Presley estate is shaping up as a real Heartbreak Hotel,' said one headline.[19] However, Apollo Global's sale of the Elvis Presley marketing rights, which included his name and likeness, and tours of Graceland, did not immediately attract the offers hoped for and Apollo had to consider whether to cancel the sale if it failed to receive what it considered a minimum bid.

Potential bidders were said to include the music-publishing company Sony/ATV, plus the investment firms Guggenheim Partners and G2 Investment Group. It was rumoured that Sony/ATV was interested in linking the Elvis estate with that of Michael Jackson to coordinate the activities of Graceland with the exploitation of the music catalogue sold by the Colonel. Since Sony Music Entertainment already handled the Presley master recording catalogue, it would no longer need to make artist royalty payments to the estate. Bids for the Presley and Ali estates were expected to be in the $100 million to $150 million range. On closer examination of what was on offer it became clear that while the annual income from licensing the brand was in excess of $30 million, the physical assets such as Heartbreak Hotel and the Graceland mansion would soon require a capital infusion in order to upgrade and maintain the properties.

As the summer of 2013 wore on, there was no news of any deal being struck and analysts feared that the whole sale might founder. No single potential buyer, it seemed, had the whole package of business skills to maximize returns from a diverse set of assets. Given these potential difficulties and following on the heels of the closure of *Viva Elvis*, the Raine Group did not have an easy task, despite the undeniable attraction that more than 35 years after Presley's death and 32 years after Ali's retirement, the two assets on offer generated revenues of about $60 million a year. Lisa Marie issued a statement supporting the search for a new owner. She confirmed that she had no plans to sell the Graceland mansion house and said that her priority was securing the best long-term deal for her family.

As the financial wheeler-dealing continued through 2013 in New York and Los Angeles, ordinary fans were given no say and indeed kept in the dark. The Elvis blogger Alan Hanson attempted to find some grounds for optimism.

> While Elvis Presley Enterprises is . . . being tossed around like the ball in a game of touch football, Elvis fans can take solace in that his image has remained in the same capable management hands throughout it all. Jack Soden, the president of EPE, remains in the position he's held for more than 30 years. As long as he's allowed to continue running the day-to-day operations at EPE, his respect for the Presley brand should keep it on sound financial ground, regardless of which conglomerate happens to own the company.[20]

At the end of 2013 a buyer was found when the Authentic Brands Group stepped forward as the new owner of the Elvis estate's exploitable assets. No purchase price was disclosed, but the New York Post speculated that Authentic had emerged as the lead bidder after upping its offer to $125 million. The New York-based company is one of a new breed of businesses that market images. Its mandate, it says, is to acquire, manage and build long-term value in prominent consumer brands. It is linked to Leonard Green and Partners, one of America's largest private equity firms, which has raised over $15 billion of private equity capital since it was founded in 1989. The people controlling the Elvis image live in a world far removed from that of the ordinary

Elvis fans. 'We're at the intersection of ideas and creation on the strategic superhighway,' Authentic declares. What would Vernon have made of that? Currently Authentic owns more than twenty global consumer brands divided into four main categories: sport, men's fashion, women's fashion and celebrity. The last category includes Marilyn Monroe as well as the newly acquired Muhammad Ali and Elvis rights. Authentic's interest is in growing the income from the licensing and merchandising rights to Presley's image, name and likeness, plus maximizing the profit from the estate's collection of music, photos, movies, television appearances and performance specials featuring the King of Rock 'n' Roll.

The rights to operate Graceland as a tourist attraction were bought by Authentic in conjunction with Joel Weinshanker, the owner of the National Entertainment Collectibles Association. NECA is a New Jersey-based organization specializing in manufacturing collectibles licensed to films, celebrities and sport. NECA itself was not involved in the deal, although it has an interest in Elvis, in that its range of novelty collectibles includes a bobblehead version of the King. 'This is an exciting day for Elvis and his fans,' Priscilla Presley said in a statement after the announcement of the deal. 'We look forward to working with the ABG team to further promote the legacy of Elvis. This is the opportunity the family has been envisioning to expand the Graceland experience and enhance Elvis's image all over the world.' 'The licensing and merchandising aspect of this business is not to be confused with the fact that the property will always remain with me and my family,' Lisa Marie Presley said. 'It is with great honor, and a profound sense of responsibility, that we assume ownership of the Graceland operations,' stated Joel Weinshanker. 'We will usher in a new era of an enhanced Graceland experience, run for the fans, by a fan. Graceland is Elvis Presley's castle, and I look forward to helping take this global landmark to new and exciting heights. We look forward to continuing to give visitors to

Graceland, whether online or in-person, whether their first visit or their 500th, a world class experience.'[21]

It was not long before the architects and builders were at work on a 450-room Elvis-themed guest house to replace the Heartbreak Hotel. It was one of the most ambitious hotel projects Memphis had ever seen, and estimates of the cost were in excess of $70 million. Plans included a grand staircase inspired by Graceland itself and a decor that would remind guests of Elvis's home. There was also to be a 500-seat theatre and VIP suites designed by Priscilla. Fans hoped that Graceland was now under secure long-term management, and that real and substantial investment would be made in the Memphis attraction to ensure a successful and prosperous future.

In his summer 'Strictly Elvis UK' newsletter of 2015, long-term Elvis fan and travel entrepreneur David Wade expressed this optimism. He had been reading in the Memphis newspaper *Commercial Appeal* about Graceland's investments in real estate around the mansion and its ambitious development programme. 'With planning like that in place Elvis fans can rest assured that Elvis' legacy to us all is in very safe hands and we, and our children, and our children's children, will be able to visit, learn from and enjoy Graceland for a long time ahead,' Wade concluded.

Under the new investors' regime a range of Elvis projects took shape away from Memphis. There were reports in 2014 of a big-budget film based on the life of the King being planned. Behind the rumours, it was said, was the Warner Brothers studio. They had already remastered the 1970 film *Elvis: That's the Way It Is*, which was re-released in cinemas and for home viewing. In 2015, together with Westgate Resort in Las Vegas, EPE unveiled a new permanent exhibition featuring hundreds of artefacts never before displayed outside of Graceland. Elvis will be back in the building, Joel Weinshanker announced. The exhibition covers an area of 28,000 square feet, and visitors not only see displays telling Elvis's life story but their visit concludes with a film featuring his greatest performances. Also in Las Vegas, a newly renamed and renovated Elvis Presley International Showroom presents Elvis-themed live shows on the very stage where Elvis performed from 1969 to 1976. And to complete the new Las Vegas attractions, there is the city's first-ever wedding venue to be operated by Elvis Presley Enterprises. When the venue's first couple were married there, Priscilla acted as matron of honour. 'Elvis is synonymous with Las Vegas,' said David Siegel, of Westgate Resorts. 'After a 40-year absence, it's time for the authentic Elvis Presley to return to Las Vegas,' said Joel Weinshanker.[22]

Across the Atlantic, an ambitious exhibition telling Elvis's life story was staged in London at the O2 arena. Items on show ranged from Elvis's birth certificate to his pink Cadillac, his family Bible and his gold telephone. It opened in December 2014 and was due to close in August 2015, but such was its popularity that it was extended several more months. The box-office ticket sales confirmed Elvis as a highly marketable commodity in Europe, and Elvis fans from mainland Europe travelled to London to see the items on show.

Expectations of the new management were high, but fans were acutely aware that Graceland's fortunes continued to be linked to those of an outside company with other substantial interests. The viability of Graceland as a business remains vulnerable as long as it can still theoretically be damaged by failure in some unrelated commercial area to which it is now linked. That the Elvis image is now in the hands of brand-focused New York financiers is again a matter of concern to some fans. Will the new owners honour the integrity of the Elvis image? Might they sanction profitable enterprises of which Elvis would not have approved? Is the residual family interest in the business sufficient to guarantee that the Elvis brand evolves in a way in which the fans would approve? With Elvis now an investment, there will be no emotional barriers to exploiting his memory. While Lisa Marie can have some influence, ultimately she can do little to prevent her father being used to generate profit in whatever way the investors perceive as most lucrative.

In August 2014 Graceland, in a new commercial initiative for the business, held the first-ever Elvis Week auction of memorabilia when 72 authenticated items owned by third-party collectors went under the hammer. Many of the lots on offer had been owned by Greg Page, one of the world's leading collectors. A gold and diamond lion's head pendant that Presley wore to meet President Richard Nixon fetched $82,500 – well above its estimated value of $25,000 to $35,000. A maroon and silver 1977 Seville, the last Cadillac Presley bought for his own use, was sold for $81,250. One of the surprises of the auction was the $27,500 paid for a paper target riddled with bullet holes, which had been fired at by Elvis Presley at his personal shooting range.

As part of the Elvis eightieth birthday celebrations in January 2015, Elvis Presley Enterprises promoted a second auction. Sixty-seven items were put up for auction and again many items sold for much more than the auctioneer's estimates. It was thought that the only surviving copy of Elvis's first recording might fetch up to $100,000, but the buyer paid three times that amount. For $300,000 the buyer acquired a unique piece of Elvis history. The 78-rpm acetate was recorded in 1953 by the eighteen-year-old Elvis, who had walked off the street into Sun Studio and paid $4 to cut a disc as a present for his mother. He sang two songs, 'My Happiness' and 'That's When Your Heartaches Begin'. When the studio receptionist took his dollars, she asked him about his style: who did he sing like? Elvis replied, 'I don't sound like nobody.' She had the presence of mind to note his name and phone number.

The auction was a success and eight months later during Elvis Week there was a third auction of what Graceland described as rare and authentic Elvis Presley artefacts and memorabilia. It should be noted that Graceland was not selling off its own family silver. The items for sale came from collectors or friends and associates of Elvis whose families had had the good fortune to inherit items of interest that could be authenticated by Graceland. What was significant is that having opposed and then taken control of the Elvis tribute competitions, the Graceland business arm was now attempting to dominate the sale of Elvis collectibles. Will the day come when investors start to sell off any of the physical assets of the Elvis business they have acquired? Obviously those still owned by the family cannot be sold without their permission, but there are other items whose ownership is more ambiguous.

A worrying rumour circulated in August 2014 of an unwelcome initiative. Elvis's private jets, *Lisa Marie* and *Hound Dog II*, were to be moved and taken off site. It was reported that the new Graceland management had notified the planes' owners that they should prepare to remove the jets early in 2015. The planes are owned by the Memphis-based OKC Partnership. In a letter to K. G. Coker of OKC, Jack Soden said the company was ending the agreement and asked Coker to remove the planes and restore the site by 26 April 2015. When the planes were parked at Graceland originally, the deal was that the owners would leave them on long-term loan in exchange for a share of the ticket sales. 'I would love to see the aeroplanes stay where they are forever,' Coker said. 'Millions of fans have toured those airplanes and there's a real connection between fans and those airplanes. Those airplanes are part of the Elvis experience.'[23]

A protest petition was started by a group of fans. A compromise was suggested by which the aircraft might be moved to a new site nearby. There was speculation as to why Graceland would want a proven attraction dismantled and the general conclusion was that the planes took up space that would be more profitably used for retail or hotel accommodation. And if the management were prepared to remove the planes, what might happen next? Might their business initiatives include, one day, allowing visitors access to the upstairs of the mansion house? Think how visitor numbers would be boosted if people could see the actual bathroom where Elvis died.

Fans started a petition in 2014 when rumours circulated that Elvis's jets were to be moved from their parking spot opposite Graceland to free up space for new retail outlets. The planes are still there.

Fans willing to dwell on the positive consequences of Elvis being sold on to business interests dream of what might happen should substantial dollars be available for a range of exciting new Elvis investments. The technology is being developed to let Elvis live again – virtually. Fans have already had a foretaste of the possibilities. In 2007 Elvis appeared on the television show *American Idol*, singing with Celine Dion. The producers had used footage taken from an Elvis show and digitally manipulated it before cunningly projecting it to give a highly convincing onstage performance. There is also a travelling Elvis Show that combines live performers, including some original Elvis band members, backing Elvis, who is seen on giant screens. For a member of the audience, especially one near the back of the auditorium, who would only see the performer as a tiny figure in the distance, and who would enjoy the show from the big screen image, it is like seeing a live Elvis show for real. The show's concept, says

EPE, is to present an 'authentic as possible' Elvis Presley concert. The producers edited together a collection of Elvis's finest concert performances that exist on film and video and removed all sound from the footage except for Elvis's vocal. The Elvis footage is projected onto a large video screen. On stage a sixteen-piece orchestra performs live with Elvis singing. The new screen show has travelled extensively to where the fans are and to places Elvis never reached. It is the world tour Elvis never managed to pull off in his own lifetime.

Yet bringing Elvis back to life electronically could go much further. When the rapper Tupac Shakur was shot and killed on 13 September 1996, at the age of 25, his fans believed they would never see him perform again. Yet in April 2012 he walked on stage at the Coachella festival and sang. He performed some classic tracks and bantered with the real life Snoop Dogg and Dr Dre. Tupac's muscular, tattooed, bare torso appeared as if in the flesh. It was weird, compelling and scary, said eyewitnesses.

What the audience saw was an image, an extraordinarily lifelike recreation by a company called Digital Domain Media Group Inc. It was, of course, says its creator and visual effects expert, Ed Ulbrich, an illusion. It was called a hologram by the media, which was not an entirely accurate description of the technology involved. It was a blend of new digital and hologram creations with a classic stage illusion known as Pepper's Ghost. As Ed Ulbrich put it, it was 'smoke and mirrors with modern technology'.

The significance to the Elvis story is that the Tupac illusion is just the start of the process. The illusion Ed Ulbrich's team is currently working on is recreating Elvis. What made the Tupac performance such a leap forward was that it was not old footage being shown, but a genuine digital recreation. 'This is not found footage. This is not archival footage. This is an illusion,' Ed Ulbrich said. It lasted only a few minutes, but came as such a surprise to the audience that 'they went wild at the magic!' It was of course pre-rendered material. There was nothing spontaneous about the performance, but one day, says Ed Ulbrich, it might even be possible to build spontaneity into the virtual act. 'One day dead entertainers will appear on stage as if they are real.'[24]

The legal and ethical implications of such possibilities are huge. Many unanswered questions arise. Would those with the current legal claim to exploit Elvis's image have the right to veto or license such recreations of Elvis? Who owns the digitally created likeness of Elvis?

The opportunities for reintroducing Elvis to future generations will be enormous, as will be the cost: there will have to be substantial investment. The Tupac illusion took several months of planning and four months of studio time, with a budget reckoned in the hundreds of thousands of dollars. The technology is currently very expensive, but so many developments that were once prohibitively expensive have become affordable, there is no telling what might be achieved.

The Followers, the Faithful and the Fanatics

Future investment in the Elvis brand will depend on how the investors assess and value the market. Will there be a sufficient number of Elvis fans in the future to justify expensive hi-tech projects and do the Elvis fans have the spending power to make such projects viable? Measuring the growth potential of the Elvis business is difficult as the size of the current fan base is hard to pin down. How many Elvis fans are there around the world? Many thousands certainly, but it might even be millions. How has that figure changed over time? Is it growing, or might interest in Elvis be declining as the generation that knew him alive fades away? Are new younger fans coming into the fold, and, if so, at what rate?

There are some useful snapshot opinions to be had. One person in a strong position to judge is Robert 'Butch' Polston, who runs one of the biggest independent Elvis businesses in the world, BK Enterprises, working for and with Elvis tribute artists. His business, which sources and provides Elvis costumes, started three years after Elvis's death.

I've watched this thing that I helped create go from fifteen tribute artists to thousands worldwide! It is growing and it has become a family event where the love of Elvis is handed down from parents to children and from children to grand-children. I see no end in sight any time soon. There are new Elvis fans every day. Some kids 4 and 5 years old see him in a movie or one of the two documentaries made about him and it is amazing to watch the beauty of life light up in their wondrous eyes.[1]

Some Elvis facts can be quantified: the numbers of visitors to Graceland, sales of records or downloads in a year. Website hits too can be tallied. It is from these figures, plus anecdotal evidence and observation, that an attempt can be made to gauge the current interest in Elvis and track how it is evolving.

At the Graceland mansion there is a steady stream of visitors all year round, either paying to tour the house and grounds or simply stopping outside for a photograph or to leave a message on the wall. The 1.5-metre-high, 140-metre-long wall that bounds the highway is covered with signatures and messages. By 2012, thirty years since opening to the public, Graceland had seen eighteen million visitors arrive through the famous music-motif gates. It is one of the five most visited homes in the United States, and it is claimed that it is the most famous home in America after the White House. The daily attendance ranges from a few hundred visitors on a weekday in the dead of winter to 2,000–3,500 visitors per day in the spring and early summer, to over 4,000 per day in July at the height of the travel season. The peak season dates from Memorial Day through to Labor Day (late May to the beginning of September). Visitor numbers hit a peak in Elvis Week in mid-August when the King's death is marked. This annual peak is especially pronounced in years marking landmark anniversaries. The traditional vigil and all-night candlelit procession around the grounds attracts in excess of 70,000 fans in a significant year. To cope with the number of visitors, approximately 350 staff are employed through the year, a number that swells to as many as 450 in the busy summer season.

The annual visitor number touched the 700,000 mark in 2005 and has since fallen. In 2010 a 4 per cent drop in visitor numbers was reported, from 540,000 in a year to 510,000, and prompted the estate to re-examine the attractions on offer. There was no evidence that Elvis himself was a diminishing attraction, but there were reasons to suspect that his home needed upgrading to meet twenty-first-century expectations. While the house and grounds remained sacrosanct, there was much scope to improve the museums, gift shops and other facilities across the road. Marketing managers were aware that as a visitor attraction Graceland was in competition not only with other heritage sites and museums, but with family-orientated theme parks as well. This was especially relevant to Americans taking domestic vacations.

For several years the Graceland management had been aware of the numbers of visitors who pass by and look but do not buy a ticket for a tour. Some will have seen the house before and will be making a brief drive-by visit to look from a distance, or stopping briefly to linger with the crowds by the wall. Sometimes wedding or birthday party groups stop by for a quick photocall using Graceland as the backdrop. Others might want to tick the 'we've seen Graceland' box but have no real interest in spending two or more hours walking around reverentially. Some visitors may be deterred from staying too long at Graceland, as parts of the surrounding neighbourhood appear run down and rough.

Like all leisure attractions, Graceland's income and visitor numbers can be affected by the wider economic conditions. Fans who once made an annual visit to Graceland may for financial reasons decide that every other year will suffice. Tickets are not cheap. In 2013 it cost an adult couple $140 to visit the mansion and all the other attractions on offer. Those who decided not to go to the museums and to forgo a look inside the private jets still had to pay $33 a head to go through the Graceland gates. Raw attendance figures do not therefore produce as reliable a guide to the waxing or waning of Elvis's popularity as might be hoped.

A special effort was made in 2012 to attract extra numbers for the 35th anniversary of the King's death. Elvis's daughter, Lisa Marie, and her mother, Priscilla, attended. The following year had no special commemorative significance; anecdotal evidence suggests the numbers were down, perhaps by as much as 50 per cent. Come 2017 and the fortieth anniversary there may be another surge and attendance records could be challenged. Until then Graceland's fortunes will most likely ebb and flow in line with the strength or weakness of the economy. And there will always be Elvis fans prevented from travelling to Graceland due to illness, disability or financial circumstances who will never be included in the count. It can be seen that exploring the world of Elvis fandom simply by counting visitors to Graceland has its limitations. What must be encouraging to the new investors is the figure that more than half of Graceland's visitors are under the age of 35 and by 2015, according to some newspaper reports, visitor numbers to Graceland were rising again and were now at more than 600,000 a year.[2]

The highlight of the Elvis year is the week leading up to 16 August, the anniversary of the singer's death. It is known by fans around the world as Elvis Week and every true fan hopes to attend at least once in a lifetime. Many fans who can afford the time and the costs of travelling and staying in Memphis in mid-August make Elvis Week an annual pilgrimage. The week culminates with a candlelit procession at Graceland, allowing fans to walk through the mansion gardens to the grave in solemn remembrance. During Elvis Week 2013 I made an assessment of the make-up of the crowd by monitoring the video feed from Graceland of the procession. Individuals could be clearly seen as they lit their candles from one of the main torches. A random sample of 350 was taken and the walkers categorized by gender and age. While gender was mostly easy to gauge, age was less so. A visual assessment was made to categorize who was over the age of 45, who was adult but younger than 45 and who was a child under fourteen. Obviously there was room for error in this process – some people look old before their time, others age slowly – but it gave a rough guide. Of the adults taking part, 69.5 per cent were women, 30.5 per cent men. Of the total number counted, 48 per cent were considered to be under 45 years of age and 52 per cent over. In the younger age group 13 per cent were men and 87 per cent women. In the older age group 43.5 per cent were men and 56.5 per cent women. Out of the total number, 5.5 per cent were children who appeared to be under fourteen years of age.

This snapshot of Elvis fandom showed participants to be overwhelmingly white, but they represented a wide range of nations, as judged from additional evidence such as broadcast interviews, inscriptions on T-shirts, flags carried and other indicators. American citizens appeared nevertheless to constitute a large majority.

The annual procession is a truly remarkable sight, not dissimilar to processions seen at such pilgrimage sites as the healing shrine of Lourdes. Over the years the evening's rituals have become so well established that they now feel timeless. The crowd gathers outside the gate as the darkness falls. As the light fails, the conversation quietens. The mood changes from that of a party to one of solemn remembrance. The act of moving in an orderly disciplined line can be compared to meditation. Everyone moves towards the same place – the graveside – and files past respectfully and prayerfully. Fan club presidents and their members stand at the entrance to the Graceland driveway as the honour guard, twenty at a time, changing every twenty minutes all through the night as the thousands of fans file past. It is an individual rite that creates a unique sense of being at one with the whole company.

Adrian Sainz of Associated Press filed this evocative copy from the scene at 11.11 pm on 15 August 2013. 'Wreaths of flowers and pictures of Presley encircled the grave, while shadows cast by the glowing candles danced along the stone wall surrounding the garden. Soft music played in the mild night, as some in the procession bowed their heads or cried quietly.' Sainz spoke to one fan making her fifth trip to Graceland. On the back of the shirts worn by her and her husband were the words, 'If you have a friend who is an Elvis fan, you have a friend for life.' 'Where else can you go where you meet people from year to year who have the same passion?' she said. To her, the vigil was a way to remember not only his career, but his generous personality and 'ability to make people happy with his music. If you were sad or happy or whatever, he was such a big part of your life.' One man in the crowd was a first-time visitor from Chile. '"It's hard to believe," he said, "that I'm here on the street where he walked, the street corners where he stood, the restaurants where he ate."'[3]

It is not, however, necessary to travel to Memphis to take the temperature of Elvis fandom. The 2014–15 Elvis exhibition at London's O2 provided one of several other such opportunities. Fans moved through the darkened exhibition halls at the pace of a pilgrimage procession, pausing to read and admire. But the mood was not entirely sombre. Some visitors started dancing when foot-tapping Elvis music was played. Attendees observed on one sample day in July were 60 per cent female, 40 per cent male. There were few children, as it was still during the school term, but under-35s appeared to be well represented and were present in numbers almost equal to those of the older Elvis fans.

A wider picture of who the Elvis fans are, and one not solely based on those attending events, can be found in the work of Professor Patsy Hammontree from the University of Tennessee, who conducted a study of Elvis fans. She made this observation about the fans as a whole.

There is a general misconception that only undereducated women on a lower socioeconomic level constitute the Elvis Presley audience. Rather, his audience is comprised of an incredibly variegated group of people from all economic and social levels.

Chronologically, the spectrum stretches from age five to 85. And large numbers of men – including construction workers and physicians – admire Elvis. It is virtually impossible to draw a profile of the Elvis Presley fan because of such diversity, a factor that also precludes any standardized label being applicable to the mass audience. Elvis's popularity was international. He had millions of followers in both Europe and Asia. There are Presley fan clubs even in the Middle East. Someone said boys and girls were wearing Elvis Presley T-shirts in the jungles of Thailand. The diversity of even a sampling attests to the Presley cultural phenomenon. In truth, the man takes on mythic and archetypal dimensions such that for some fans only Christ is greater.[4]

Elvis's appeal to many women might be thought relatively simple to explain. He had sex appeal and female fans simply feel in love. Yet, if that is the extent of his appeal, it leaves a huge unanswered question. What was, and remains, his attraction to men? 'He had that amazing voice – which was sexy for women', said the songwriter Doug Flett, 'but reached guys as well.'[5]

Elvis was a role model like no other. What Elvis had, whatever it was, other men wanted. Therein perhaps lies part of the explanation. This desire to be Elvis-like is not restricted to the generation influenced by the early Elvis, when to be like Elvis was a guaranteed way to annoy the adults, something many teenagers of the time were delighted to do. A 2010 survey conducted by a shampoo company identified Elvis's quiff as the most iconic 'classic' men's haircut of all time, with 50 per cent of men voting the King's haircut as their favourite. The David Beckham look had only 17 per cent support.

It can be said too that the intimacy of his voice transcended gender. He sang to women as if he were whispering private endearments; he sang to men as their best friend sharing something privileged and confidential. Some men have taken on the role of Elvis substitutes. They nurture the Elvis look, not only because they are fans, but because it is a way to capture the attention of Elvis's female followers. Many Elvis tribute artists enjoy the attention, and in some cases adoration, they receive when in character.

If it was once assumed that Elvis fans defined themselves by class, and were predominantly from what are perceived as the lower classes, this is an assumption that has long been confounded. In May 2014 Graceland, the home of the King, received a visit from a future king. Prince William, the Duke of Cambridge, his brother Prince Harry and their two cousins Princesses Beatrice and Eugenie were in Memphis for a friend's wedding. The opportunity to pay their respects to Elvis was not to be missed by the party of young British royals. Prince William was born in 1982, five years after Elvis died; Prince Harry in 1984. But nevertheless the power of the Elvis myth drew them and they made the same pilgrimage to Graceland that millions of others have done, one royal dynasty paying court to another. Among the best-known

Elvis is a name recognized around the world. Say 'Elvis' in Moscow, Soweto, Rio de Janeiro or Bangkok and there will be immediate recognition.

Elvis fans are presidents and prime ministers as well as princes. 'Elvis Presley was the first and the best. He is my favourite of all time,' famously claimed that celebrated alpha male Bill Clinton. When in 2013, Sir Paul McCartney of Beatles fame visited Graceland, he left a guitar pick on Elvis's grave, 'so that Elvis can play in heaven'. In 2006 the Japanese prime minister Junichiro Koizumi was given a personal tour of Graceland by Priscilla and Lisa Marie Presley and is reported to have burst into song with a few bars of 'Love Me Tender' in the Jungle Room. He had flown to Memphis with President George W. Bush, who arranged for him to be served with fried peanut butter and banana sandwiches on board Air Force One. The prime minister and his brother, Masaya, had been members of the Elvis Presley fan club in Tokyo for more than thirty years. The premier and Elvis also shared the same birthday. In 2001 a Japanese record label produced a charity CD of Junichiro Koizumi's favourite Elvis songs. A digitally altered image on the cover showed the politician standing alongside Elvis at Graceland.

Why is Elvis still so influential, nearly forty years after his death? It's a question the British journalist Harry Mount posed in a short book, *The King and I* (2013), which he described as 'the story of my obsession with Elvis'. Harry Mount is blue-blooded, British establishment to the core. He is a cousin to the prime minister David Cameron. He went to the same school as Cameron's one-time deputy Nick Clegg and then to the University of Oxford. He is a self-confessed lover of the languages of the ancient classic cultures. He was barely six when Elvis died, although was aware of the impact of the event in that he saw the mother of a school friend in tears. He admits to having been obsessed with the singer from an early age. He acknowledges that it was unfashionable when he was young to admit to liking Elvis. He rehearses all the old justifications of the hardened Elvis fan – mentioning the allure of the voice and, despite the years of decline, the charisma – but ultimately fails to truly describe why Elvis took hold of his

Fans on pilgrimage to Memphis leave thousands of messages every year on the wall outside of Graceland. They include prayers to Elvis asking for healing and blessings.

soul. He visited Graceland as a young man and pretended not to take it all too seriously, yet admitted almost 25 years later how he was in truth profoundly moved by the visit.

Without quite knowing why, Mount and Koizumi and their like are serious Elvis fans. Many musicians are not only fans, but own up to Elvis being the major influence in their lives and careers. 'Hearing him for the first time was like busting out of jail,' said Bob Dylan. 'When we were kids growing up in Liverpool, all we ever wanted to be was Elvis Presley,' recalled Paul McCartney. 'I grew my hair like him, imitated his stage act, once I went all over New York looking for a lavender shirt like the one he wore on one of his albums,' Paul Simon recalls. Elvis was the big brother to be looked up to, admired for his style and imitated.[6]

Yet in trying to assess how many fans there are worldwide, how does one define a fan? Are fans those who simply like his music? Does a fan also need to have bought an Elvis item at some time to qualify? Is a true fan only someone who has made the trip to Graceland or been to hear a tribute artist?

There are clearly some fans so utterly obsessed with the King that Elvis has taken over their lives. The late owner of Graceland Too at Holly Springs, Mississippi, Paul MacLeod, lived and breathed Elvis Presley in a house that was filled with souvenirs from top to bottom. For many years he, and for a while his son, made himself available to show visitors around 24 hours a day, keeping himself awake with high-caffeinated cola. There was not a room, wall or space anywhere in the house that did not contain something of relevance to Elvis. Paul and his son, who was of course named Elvis, described themselves, apparently in all seriousness, as 'the universe's, galaxy's, planet's, world's ultimate number one Elvis fans'.[7]

MacLeod died in July 2014 in tragic circumstances, indirectly as result of defending his home and life's collection. His death, from natural causes, occurred just two days after an incident at Graceland Too in which an intruder had forced his way in and demanded money. MacLeod shot and killed him. The Holly Springs police said that MacLeod would not face charges, but the strain and shock of the events proved too much for him. He was 71 and had been in poor health for a while. As a tribute to his enthusiasm and dedication, fans made a special trip to his house for a vigil just before Elvis Week a month later.

There is however a spectrum of enthusiasm: Paul MacLeod and his like are at one far end of a spectrum that extends through to the many thousands of people worldwide who listen to his music with enjoyment, but do not allow Elvis to dominate their lives. Of the thousands of Elvis fans worldwide, many fell in love with the King when they and he were young. Over the ensuing decades they have never deserted him. The lucky ones even saw him in concert. They might still own and treasure an autograph, a scarf or even a ring as an irreplaceable souvenir of the day. Today these fans are no longer besotted teenagers, but mature women with husbands, homes, children and grandchildren, or ageing men with paunches and receding hairlines. To them, why Elvis? is a question they would never think of asking. The answer is so obvious. He is the air they breathe. For some, he is their reason for living. 'If you're an Elvis fan, no explanation is necessary; If you're not an Elvis fan, no explanation is possible,' observed Elvis's friend George Klein.[8]

Yet the Elvis generation is an ageing generation. If the appeal of Elvis were restricted to his contemporaries, the Elvis phenomenon would now be on the decline. That, however, is not the case. All the evidence suggests that Elvis is not fading from memory. Whether judged by music sales, visits to Graceland, trading in souvenirs, attendance at tribute concerts, website hits or any other indicators, it appears that as the old fans age and die, new fans are emerging to take their place. The new fans are young men and women who had not been born when Elvis died in 1977. Indeed, today 60 per cent of the population of the world falls into that category: the post-Elvis generation.

Certainly knowledge of and enthusiasm for Elvis is being passed from generation to generation through families. In the same way that children of Conservatives or Democrats are likely to 'inherit' their parents' political habits and children of Methodists or Mormons are likely to share their parents' religious affiliations, so the descendants of Elvis fans are more likely themselves to be followers of the King than if they had not been brought up in an Elvis household. The influence is felt young. A 2013 video clip that was seen by thousands, having done the rounds of the social networks, showed twenty-month-old toddler Ella Mae receiving a good Elvis education. From the moment her father plays 'An American Trilogy', she starts singing along. On the Internet clip she is seen in her car seat shouting 'here it goes, get ready' just before the flute solo.

Family ties do not explain everything. Inevitably some children kick against their parents' enthusiasms and would rather be punks or goths: anything but Elvis! What also seems to be happening is that Elvis is acquiring converts: people with nothing but a casual awareness of Elvis are discovering him for themselves.

That wider casual awareness of Elvis is not fading. There is much evidence for this, but one of the more light-hearted examples comes from the American game show *Family Feud*. The show posed this question for one of its surveys. 'When someone mentions the King, to whom might he or she be referring?' Eighty-one out of a hundred respondents said Elvis: Jesus scored seven and Burger King two.

Perhaps one way to gauge the breadth and depth of fandom is to look at various kinds of enthusiasts: there are the fan club members, the consumers of Elvis music and art, the Elvis tribute artists and the growing army of online devotees. Some of the ways fans appreciate Elvis were, thanks to modern technology, utterly inconceivable in Elvis's day.

One of the defining Elvis rooms seen by visitors on the Graceland tour is his television room. The famous Jungle Room in the mansion house demonstrates how fashions in interior design have moved on since Elvis's day, but the television witnesses the huge technological changes over the last three and a half decades. It must astonish younger visitors to see how basic the technological equipment was in his day. To him it was the latest and most up-to-date electronic gadgetry on the market; to the modern generation it looks as heritage as a Model T Ford or steam train. The chunky analogue television sets, pre-dating wide- and flatscreen televisions by forty years, are as dated as the decor, with its settees and scatter cushions, where Elvis lounged with his entourage. It is like an exhibit in a museum of social history, for when Elvis died the technological revolution that has created the Internet, the World Wide Web, mobile phones, iPods and multiple high-definition television channels was still far in the future. As the technological changes have taken hold, they have had an impact on Elvis fans. Today fans still meet up to enjoy Elvis moments in each other's physical company, but between times they are prolific users of social media such as Facebook and Twitter to swap Elvis stories and experiences.

Even though online social networks are gradually replacing the old fan clubs, the clubs remain an integral part of the Elvis network. There have been Elvis fan clubs since the first years of Elvis's career, when they were encouraged by his manager Colonel Parker. He saw them as a useful marketing network to promote the star and through which to sell merchandise. Local fan clubs helped spread the word about upcoming performances in their area. Today the Elvis estate is similarly encouraging. New clubs can apply for official recognition by contacting the Graceland head office and filling out a registration form. Some clubs like to include the fact that they are 'official' in their title. The Official Elvis Presley Fan Club of Great Britain is one of those. Other clubs choose more exotic titles to reflect the particular interests, or sense of humour, of the founding members. There is the All Shook up N Vegas fan club, the Burning Love 4 Elvis club, the Can't Help Falling In Love With Elvis club, the Kentucky Rain Keeps Pouring Down club, the intriguingly titled Memphis Teddy Bear Project and a club for fans with disabilities called, after the Elvis song, Walk a Mile in My Shoes, to give just a few examples. Individual fans may also decide to invest in Graceland's Elvis Insider membership, joining 'Elvis fans around the world in the ultimate Elvis fan group!', as the members' website claims. In doing so they are also offered, in the true spirit of the enterprising Colonel, a range of money-saving deals, the club also helps to promote Elvis events on behalf of the organizers.

The geographical spread of fan clubs has been wide, with officially approved fan bases in 31 countries. The Canadian-based Wonder of Elvis Fan Club offers practical advice to fans visiting Graceland. 'Make sure you bring a Sharpie marker with you so you can sign the wall surrounding Graceland!' 'Purchase the VIP Tour of Graceland. You can go through the Mansion as many times as you like in one day. Take the last tour of the day. This is normally a very quiet time and it is incredible to have the house to yourself!'

In addition to the officially approved clubs there are numerous other Elvis groups of varying size that prefer to have no formal links with the Graceland organization. Some of these unofficial Elvis clubs are openly critical of the estate, accusing it of demeaning Elvis's memory in a relentless pursuit of profit. In 2010, for instance, one dedicated Elvis fan, Steven Roberts, expressed 'disgust' at a sales catalogue that had been mailed to him. The Elvis 75th Birthday Popcorn Tin advertised as coming with 'banana flavored popcorn and peanuts'. He called it 'hideous in appearance. The sheer idea that people are going to be eating popcorn out of this thing while watching his movies dressed head to toe in images of Elvis, is just downright insulting.' He also highlighted what he called 'the ugliest stupidest T-shirt I have ever seen'. His list went on for several pages, ending with a message for the Graceland marketing department. 'We are not going to stand for this garbage and the smearing of our favorite singer.'[9]

There is no need to travel to Graceland to see Elvis fans en masse. They gather at the huge variety of Elvis festivals held through the year and around the world. In the USA fans have several to choose from. In October, for instance, Indiana welcomes Elvis fans with the Elvis Fantasy Fest in Portage. In Georgia, fans are able to attend a Christmas celebration of the King in Dublin, and four months later enjoy another Elvis festival at Brunswick. The annual Las Vegas festival is a July event, where fans can find out who wins the Heart of the King Awards. Then, after the Memphis Elvis Week, dedicated fans can move on to South Carolina for a festival at Newberry in September or travel to Europe's biggest Elvis event at Porthcawl, UK. Elvis fans descend on the Welsh seaside town in their thousands to celebrate the King. In 2014 the local police estimated that over the four-day event the town had 30,000 visitors, although not all were attendees. The featured events take place in the Grand Pavilion, but there are over twenty other venues, making Porthcawl the largest Elvis event in Europe. It's an opportunity for dancing, dressing up, drinking, meeting friends and some serious party-going. The evidence of video footage posted online suggests the participants average just over forty years of age and are overwhelmingly white. Porthcawl is even larger, it is claimed, than the Elvis gathering at Bad Nauheim, where Elvis began the German stint of his military service in October 1958. Every year since 2002 the town has marked the anniversary of his death and while thousands of fans gather at Graceland, many who are unable to cross the Atlantic go to Bad Nauheim. Over several days in August Elvis takes over the town. There are Elvis tribute artist concerts, screenings of films and a parade of Cadillacs. Even allowing for some fans attending more than one festival, it is estimated that in excess of 100,000 Elvis fans travel to at least one of the Elvis events every year. Around 1,000 fans attend the annual Elvis Festival at the English seaside resort of Great Yarmouth, which 'just keeps getting bigger', say the organizers.

Elvis is now available 24 hours a day to fans courtesy of the Internet, DVD players and personal stereos, but there are still times when the main broadcasters decide to hold an on-air Elvis event, not just for the fans, but for the wider population. In November 2013 the UK commercial network ITV1 ran a ninety-minute countdown special of the top twenty Elvis songs. The programme attracted 4.6 million viewers on the night, 22 per cent of the entire television audience at that time, a figure with which the broadcaster declared itself very satisfied.

That the number of Elvis fans in the UK and around the world is substantial is borne out by the Elvis Facebook page, which has been 'liked' nine million times. On Facebook a reader of a page has the option to press the 'Like' button to register their support and approval for it. In addition, separate stories posted on the page attracted their own likes: 21,000 Facebook members liked the 2013 candlelit vigil; the Ultimate Elvis Tribute winner received 13,000 acknowledgements.

Elvis does not lead the field when it comes to Facebook endorsement, however. President Obama has 36 million likes, Manchester United has 34 million and both are well behind Bob Marley with 48 million and Michael Jackson with 63 million.[10] The tallies of Facebook likes are governed by several factors: how long the page has been in existence, and how adept at, and interested in, social networking followers might be. Facebook likes, while a useful indication of interest, are not a definitive guide. There is a huge appreciation of Mozart worldwide, but his Facebook page has fewer than three million likes. The page is not in any sense an 'official' page and lovers of Mozart are probably of a generation or social group disinclined to network in cyberspace. But surely Mozart is not less popular or influential than Michael Bublé, who has 6,500,000 supporters?

Elvis's online presence makes him the King of Digital, claims Elvis Presley Enterprises. Together with app downloads, Facebook likes, more than five million unique visitors annually to Elvis.com, and significant activity on Twitter, YouTube and other social media, the King rules over a new virtual kingdom. The online radio stations devoted exclusively to Elvis's music broadcast in a variety of languages and are examples of a new phenomenon: that of specialist audio stations that only became possible with the Internet. There are an estimated 51,000 online radio stations targeted at listeners with specialist interests and not surprisingly several of them are devoted to Elvis.

A popular one is Elvis Matters Radio, which broadcasts Elvis music 24 hours a day around the world from Amsterdam. The official Elvis Radio broadcasts from a studio at Graceland via a satellite network. It has speech as well as music content and programmes Elvis thematically. A Sunday morning gospel show is described as two hours of the best Elvis Southern gospel music ever recorded, 'guaranteed to keep your weekend positive in the most righteous manner', the schedule notes promise. There's also a daily Elvis show with a Hollywood theme and a regular Elvis quiz. Once an Elvis fan had to place stacks of single records physically on a turntable to listen to the King. Today a fan can have Elvis in the ears all day and all night via a personal selection of music chosen online and downloaded or via one of the non-stop Elvis channels.

Elvis also remains popular in the live theatre, and several musicals with an Elvis theme have been staged. In 2015 a new musical based on Elvis's music, *Love Me Tender*, made a UK tour, visiting fifteen cities. The musical, which weaves Elvis music into the action, is set in a small American town in the 1950s and is based around a guitar-playing, hip-swivelling stranger who rides his motorbike into town. It is one of several Presley-themed musicals to have been staged, a theatrical tradition that goes back at least to 1977, when a jukebox musical entitled *Elvis* ran in London's West End. In 2004 *Jailhouse Rock*, based on the film of the same name, ran at London's Piccadilly Theatre, and the show *Million Dollar Quartet* featured Elvis Presley tunes and others by rock stars of the same era.

If Internet statistics and theatre bookings give a guide to quantity of fandom, they are not so reliable when judging quality. How does one quantify the intensity of the devotion of an Elvis fan? One measure of the obsession is the depth of grief felt at that unique moment in history when his death was announced.

I was listening to the radio. Suddenly a lady came on . . . with the news that Elvis had died. It was as if something hit my head. Something crashed inside me . . . The cups in my hand fell into the sink. For that day I was like a robot. I had no appetite for anything.[11]

It was on the news and I just sat and cried all day. I couldn't believe Elvis had died. I sat and watched the television over and over again. I cried. I couldn't believe it. I took my children to school, came back and cried. I couldn't go to work. It was too emotional, too upsetting. Horrible.[12]

We said we would kill ourselves. I was 10 and my sister was 11. If Elvis died we would kill ourselves. It seriously crossed our minds. Very seriously.[13]

Thankfully, many, many more people live for Elvis than have died for him. They do not just live for him, but live through him. They choose their clothes to match the Elvis style. They dye their hair, wear Elvis jewellery and mimic his gait and speech. Elvis fans have changed their names and named their children in honour of the King. They listen to no other music but that of Elvis. Their social lives revolve around Elvis events, they turn to Elvis at times of anxiety and their purchasing decisions are dictated by the Elvis merchandising industry.

The Billion-dollar Question

When he died, Elvis's earning power as a performer was declining steeply. Today the dead Elvis is taking care of a vast business whose size is a good guide to both the extent and the intensity of his contemporary following. In 2013 Forbes, the leading business information company, reported Elvis as being second in the ranking of top-earning dead celebrities. With $55 million in earnings, the King of Rock 'n' Roll pulled in the same amount as he had done both in 2011 and 2012, despite the Cirque du Soleil Elvis show in Vegas producing disappointing returns. Top of the list, with earnings of $160 million, was Michael Jackson. Unlike Elvis, who sold off the royalties to his music, Michael Jackson bought up rights. His estate not only earns from sales of his own music, but from a 50 per cent stake in Sony's ATV catalogue, which includes artists such as The Beatles and Lady Gaga.

In terms of overall earnings, the King of Rock 'n' Roll may have been runner-up to the 'King of Pop' over the past few years, but Elvis's estate is still earning steadily and what the Forbes figures did not reflect were the unofficial Elvis earnings. The combined incomes of the tribute artists were not collated; neither was the income accumulated by independent Elvis traders who sell souvenirs, Graceland trips or memorabilia. Not included, for instance, was the $37 million raised at auction when Andy Warhol's *Double Elvis* picture was sold. Undoubtedly those of

Elvis's financial affairs which have remained in the hands of his estate have improved considerably over the years since his death. One can only speculate as to what his income would be if he had been managed as shrewdly as Jackson in the first place. What can be said is that while Jackson's earnings are made up of a portfolio of business interests, Elvis's main asset is himself and his enduring appeal.

Putting a value on Elvis's appeal is almost impossible. It is even difficult to calculate just how much Elvis music has been and is still sold. Not only are marketing campaigns often based on national or local strategies, but there are considerable overlaps when it comes to the production of new albums, with tracks appearing in various permutations in several different compilations and box sets. The way music is distributed since Elvis first hit the big time has also changed radically.

Is he the most popular recording artist of all time, as his fans claim? Is he the only artist to have sold one billion recordings? Nick Keene researched the claims for Elvis Australia.

The Presley figures have not been immune to the odd spot of massaging over the years. Elvis did not sell 1 billion records by 1982 which claim first appeared via an article in the Washington Post dated 12 July of that year and quoted RCA as its source, nor is there any validity in the current claim of 1.5 billion – whatever Sony BMG may say in the liner notes on the back of one or two recent DVD releases. Rest assured my investigations reveal that Elvis is still by some distance the greatest record seller of all time, but even 26 years later it is no easy task trying to establish whether or not his sales have actually exceeded one billion copies.[1]

Or, as the Graceland website put it, 'no statistics should ever make us feel different about Elvis or any other artist. We don't judge Chopin, Charlie Parker or Bob Dylan by their sales figures.'

Whatever the figures of historical sales might be, in the context of Elvis's posthumous legacy, it is current sales that matter. In 2005 Elvis topped the UK singles chart three times. In 2015 Elvis topped the UK album charts for a twelfth time, more number ones than any other male solo artist. *If I Can Dream* was a collection of Elvis classics featuring orchestral reworkings by the Royal Philharmonic Orchestra. Recordings come as limited editions, special sets and themed releases. He is sold in all formats. Even new vinyl versions of his classic recordings attract buyers. Elvis is constantly re-released, remixed and recycled by the industry, because they know his music continues to sell.

Many Elvis sales illustrate what in recent years have come to be known in business circles as long-tail sales. This phrase was coined to describe how products that appeal only to a specialist market can nevertheless rival bestsellers in profitability if the sales continue over a long period of time and are relatively cheap to market and distribute. The long tail is the shape of the graph of the U.S. sales figures correlated with time. It can be seen in the sales and chart positions in January 2013 of three Elvis reissues: *Elvis Uncovered* remained at 153 on the physical album chart, selling some 1,942 copies, but its total sales to date were 59,178. Similarly, *Viva Las Vegas* rose from 68 to 56 on the top soundtrack album chart, selling some 809 copies, bringing the total sales tally to 47,787. And *He Touched Me/An Evening Prayer* (volume one) re-entered the top music video chart at number twenty after selling 468 copies, taking the running sales total to 216,432.

The canon of Elvis music is not fixed. He can no longer enter a recording studio, but thanks to modern technology and capitalist entrepreneurship Elvis's recordings are constantly being reissued and repackaged. The year 2013 saw the fortieth anniversary of Elvis's two recording sessions at Memphis's Stax studios. This was as good an excuse as any for the Graceland marketing department to highlight Stax in its promotion of Elvis Week and for RCA Legacy to release a three-CD box set, *Elvis at Stax*, the first time Presley's songs recorded at Stax were brought together in the same release. Fans could also buy out-takes and relevant photographs. On 13 August what was described by the promotional material as 'a very special listening party' was held at the Stax Museum of American Soul Music. Fans had the opportunity to stand in the very same spot where Elvis recorded the music they were hearing and to hear from some of the people who were there on the day.

In 1973 Elvis's concert 'Aloha Hawaii' was also shown to millions via satellite around the world. Not surprisingly Elvis Week 2013 featured a special screening of the show in Memphis and full advantage was taken of marketing opportunities, as happened the same year when a British television network polled viewers for their favourite Elvis numbers. The list produced tied in nicely with a Sony album.

Whatever happens in the future, however many times the Elvis brand is sold and traded, the fans hope that the business will be ringfenced. If it is subsumed into another empire it will run the risk again of being linked to the fortunes of other unconnected enterprises. What the core business at Graceland needs is to be protected from a situation where investment in the essential Elvis attraction suffers.

One future for the business could one day be as a fan-owned venture. Might it be bought by a consortium of fans? Could the worldwide network of clubs and Elvis supporters collectively supply the capital needed to buy the business and take control? It would take a group of motivated individuals to get involved and act as a catalyst. They might market shares in Elvis Presley Enterprises to fans to raise the millions of dollars needed to secure ownership. Thus fan-owned and protected, the Graceland business could consolidate and expand. Growth and profit would not be the primary goal, however. The main aim of the business would be the promotion of Elvis and the stewardship of his memory and assets. It could be a not-for-profit organization and thus benefit from tax advantages. Yet for this to happen, the current commercial investors would need to have lost faith in their investment and be prepared to offload it at an irresistible price. A thriving and profitable Elvis brand will not be offered to fans for a price they can afford.

Whatever form the future takes, it can be said with certainty that without Elvis being marketed to, or discovered by, up-and-coming generations, there will be no future. It could be argued that the strategic marketing of Elvis to the younger generation is what truly lies behind his enduring success. The Elvis entrepreneurs have not limited their activities to licensing nostalgic merchandise for ageing fans to buy, or reissuing boxed sets of golden oldies. They have been and remain proactive in growing a youth market. It has been the deliberate policy of Elvis Presley Enterprises since the 1980s to introduce Elvis to younger audiences. When the Disney animation *Lilo and Stitch* was released in 2002, the soundtrack included no fewer than five Elvis tracks. The film was an ideal medium to introduce Elvis to a new audience. 'Because of that we have eight, nine and ten year-olds who are dyed-in-the-wool Elvis fans,' Jack Soden told *Billboard* magazine in 2004.[2] Today those children are the twenty-year-olds who wait in line at Graceland. Ahead of them are the thirty-, forty- and fifty-year-olds who watched Elvis videos via Disney back in the 1980s and '90s.

'We make the introductions, and the rest happens without much more of a push from us,' observes Soden. 'It is part of our responsibility to reach new eyes and ears, though it's an easy one.'[3] 'His flame will forever burn' says Robert 'Butch' Polston, 'and that flame will forever create new followers for him and his legacy until the end of time . . . The young fans who were not born when Elvis was performing are in awe of the older fans who actually saw him perform.'[4] Polston regrets however that the new fans will never know the full effect of the real Elvis and instead will become fans of tribute artists, unless, of course, a virtual Elvis is the comeback King.

Elvis Presley Enterprises has made it a policy to be proactive in several online formats, establishing a presence on websites where young people are to be found. The target group is from age twelve to eighteen. Although fans post a lot of Elvis material online themselves, EPE has exclusive access to a lot more and ensures it is made accessible via such sites as YouTube and iTunes. Similarly Elvis ringtones are now available and EPE is well into the business of apps. Features of a recent Elvis smartphone app even included a 'Live-Cam' section, which gives fans a real-time look at Elvis Presley's Graceland mansion.

As personal online testimonies from various social media fan sites confirm, Elvis continues to attract young fans: 'I became an Elvis fan at 9 years old. CBS was showing a mini-series about him. I watched it and became an instant fan,' writes sixteen-year-old Taylor. 'I first discovered Elvis when I went over to a friend's house,' writes Ruhi, aged thirteen.

> They told me they had to show me a funny song – it was Elvis Presley's 'Viva Las Vegas'. The actions were a little wacky, but when I heard his voice, I was shocked; he had such a beautiful voice! So when I went home that evening, I went on YouTube there he was, Elvis. My heart jumped out of my body, and I thought, 'Wow, what a gorgeous man!!'

The unique qualities found in Elvis's voice transcend the generations. The core sound, remixed and rearranged musically to match contemporary musical fashion and tastes, has retained its appeal sixty years later. Mary Hancock Hinds, who admits to being 'at the tail end of the generation who saw him', sees a new generation of fans being brought along. 'The clothes they sell in the mall at Graceland with Elvis logos are designed or made not for menopausal women but to fit the younger ones.'[5]

There is no need for the hard sell. Indeed for most of the years EPE has been in charge of the Elvis image, it has had to do very little – just make Elvis available – which until very recently it did very sparingly. For instance, before 2002 EPE had been approached many times by producers wanting to remix Elvis tracks, to give familiar Elvis numbers an extra contemporary something. Permission was never granted. Eventually, when the Dutch producer Junkie XL made an approach to EPE for permission to remix one of Elvis's lesser-known numbers, 'A Little Less Conversation', for a high-profile Nike advertisement, it was granted – to his surprise.

> They had knocked back so many other proposals over the years. I'm not sure why they accepted mine. When Nike approached me to do the music for its soccer commercial, a group of us sat down and brainstormed what tracks might work. It was a team-based decision. We knew the vibe from 'A Little Less Conversation' would work in any culture. Nike thought it was 'spot on' for what football is all about.[6]

A minor hit taken from one of Elvis's more forgettable films was turned into a worldwide dance club hit and advertising triumph. It topped the singles charts in nine countries. In the film *Live a Little, Love a Little*, released in 1968, Elvis is seen at a poolside party in the company of dancing and smooching partygoers. They are all dressed in eye-catching 1960s fashions, and a smooth, immaculately groomed Elvis oozes sexist charm. The videos that accompany the 2002 remix are utterly different. To begin with, there is no Elvis performing. One video is shot in monochrome, with only a hint of colour. It shows a spooky gladiatorial game of soccer being played in a confined space enclosed within a wire wall. It looks like football crossed with cage wrestling. It is surreal advertising at its most obscure, all choreographed to the pounding Elvis remix. Another video shows a wall of dancers, each in their own box-like cell, stacked on shelves. Sometimes a cell is lit in red and sometimes in white. Some dance solo, others with partners. A range of dancing styles is represented from jiving to breakdancing. As with the soccer video, the remixed sound keeps the distinctive Elvis quality, but the beat and backing is a vast improvement on the original. It gives the number far greater body and power. It is easy to understand how it became a worldwide hit. Several young Elvis fans have said that hearing the remix and seeing the videos was what turned them into Elvis fans.

Some aspects of Elvis do date. The films he made have never come back into fashion. They are watched by the old fans, but cinema has moved on since Elvis's time and his movies have not worn well. What does not date is the essential quality of the voice. 'Thousands of people who were not born when Elvis died have discovered Elvis and are every bit as intense and devoted as the original fans,' Jack Soden said in an official 2013 Elvis Week interview. 'There is a tremendous regenerative power. It is not something we could have created – only Elvis. Elvis just grabs people with his charisma, good looks and, of course, his music.'[7] As a commercial enterprise, that is all the explanation Jack Soden and his team need.

In 2008 the Italian DJ and record producer Agostino Carollo, known as Spankox, produced a new version of Elvis's 1954 Sun recording 'Baby Let's Play House'. It became a moderate international hit. A few months later Spankox released the first Elvis Presley remix album to be supported by the Elvis Presley Estate – *Re:Versions*. In October 2009 another album was released, called *Re:Mixes*, with fourteen revamped tracks. The packaging was designed to have a retro feel and there was even a vinyl version. The album became, in the words of the promotional material, 'a must have for every true Elvis fan and for all music lovers that not only like good music but also like to touch and feel the music they own'.

In the same vein came *Re:Volution* in 2011, *Re:Loaded* in 2012 and in 2013 *Re:Born*. Its promoters called it 'a new milestone in Elvis' career. The idea behind this new album is to rediscover the King of Rock 'n' Roll with a new sound and introduce Elvis to a new generation of fans.' Spankox, it was claimed, had 'brought the King back to the top of the international record sales charts. All the tracks feature the original Elvis Presley vocals, restored and enhanced using modern technology for the best possible listening experience, and are newly arranged in a very clever way, capturing and enhancing the feel and excitement of the originals.'[8]

New technology has also enabled Elvis to perform duets post mortem. In September 2014 a recording was released of Barbra Streisand singing 'Love Me Tender' as part of her new album, *Partners*. Forty years ago, Elvis Presley is said to have insulted Streisand and snubbed her offer to co-star in *A Star is Born*. Any history of bad feeling was overlooked when the great showbiz diva and the King of Rock 'n' Roll finally made music together. The pairing had the approval of the Presley family and of course was not Elvis's first posthumous duet. As previously mentioned, he had performed 'If I Can Dream' with Celine Dion, thanks to some cunning video and audio trickery, for the *American Idol* telethon in April 2007. He has also sung with his daughter, Lisa Marie. There wasn't a dry eye in the house when Lisa surprised a crowd of 20,000 fans at Memphis's Pyramid Arena with a duet of 'Don't Cry Daddy' during Elvis Week 1997 on the twentieth anniversary of her father's death. This was followed up in 2007 with 'In the Ghetto', and in 2012, on the 35th anniversary, Lisa Marie launched a video duet featuring family photographs, giving fans an inside glimpse of the private lives of the Presley family.

While some fans are purists and dislike the liberties being taken with their hero, others rave. As one fan review on Amazon declares, 'I discovered that not only do I like these remixes, I love 'em!! Why? Because they sound like Elvis recorded them today . . . We may not prefer these over the original gems but boy do they sound good too. And here's the trick – they still sound E L V I S.'

Announcing the Barbra Streisand duet in 2014, a Graceland statement acknowledged the differences of opinion. Remixes and duets, Graceland said, are something that irritates a sector of the Elvis fan community, while other fans see it as a welcome adaptation of a classic, made new again and shared with future generations of fans. Regardless of what side you are on in the debate, you have to admit, it is pretty amazing what can be done with modern technology. Elvis was an innovator who always embraced and created the latest trends of his time, and still does today.[9]

Authentic, the new legal owners of the Elvis legacy, will be looking for ways of matching the Elvis brand with appropriate marketing campaigns. This is where the money lies. The money to be made from licensing Elvis to souvenir makers is peanuts compared with linking the Elvis sound to worldwide promotional campaigns. Nike took a gamble that paid off. Not only did Elvis make their advertisements memorable, the company benefited additionally from its association with the music when it went global. Other international marketing campaign managers watched with interest and took note.

Elvis's potential in advertising had been left largely untapped by Colonel Parker, who usually knew a marketing opportunity when he saw one. However, the Colonel was unfamiliar with the rarefied world of media creatives and advertising agencies. Only once did Elvis make a broadcast commercial, and that was for his favourite store, Southern Maid, who supplied him with jelly doughnuts. The commercial went out on the *Louisiana Hayride* radio programme in 1955.

Once EPE had been persuaded to take the plunge into the world of advertising, there was no stopping them. Over the following years Graceland's attitude to renting Elvis's image to sell other products changed radically. By 2014 EPE, now a subsidiary of Authentic, was openly touting for business from corporations and advertising agencies from all over the world to incorporate Elvis Presley and Graceland into their marketing messages. 'Making

The King of Rock 'n' Roll an effective part of your next advertising or promotional campaign is just an e-mail away. We will be happy to consider your request to use the name, image, likeness or voice of Elvis Presley or the name, image and likeness of Graceland or other EPE-owned trademarks. Please contact us with your proposed use, term, territory and other pertinent information,' said the Graceland online promotional message.

The remixed track of 'A Little Less Conversation' became popular with advertisers. In 2012 BMW used the track in a promotional video. In 2011 Coca-Cola used it in a new Japanese television campaign to promote a canned coffee product. The visuals were carefully pitched in mood and style to attract younger male customers and Elvis provided the ideal soundtrack. Coca-Cola wanted to 'add pep to flat sales'. The *Wall Street Journal* reported that every scene included at least one attractive woman. 'The TV ads depict groups of mostly young males goofing off (usually in front of one or more beautiful women) while Elvis Presley's "A Little Less Conversation" plays in the background.'[10]

Another obscure Elvis song found on the soundtrack of an old Elvis film and given the modern treatment was 'Pocketful of Rainbows'. It was chosen for a stylish advertising video made for the Irish National Lottery. The slushy strings of the 1960 *GI Blues* film version are replaced by a hard techno beat. The image of Elvis in military uniform wooing the Hollywood starlet Juliet Prowse on a mountain chairlift is replaced by shots of rainbows being seen through jets of water shooting from two fire-service launches on the River Liffey. *GI Blues* was originally made to cash in on the new, clean, reformed reputation Elvis acquired after being called up to the army. That its music is now being used to promote gambling in Ireland is something the Colonel could never have imagined, although, given his own interest in gambling, he may well have approved.

It has not just been lesser-known Elvis numbers that have been revitalized. '(You're the) Devil in Disguise', recorded in 1963 at the height of the Cold War, was one of Elvis's many number ones, even though John Lennon voted it a 'miss' on the BBC record review show *Juke Box Jury*, saying that Elvis had turned himself into Bing Crosby. In 2011 Russia's largest telecommunications company chose this Elvis number to promote a mobile phone service. 'Can't Help Falling in Love with You' has been borrowed to sell bathroom fragrances; a Greek dairy company chose 'Always on My Mind'; and an Australian drinks company called Spring Valley has opted for 'Spring Fever'. The year 2011 saw another Elvis classic being reused; this time the 1956 hit 'Hound Dog' was used to promote a Hyundai car in South Korea. Unusually, this television advertisement featured vintage footage of Elvis himself.

In a 2011 commercial seen in Brazil, clips have been edited from a long-forgotten 1966 film, *Spin Out*, showing Elvis partying and flirting. The music that goes with it has nothing to do with the film but is from a 1960 Elvis cover version of 'Fever'. Elvis purists might wince at some of the liberties taken with the King's voice and image, but Graceland's new owners are quite happy for creative directors to take a mix-and-match attitude.

A cheaper and cheeky option adopted by some advertising teams is to use an Elvis impersonator, but presumably there must be a benefit in having the genuine article associated with a product, otherwise the impersonators would attract a larger proportion of the Elvis endorsement market. And the Elvis endorsement comes for free in some countries, including the UK, where the law allows for images of dead celebrities to be digitally manipulated without royalties being owed to the estate.

Elvis is even used by the political right to reinforce campaign messages. Candidates in both the USA and the UK have borrowed the music and lyrics of 'A Little Less Conversation' to imply that they are politicians of action, while their opponents just talk about getting things done.

Although the reuse of Elvis material by advertisers is usually shaped towards the country or demographic group that is the prime target, Elvis can be relied upon to resonate with those out-side the target group as well. Therefore money spent on buying advertising time has both a prime and an added value. The Junkie XL Elvis remix was designed to create interest in soccer. This it did, but then had a secondary life selling canned coffee and yet a third incarnation selling a political message.

You Too Can Be Elvis

There have been Elvis impersonators for almost as long as Elvis himself has been a star. Back in 1956 a sixteen-year-old Canadian named Jim Smith was seen on the television show *House Party* with a guitar in hand, miming to Elvis songs. Jim is now widely acknowledged as the very first of thousands of Elvis aspirants. In Elvis jargon the preferred term for an Elvis mimic who performs as the King is 'tribute artist'. Other terms such as 'impersonator' or 'lookalike' are regarded by many as disrespectful to the memory of the one and only Elvis. Not that such niceties bother every tribute artist. Alabaman army veteran Rob Langford is quite happy to be called an Elvis impersonator, although he is aware that in some circles 'it's not politically correct'.

There are now so many impersonators around the world that the total number is probably unquantifiable. To begin with, how would one be defined? Is every middle-aged man with sideburns, dyed hair, an open-necked shirt and medallions to be included in the count? Should the tally be confined to those who are paid to perform Elvis tribute concerts, or include anyone who dons a spangled jumpsuit and does a karaoke set? Are tribute artists who sound like Elvis but don't look like him to be included? What about the lookalikes who mime to Elvis tracks? Should Elvis parodies be put on the list and what about female Elvises, like Anita or Elvis Herselvis? There are also the boy Elvis lookalikes seen

When Elvis died there were already 170 Elvis tribute artists at large. By the year 2000 it was calculated that this figure had risen to 85,000. At that rate of growth, by 2043 there will be 9,447,645,907 Elvises on the planet!

outside Graceland having their photographs taken by proud parents as a kind of rite of passage.

Given the difficulties in finding a definition, it is not surprising that no precise description of an Elvis impersonator was given when in December 2000 the radio show the Naked Scientists estimated there were 85,000 Elvises around the world. At the time of his death in 1977, it's claimed, there had been just 170. Mathematicians have had fun using these two figures to show that the world population of Elvis tribute artists is growing at a rate of 27 per cent a year. 'Here's the bit that will leave you all shook up. If you've got a suspicious mind, try working out how many Elvis impersonators there will be in the year 2043.' Assuming the current rate of increase, there will be 9,447,645,907 Elvises on the planet. 'The population of the Earth in 2043 is expected to be slightly less than this number. So that means everybody on earth, including people in the ghetto, will be a guitar man just like Elvis. And a few extra Elvis impersonators will have arrived from elsewhere.'[1]

But from ludicrous extrapolation back to the real world – Rob Langford, who knows his local scene well, reckons that in Birmingham, Alabama, there are twenty Elvises who are paid to perform. One man in 5,000 in the city is a sometime Elvis. There are in fact just over a hundred listed Elvis impersonators who live in, or are willing to travel to, Birmingham to perform. Bearing in mind that they are mostly white and Birmingham has a high African American population, the proportion of Elvises among the city's white males is likely to be significantly greater than one in 5,000.

The Yahoo Music site suggests there are 84,000 Elvis tribute artists in the USA. This seems a ludicrously high figure – one in every 1,400 adult white males (assuming the majority are adult white males, although the tribute artists do include women and span several ethnicities. There is a popular Chinese Elvis who performs in London). The quoted figure can be traced back to a claim made by Robert Sillerman, who bought Elvis Presley Enterprises in 2004. In the course of a television discussion on the continuing popularity of Elvis, he cited a 2002 BBC finding that over 84,000 people claimed 'Elvis impersonator' as their main occupation on their tax returns. No primary source for the claim can be found and it is probably a folk tale based on guesswork; nevertheless it and other estimates suggest that there are many thousands of Elvises performing around the world. Sillerman, as a successful entrepreneur, would not have bought the Elvis brand had he not researched the potential income base and been satisfied of its size and potential for growth.

There are many unofficial estimates as to how many Elvis tribute artists there are in the world, ranging from 50,000 to 200,000.

There is no verifiable figure. Butch Polston supplies many of the Elvis performers with their stage costumes, yet when asked to estimate numbers and to break the total down to those who made a living from their act, and who were the keen amateurs, he admits,

> I truly have no idea. Several sites have come up with figures. I would say that, knowing thousands of these guys as I do, if you took a hundred Elvis performers, 50 per cent would probably tell you that they do it as a hobby because of their love for Elvis, 35 per cent do it full time, either with their own venue or in a travelling show, and the remainder do it a little of both – as a hobby, but they also have the flexibility with their full-time jobs where they can take several weeks off to do a particular theatre or do weekends at nursing homes or other places to add to their income, just to keep Elvis's memory alive.[2]

The Reverend Dorian Baxter is a Canadian Anglican priest who pursues a parallel career as Elvis Priestley. His interest in Elvis stretches back almost to the genesis of Elvis time in the mid-1950s. Asked how he gauged interest in Elvis – was it growing, decreasing or static? – he was unequivocal in his reply. 'In my view it has grown exponentially and in a special way I feel it bears some resemblance to the ever-expanding universe connected to the Big Bang Theory.'[3] In particular he noted a new generation of Elvis fans coming to his shows, fans who are far too young to have known or seen the King in life.

It might have been very different if Colonel Parker, and later the Elvis estate, had been successful in obtaining legal control over the growing number of singers performing Elvis songs in the style of the King. The whole genre of Elvis tribute shows that has grown up over the years might never have been. In his lifetime, Elvis had viewed the pastiche Kings with wry amusement, but generally advised them to develop their own acts rather than mimic his. The Colonel however viewed them as fake Elvises, little different from bootleg records. They were making money from the public, but without him getting his cut. In February 1978 he collaborated with Broadcast Music Inc. to see if they could devise a scheme whereby anyone wanting to sing more than three Elvis songs in any one show would need a special licence. As BMI did not have rights to the whole catalogue this proved unenforceable. But the issue did not rest there. When Priscilla took control of the estate she too decided that the ersatz Elvises needed to be brought under some sort of control. It was claimed that the estate merely wished to protect Elvis's image. At first Elvis Presley Enterprises tried writing to the impersonators demanding they cease performing without official sanction. Generally, however, the Elvises ignored the communication, according to Sean O'Neal, author of *Elvis Inc*.

Ten years after Elvis's death, with the tribute acts becoming increasingly popular with fans and lucrative to the performers, Elvis Presley Enterprises decided to take serious legal action against one of the most popular, Johnny Spence. He had been among the first tribute acts on the scene, having started swivelling his hips and curling his lip in the early 1970s, performing in clubs in his home town of Rockford, Illinois. He was also one of the first Elvis tribute artists to generate his own fan base and following. In 1987, to celebrate the tenth anniversary of Elvis's death, Spence was billed to appear as an Elvis in a concert at a 12,500-seater stadium. The *Chicago Tribune* reported that he applied for official EPE approval, but was turned down. When EPE heard that he intended to go ahead without their approval, their attorney wrote to Spence saying that if he did not cancel his scheduled *Elvis the Way it Was* show, he would seek a court injunction against the performance. 'We own exclusive right to the name, likeness and image [of Elvis] . . . You are not authorized to use the name Elvis or to perform any Elvis impersonation or act, and you are advised to immediately cease and desist.'

'They can't do this to me,' protested Spence. 'They can't take Elvis out of me because the whole image inside of me is Elvis. It just comes out.' Spence said that he considered the lawyer's notice a threat to Elvis impersonators everywhere. Spence's attorney, the entertainment lawyer Jay Ross, who had previously represented other Elvis impersonators, said that he considered the notice a threat, not just to Elvis tribute artists, but to all performers who do imitations. 'How far can they take this?' he asked. 'It concerns the degree to which a performer or a performer's estate controls the commercial use of the performer's voice and image . . . We can't get ridiculous about this. What happens if George Washington's heirs start demanding a two-cent royalty every time we use a dollar bill?'[4]

In the end the dispute was settled out of court, yet what the Elvis estate lawyers really wanted was a case to go to court and establish its rights, in legally enforceable terms, over all Elvis impersonators. The test case that eventually came to court involved Rod Russen, the producer of *The Big El Show*, a travelling stage show dedicated to the memory of Elvis, starring tribute artist Larry Seth. The show also produced merchandise showing an image very similar to Elvis. It had started life in 1975 before Elvis's death and was promoted as 'Reflections on a Legend . . . A Tribute to Elvis Presley', 'Looks and sounds like The King'. The show opened with the familiar Strauss fanfare used by Elvis and even had its own live TCB Band. Just one week after Elvis's death more than 50,000 fans turned out in a driving rainstorm to see *The Big El Show* perform an outdoor concert on the riverfront in Philadelphia.

EPE accused Rod Russen of engaging in unfair competition and infringing trademarks. It alleged *The Big El Show* damaged its ability to license Elvis and might lead audiences to believe the show had official approval. The Elvis company demanded damages and that the show be stopped. The case went to court and at first sight it would seem that Graceland won. The judge reaffirmed that Elvis's name and likeness had been inherited by the estate and issued a restraining order prohibiting the show from using the 'Presley logo, sketch, likeness or picture.'[5]

However, the key finding that has enabled all American Elvis tribute acts to remain in business is that the judge ruled that the show was

> not unfair competition . . . there was no likelihood that Larry Seth would be confused with Elvis Presley. He disagreed with the argument that The Big El Show diminished Elvis Presley Enterprises' ability to license Elvis. In the Judge's opinion, an Elvis impersonator did not need a licence from anyone to perform. An impersonation is an exercise of free-dom of speech.[6]

The Graceland estate's legal team did not give up. It next targeted a Las Vegas show called *Legends in Concert*. The show's attorney, Mark Trator, who had himself been involved in the passing of a state law in Nevada specifically allowing impersonators to perform without permission from the heirs of the subjects impersonated, made a telling observation. He noted that Elvis Presley Enterprises ignored 99 per cent of Elvis tribute acts, focusing their efforts on the most financially successful ones. This suggested to Trator that the estate was more concerned with making money than protecting Elvis's image. While he did not object to their pursuit of profit, 'he did not admire their hypocrisy'.[7]

After finding it could not control the tribute acts by legal means, EPE changed tactics and for a while ignored the growing phenomenon. Gradually this approach gave way to the current policy. The company sanctions, encourages and indeed organizes tribute act competitions, viewing the contestants as money-spinners to be turned to their advantage, as opposed to a threat to their business interests. A good Elvis impersonator attracts his own following and sells his own merchandise and recordings, yet at the same time he acts as a shop window for all the other Elvis material available. An Elvis fan who goes to a tribute show may well be inspired to go online and search out a new record box set or Elvis poster; or, Graceland hopes, book a ticket to Memphis and a Graceland-owned hotel room. The fan may well opt to travel to Memphis for Elvis Week and book tickets for the official Ultimate Elvis Tribute Artist final held in Memphis every August. Indeed the fan's favourite Elvis artist might even be a finalist.

The first Elvis tribute act contest held in Memphis was in 1987 and was an unofficial affair. The idea of holding competitive events is credited to Dr Ed Franklin, who had been the veterinary surgeon who looked after Elvis's horses. Polston recalls how it came together at a place called Bad Bob's Vapors Nightclub, which was owned and run by Franklin. 'I had already been selling Elvis costumes, which I created the market for,' recalled Polston.

I wanted to basically find a venue to set up a display to sell them. Prior to the first contest, Doc was only letting people get up and sing a song or two with the band if they thought they sounded like Elvis, and giving them a free drink or dinner. It was graded by the applause that the individual received. I went in and saw this going on and thought 'This is where I need to be,' so I approached Doc and laid the plan out for him. I told him that he could come up with some prize money from selling tickets to people to get in to it, plus he could make money selling drinks and dinners, and I would offer a free item to the contest winner. He told me it was a crazy idea and it wouldn't work. Approximately eight months later, he called me and said 'Hey Polston, I've got this idea for a contest!' So, basically, if it wasn't Doc's idea, it was not gonna fly. That's just the way Doc was. So I say, good for the Doc.[8]

It was in 2007 that Elvis Presley Enterprises first launched what has become an annual event to find the singer who offers the 'best representation of the legacy of Elvis Presley'. Twenty-four of the best acts from around the world, each of whom has won a preliminary round, travel to Memphis to compete. Shawn Klush of Pennsylvania won the first-ever ultimate title in 2007.

The first non-American to win the international title was England's Ben Portsmouth in 2012. Dean Z from Missouri was acclaimed the ultimate Elvis in 2013 and immediately after his victory it was officially announced that the 2014 winner would not only succeed to the title, but bank a cash prize of $20,000, a contract to perform with 'Legends in Concert' and a unique Elvis belt. While the Memphis title is the most coveted, there is an Elvis competition underway somewhere in the world almost every week of the year.

EPE is now so committed to promoting Elvis in this way that it is constantly on the lookout for new locations for competition heats, appealing to potential new venues with the line that the Ultimate Elvis Tribute Artist Contest 'has become one of the fastest growing entertainment opportunities available'. Venues targeted as potential locations include music festivals, theatres, even casinos, indeed anywhere that can stage 'a unique entertainment experience combining the excitement of Elvis' music and showmanship with the thrill of a high stakes talent competition'. The opportunity is sold as 'a great way to provide a complete entertainment package for your audience and draw for music fans of all ages'. In effect the Elvis estate is selling a franchise to a money-spinning format, as the contest allows organizers 'to join forces with the most recognized entertainment force in the world. You will be provided with tools you need to take full advantage of this opportunity and you'll have instant media attention in both your region and around the rest of the world.' Competitors are judged according to strict criteria, which are listed as singing ability, the presentation of the look and style of Elvis, stage dress and the ability to recreate the charisma of Elvis. At the Ultimate Elvis final, the greatest emphasis, 40 per cent of each judge's votes, is placed on the vocal aspects of the act.[9]

The 29-year-old Dean Z has travelled the world with his act and has appeared regularly at the *Legends in Concert* show at Branson, Missouri, alongside a Johnny Cash, a Celine Dion and several other look- and soundalikes. Dean says he has dedicated his whole life to Elvis and has been performing professionally for twelve years. He was three years old when he first saw the television documentary *This is Elvis*. There was an instant connection, he recalls, and soon he was up on the coffee table gyrating as the King. His mother had a jumpsuit made for him and he performed 'Jailhouse Rock' at his sister's school talent show. At the show, he sang along to an Elvis record and every time he shook, the crowd screamed. At that moment, he was hooked. Fellow 2013 finalist Jay Dupuis from Louisiana has also described discovering Elvis as a child. At the age of three he would dress up in white trousers and a shirt, flip up his collar and pretend he was the King.

A high number of performers admit to discovering Elvis at a young age. More than thirty years before the young Dean Z first heard the King, Dorian Baxter had a similar experience. It was his fifth birthday and he was playing with a new red fire truck when Elvis came on the radio singing 'Heartbreak Hotel'.

I just dropped the fire truck on the carpet and stood motionless and mesmerised looking at the hi-fi and listening intently to the voice and music being produced by Elvis Presley. The very next day I had my first Elvis record and I have been trying to sing like Elvis for the last 58 years. Right from being a child of 5 years old Elvis became rather like a personal friend. When I saw my first picture of him I felt I knew him. It was a moment I will never forget.[10]

Top Elvis acts are sold with razzmatazz and hyperbole of which the old fairground hustler Colonel Tom Parker might have been proud. Ben Portsmouth's agent, John Bedford Entertainments, says of Ben and his band: 'In the blink of your eyes you'll be taken back to what it was like to see, hear and experience the young and sexy Elvis when he first burst on to the U.S. music scene in 1954 right through to 1977.'[11] Dean Z's promoters claim, 'women spontaneously erupt into screams when they witness the same look, sound and swivel as the Memphis Flash himself.'[12] And after the show they can go online and buy Dean Z T-shirts for $20 each, as well as Elvis merchandise.

The world of Elvis tribute acts is easy to enter – just buy a jumpsuit – but a tough one in which to succeed. Behind the scenes at the contests there is a superficial appearance of fraternity, but it masks a real cut-throat competitiveness. After all, not only are status and glory to be won, but lucrative contracts are awaiting the most successful.

In Elvis Week in Memphis the place is heaving with Elvises, all aspiring to be the ultimate King of the World. One experienced Elvis tribute artist, however, has given up taking part in competitions. Army veteran Rob Langford from Alabama, the middle of 'The Elvis Belt', as he describes it, appeared on stage in Memphis in 2007. But now he has tired of competitive Elvising. Elvis impersonators are so very competitive, he says. 'You go into the dressing room before a contest and see all these guys putting on sequined jumpsuits and make-up. It's like barging in on a group of teenage girls at a beauty pageant.'[13]

One fan who has been involved in the world of Elvis fan clubs for many years says that being a fan has changed over time, partly due to the rise in the profile of the tribute acts. 'In the old days fans were pure Elvis, his recordings and films, now the tribute artists have followings. Young girls talk about them and have their favourites. The competitions have raised the bar and the standard of performance. Some guys today are absolutely magnificent.'[14]

'The wonderful thing about the tribute acts is that they have kept his name alive,' says Polston. 'If it was left strictly up to Elvis Presley Enterprises, they don't have a far enough reaching effect to people all over the world. With the Elvis acts being out there, they are helping to promote Elvis to the younger fans.'[15] There is some evidence, however, that while members of the younger generation have discovered Elvis for themselves, the Elvis tribute acts may be less popular with them than with their parents. Brad Tuttle, writing in *Time* in 2013, reported that while there were an impressive 198 Las Vegas-area Elvis impersonators listed by one entertainment-booking site, the number of Elvis Presley impersonator bookings fell by over 20 per cent from 2011 to 2012. For 2013, he noted, 'Elvis bookings have remained flat, roughly on pace with last year's underwhelming numbers.' One wedding planner suggested that for younger clients in the market for Vegas nuptials, Elvis had left the building, so to speak. 'The whole Elvisy Vegas red carpet thing is, in my opinion, going out the door,' said Carrie Gaudioso, wedding coordinator for the Mon Bel Ami chapel. 'That whole era is getting older. Almost all of our older renewals want an Elvis wedding. Our younger brides do not want cheesy, flashy, Elvis Vegas. They want something nice in their budget.'

Internet searches for Elvis impersonators, as calculated by the search engine Google, have been declining in the years up until 2013. Internet users tend to be younger rather than older and this trend reflects, perhaps, the declining interest among younger fans in the impersonators. 'The number of Elvis impersonators or Google searches for Elvis impersonator aren't reflective of interest in Elvis,' Gary Hahn, the EPE vice president of marketing and media, was quoted as saying. 'Our business, here at Graceland and around the world, is thriving.'[16]

Important as the tribute acts are to keeping the memory of Elvis alive, there are many older followers of Elvis who ignore that side of Elvis fandom entirely. Mary Hancock Hinds is a regular visitor to Memphis during Elvis Week. She comes to see old friends, eat good food, have fun and remember Elvis. The Elvis tribute acts and the Ultimate Elvis competition are of no interest to her. 'It's another sub-culture,' she says, and 'we ignore them.'[17]

Furthermore there are many thousands of fans who are positively hostile in their attitudes towards the tribute acts. They find them insulting to Elvis's memory. Robert Alaniz, who is a collector of and dealer in Presleyana, is disdainful of them, calling them 'Mickey Mouse Elvises' and 'Halloween Elvises'. 'They create real damage to his memory,' he believes. Having turned from harassing to embracing the Elvis tribute artists, Elvis Presley Enterprises has come in for criticism from fans who think they have gone too far in promoting them. Many were furious when Graceland announced its programme for Elvis Week 2013 and 'everything had an impersonator. Some old ladies want to relive their youth and like impersonators for some bizarre reason,' says Alaniz. 'They go to see impersonators and won't let Elvis die.'[18]

Pilgrims travelling to St David's Cathedral in Wales pass by an unexpected sign at the entrance to a farm track. There really was a St Elvis and he is said to have baptized St David, the Welsh patron saint.

Some people do 'turn their noses up at impersonators', Rob Langford admits, and there are limits, he believes, to what impersonators like himself should allow themselves to do. As long as he shows Elvis respect, Rob is quite relaxed about how he portrays the King. 'When doing a show,' he says, 'it is more important to be an entertainer than to get all the details right. No one will ever exactly replicate Elvis. What people want to see is an enjoyable show.'[19]

Websites such as Elvii.com offer a service to fundraisers, events organizers and trade shows to find them an Elvis. They even offer a range of Elvis styles, from 1950s to the army days to the '68 comeback to the Vegas years. For some fans authenticity is paramount. They criticize the smallest details. An artist wearing a costume from the early years but singing a latter-day song might find himself being sternly corrected. Geraint Benney from Wales, who performs as Elvis Preseli, even claimed in 2006 that he had received death threats 'from extreme Elvis fans who claimed he was showing disrespect to The King'.[20] One fan had threatened to shoot him. And his 'crime'? Geraint is bald! Possibly fans were more angered by Elvis Preseli's stage show, in which he is accompanied by a band called The Undertakers, climbs out of a golden coffin and cooks burgers on stage. Nevertheless, death threats are hardly warranted for breaches of good taste.

Some Elvises, like Elvis Preseli, are joke Elvises. They play the part deliberately for laughs. Others take their calling far more seriously. Indeed the majority of Elvis tribute acts fall into this latter category. As well as attempting to replicate the experience of seeing and hearing the original King, they use their Presley personas to raise money for charities and spread the joy they find in Presley's music. Being Elvis undoubtedly gives them a high. 'I can go into a room as Elvis and folk go nuts,' says Rob Langford. 'But no one would turn up to hear me sing. To be Elvis you sacrifice your own identity.'[21]

David Moore, who performed for several years at Memphis's Heartbreak Hotel, said that he sings Elvis because 'I want people to know what Elvis was all about: the giving, the sharing, never forgetting where he came from.' David says he has felt committed to Elvis since the age of five. 'It is a gift God has given me. I've had people coming up to me and saying it was like Elvis talking to me. People who say, I lost a son six months ago and you gave me hope with that song. I've had some beautiful experiences, sad experiences and some strange experiences doing Elvis that I can't explain.'[22] He tells a story of performing at a home where there was a quadriplegic man sitting in a chair surrounded by Elvis pictures.

> The moment I walked into the room a light went on in his eyes. It was hard to get through the songs I was so moved. As God is my witness I heard God's voice saying to me, 'This is why I have you do this.' I see it as a ministry, a ministry of healing. If I can take a person dying, a person with no hope, a child with no love and show them love and compassion, what more in life is there?[23]

Impersonator Clayton Benke-Smith has said that any Elvis performer who is dedicated to recreating Elvis's mystique has 'to eat, sleep, feel and act like the King.'[24] Patty Carroll met many Elvises in the course of a photography project that led to an exhibition of her collection of Elvis pictures. 'Once they put on the costume and the music starts something happens inside them,' she says.

> There's a transformation and they definitely feel a different kind of energy than they feel in their everyday lives. I know every single one of them has certain things they have to do to psych themselves up ready to feel Elvis. One impersonator told me that being an Elvis impersonator is not something you start out to do, but something happens and you follow the calling.[25]

Many Elvis impersonators talk of feeling Elvis inside them and the transformation that takes place. 'When I am waiting in the wings,' impersonator Bert Hathaway said, 'I can actually feel Elvis's presence with me and I become Elvis.'[26] This sense of spiritual empowerment can be felt by the audience as well. The journalist John Strausbaugh described watching impersonator Gregg Peters one winter's evening in a restaurant in the New York borough of Queens.[27] As Gregg Peters prepared his set, there was no hint of anything special to come. The place was 'a dowdy, drop-ceilinged, hangar-like working-class eatery'. Peters was 'a smallish guy with hair that looks dyed black and side-burns that looked pasted on'. His equipment was set up 'on the old tartan-patterned industrial carpeting'. There was no band, just a small digital tape machine. When he began all that was on offer as entertainment was 'a little guy singing to tapes at the back of a Queens restaurant'. Then suddenly, midway through the show, something happened.

Something enters him. It is the King's spirit filling him up like an empty vessel, transforming him into something taller, sexier. For a few amazing moments the Sunnyside Brauhaus is the Las Vegas International Hotel circa 1970, and little P is fully his Kingship, completely in command of the room, drawing wild cheers from what had been a polite but bored, sauerkraut-sated audience, drawing ladies toward the front to be blessed with the gift of sweaty scarves, drawing us all to our feet for the mighty 'Trilogy' finale. A tiny little boy who can't be more than 4 years old stands to the side of the stage area, just outside the spotlights. He's dressed in a miniature version of the Aloha-era jumpsuit, complete with little cape and big belt. He's studying Peters' moves intently, mimick-ing the Shaka gestures. At one point Peter goes down on one knee, reaches out a hand spangled with costume rings that glitter in the spotlights. The little boy reaches out his own tiny hand and their fingers touch like God and Adam in the Sistine Chapel. You can almost hear the spark of something being passed on. And then it's over. As suddenly as he had descended upon it, Elvis has definitely left the building. The spirit leaves the room in a palpable whoosh, like a pressure drop in the cabin of a jet . . . The King's spirit has rushed off to another faithful impersonator, another empty vessel who needs to be filled up.[28]

The Professional Elvis Impersonators Association talks on its website of 'The Grit and Glory of Being an Elvis Impersonator'. It defines an impersonator as 'an artist who copies or imitates the iconic American musician in looks and mannerisms. Elvis impersonation constitutes imitating his visual image by wearing an Elvis wig with the trademark sideburns and quaffed hair, putting on a rhinestone-studded jumpsuit and assorted jewelry. The artist also impersonates Elvis by singing and talking just like him.'[29]

For those who earn money by appearing in the Elvis style to entertain at a birthday party or corporate function, it is an adequate working description. Those who stage complete shows as Elvis too will fit the definition, but probably feel in themselves that the definition is limited. Being Elvis on stage involves making a real connection with the King. The tribute artist subsumes himself into the icon, or the spirit, of his hero – a hero regarded by some as their idol, little short of a god.

In wider cultural terms contemporary Elvises might be seen to be following an ancient pattern of human behaviour known as *imitatio Dei*. It is a concept found both in Christianity and Judaism and suggests that by attempting to imitate certain aspects of the divine, the believer him or herself comes closer to God. It stems from the teaching that humans themselves are made in the image of God.

From a very early date in the history of religion people developed the practice of imitating the gods, says the theologian Karen

Armstrong. 'They would reenact in ritual form what the Gods had done, either in the heavens or in their activities here on earth. And by imitating them you were creating a replica in which the Divine could be apprehended again.'[30]

When the Christian priest stands at the altar and recites the prayer of consecration over the bread and wine he or she reenacts the words and actions of Jesus at the Last Supper. 'Do this in memory of me.' Similarly the tribute artist 'becomes' Elvis for a while to bring the message of Elvis to his audience. 'The vast majority of human beings experience the divine in something earthly and in a human being, a man or a woman,' Karen Armstrong contends.

> It is very common for people to experience the divine in what can only be an inadequate human being. The essential and amazing thing about the spiritual quest is that the divine is able to be apprehended at all. So of course we think that Elvis is a grossly inadequate symbol of the divine, but one could have said the same of Jesus, after all he died the death, the very common death, of a disgraced criminal.[31]

Gregory Reece from the University of Alabama has studied the Elvis phenomenon and describes the tribute artists as more showbiz than priesthood.

> I found a lot of people dressed in white, repeating the words of a deceased idol and laying hands, and scarves, and lips upon an adoring crowd. I'm not sure that any of the participants, either performers or observers, would describe any of this activity in religious terms. It is show business, it is performance, it is rock 'n' roll, it is sexy, it is hilarious, but it is not necessarily religious.[32]

Reece goes on to claim that if the Elvis tribute artists were forced to identify the essence of their craft, 'I have no doubt that they would use essentially show business terminology to do so.' That is clearly not the case. Veteran tribute artist David Moore talks of a God-given gift. Other impersonators have talked of 'committing themselves to Elvis' and 'his spirit entering into them'. It is religious talk, not showbiz jargon. The reverence displayed by fans for Elvis was described as a form of worship by William Brown and Ben Fraser of Regent University, Virginia Beach, Virginia. They interviewed fans and tribute artists and concluded that for some fans who idealize and idolize Elvis

the fabric of their self-identity is intricately interwoven with their image of Elvis, not only as an entertainer, but also a friend, lover, husband, father, patriot and citizen. They may not call it that, but it's worship, People have a great need to worship, and if they don't believe in God or their belief isn't really strong, they can tend to worship a person. There's no doubt . . . that's what is going on.[33]

There are several examples of priests and pastors of religion who have combined Elvis impersonation with their Christian ministry, without themselves believing in the priesthood of Elvis. The priestly aspects of impersonation, they find, fit with their Christian vocation. Being Elvis has become a dimension of their Christian priestly calling. The Reverend Ravi Holy serves a benefice of eight churches based around the village of Wye in Kent. Before being ordained as a priest in the Church of England, Ravi was a member of a rock band. As a curate he had discovered a talent as an Elvis impersonator almost by chance. He was cast as Pharaoh in the musical *Joseph and the Amazing Technicolour Dreamcoat*, a part that is required to be played in Elvis style. He has also been to the local school as Elvis. 'Elvis is universally recognised and unites all ages and classes. He is so iconic. The children loved it when the vicar turned up in Elvis wig and glasses.'

One day he was talking with a family about the funeral arrangements for a much-loved local figure who had died while still quite young. They did not want the service to be too sombre and sad. It should have a party atmosphere, they suggested. 'But don't forget it is a funeral,' Ravi said, 'you wouldn't want me there dressed as Elvis.' 'That is exactly what Mum would have wanted!' came the unexpected response. The family insisted Ravi conduct the service as Elvis. He checked with his colleagues. Some parishioners were very dubious. Some were horrified. Was it really in good taste? Ravi spoke to his bishop and was offered enthusiastic support. The bishop saw it as an opportunity to reach out to people in the village who did not identify with the Church.

On the day the parish church was packed. The coffin was carried in to the Strauss fanfare, which on cue segued to 'That's All Right, Mama'. Ravi was dressed in gold lamé jacket, sunglasses and wig. He wore a clerical collar, but otherwise was Elvis. He explained that the service was the family's idea. He saw in it a Christian message. 'If Jesus were alive today and there had been a pastoral need to dress up as Elvis, he would have done so.' He was careful not to take his Elvis act too far and removed the wig and reverted to being Ravi for the prayers and committal. Afterwards some members of the congregation, who had previously been opposed to the idea, and thought him mad to consider it, agreed the service had been 'uplifting'.[34]

The Reverend Ravi Holy's Elvis impersonation remains a limited part of his total priestly calling. The Canadian Anglican priest Dorian Baxter, Elvis Priestley, has turned his Elvis act into an eye-catching public ministry, however. His Elvis persona did not emerge until 1996, when he entered an impersonator contest at the urging of his daughters. He won a top prize, and when organizers found out he was a priest, they asked him to be their chaplain. That night, he says, the throngs lined up from midnight to 4:30 in the morning. Many wanted to get back to the Lord – all because of Elvis. After that, the demand for Elvis Priestley grew. Everybody loves Elvis. The King of rock 'n' roll worshiped the King of Kings, Jesus Christ. There's something about Elvis that just breaks down barriers.[35]

Dorian Baxter's superiors were not as encouraging as Ravi's bishop and he was forced to set up his own church. Today Dorian Baxter officiates at the Christ the King Graceland Independent Anglican Church of Canada. In 2003 he was consecrated a bishop in the Communion of Evangelical Episcopal Churches and later that year established the Federation of Independent Anglican Churches of North America with himself as archbishop. Elvis Priestley is a well-known and colourful character and like many modern-day Elvises has attracted his own followers. His Facebook page has 5,000 friends, of whom over 4,000 are professed fans. But, he says,

I shy away from even the thought of a 'fan club' for me as it just leaves a bad taste in my mouth. I am an Elvis fan. How could I or any Elvis tribute artist be so arrogant to start a fan club of our own? It just doesn't sit right with me. After all there is and for ever more shall be only one Elvis Presley.[36]

One Elvis priestly role that is now widely recognized is that of officiating at weddings. Hundreds of Elvis couples have opted for a Las Vegas wedding at one of several wedding chapels where an Elvis lookalike can be hired to perform the ceremony. The basic deal at the Las Vegas Graceland Chapel is called the 'Loving You' package and costs $329. For that the couple and their friends have the use of chapel. 'Elvis' escorts the bride down the aisle and gives her away. Elvis sings three numbers and the new Mr and Mrs get a holder for their marriage certificate that shows a copy of Elvis and Priscilla's marriage certificate.

One of the many Elvis Presley-themed wedding chapels in Las Vegas, Nevada.

At the Viva Las Vegas venue a couple might choose the option promoted as

one of the most sought after Elvis wedding chapels in the world. Our Elvis ceremonies are affordable and a hunka hunka burning fun! Featuring the one and only Pink Caddy wedding, complete with theatrical lighting and fog, with a 1964 convertible pink Cadillac that makes a grand entrance into the chapel escorting the bride and groom in tow with Elvis driving. The Pink Caddy wedding is a one of a kind, once in a life time platinum hit at the chapel and our most popular.

You may choose our popular Elvis Blue Hawaii wedding. This package is highlighted by a lush tropical set, hula girls dancing to Elvis' rendition of the Hawaiian wedding song, and theatrical fog and lighting effects. Or what about stepping back in time with Elvis in our DooWop Diner! There are more than twelve Elvis wedding packages for you to choose from.[37]

At Graceland, which always has an eye for a business opportunity, there is now a wedding chapel, The Chapel in the Woods. Couples can marry in the shadow of Elvis's home, although having an Elvis take the service is not considered respectful. 'Whether it's just the two of you or up to 50 of your friends and family, Graceland's Chapel in the Woods will complement the ceremony of your dreams.' It comes at a hire cost of almost $800, cheaper on some days of the week, for half an hour plus fifteen minutes for photographs on the Graceland steps. A photographer is an extra $350.

A priest is a go-between who can channel an eternal mystery through his person to the people. In many religious traditions he is considered to be called by God and must undergo a long period of study. Similarly Elvis impersonators talk of being called. They too must undergo a long process of learning the many Elvis songs and practising the gestures. The repertoire is over 600 numbers, and all of the best-known must be memorized to perform a credible act. A select few of the first generation of Elvises are like the first Christian apostles in that they feel they have been granted an authority to perform by Elvis himself. Douglas Roy was once invited on stage by Elvis himself to sing 'Hound Dog'. He was given a rabbit's foot as a souvenir. Dave Carlson was seen by Elvis on stage in 1975 and Elvis declared afterwards of the resemblance to himself, 'I saw it, but I couldn't believe it.'[38]

The Roman Catholic tradition is that priests should not marry, as wife and family would distract them from their vocation. Most

Elvis artists are married and partners discover it is a strange relationship being married to a man whose public act requires him to exude an aura of sexuality. At a performance in 1989 Clayton Benke-Smith was mobbed by the audience screaming 'Elvis! Elvis!' Security guards had to protect him when he was almost dragged off the stage. Clayton said of the episode that it was scary, but exhilarating. Some wives are tolerant of their husband's alter ego. Linda, the wife and manager of Bert Hathaway, was quoted in 1991 as saying, 'they are not kissing Bert; they are kissing an image of Elvis. It is exciting seeing the women go after him like that.'[39]

Some partners, however, have experienced strains in their relationships, with wives being unprepared for the consequences of having a husband who is also Elvis, especially when the role takes him over completely. It must be very difficult sitting in the corner of a venue watching dozens of women demanding and absorbing his attention.

Understanding the Elvis phenomenon is not simply a matter of examining statistics, nor even the intensity of the emotions felt by fans. It also involves examining the nature of those emotions, which in many ways appear to be religious, or quasi-religious. Many fans talk of their devotion like Christians who have found fellowship or koinonia within the walls and embrace of their church; or, when visiting Graceland, like pilgrims walking in the footsteps of Jesus in the Holy Land.

Worship the King

At the climax of an Elvis Festival at Hemsby in Norfolk, UK, in the late 1980s, the compere took to the stage in front of a crowd of several hundred and shouted into the microphone.

'Give me an E.'

'E', the fans roared back.

'Give me an L, give me a V, give me an I, give me an S'. With each letter the response grew louder.

'Who's going to live for ever?'

'ELVIS!'

And then the chant began, 'Elvis, Elvis, Elvis, Elvis . . .'

Many in the audience swayed as they chanted and held their hands in the air as if at a Pentecostal service. They called the name 'Elvis' in the same manner that, at large gatherings of Christians, the name 'Jesus' is called. In fact the whole 'E-L-V-I-S, who's going to live for ever?' routine was a direct copy of a well-known Christian rallying cry, with the name of Elvis substituted for that of Jesus.

'In the beginning there was the Word and the Word was Elvis', proclaimed the impersonator Clayton Benke-Smith. From the misappropriation of the opening words of St John's Gospel to the Elvis nativity story, many fans have found ways to create a religious aura around Elvis Presley, frequently fusing and confusing Elvis and Jesus.

Some fans talk of Elvis and Jesus in much the same way. One fan had in the bedroom of her apartment in Memphis a large picture of Elvis alongside one of Jesus. 'They were both betrayed in the end and suffered. Both gave out love without asking for anything in return. They wanted people to remember them and follow their example. God preached through Jesus. Elvis did not preach, but sang.'[1]

There are several ways in which the things Elvis fans do mimic traditional religious practice. Elvis fans visit Graceland in a spirit of pilgrimage, not simply as tourists. There are examples of dramatic conversion stories. Parallels have been noted between the trade in Elvis souvenirs and the sale of holy relics in medieval times. Examples of prayers are found among the messages to Elvis written on the wall fronting the Graceland grounds. The practices of the Elvis tribute artists have, as explored earlier, turned their calling into a kind of priesthood.

It all possibly goes further than mimicry. It might be that a new religion is taking shape, based on and around Elvis Presley, an idea first suggested in my *Elvis People: The Cult of the King*. Three years after the book's publication, an article by Ron Rosenbaum appeared in the *New York Times* arguing that Elvis's popularity had 'transcended the familiar contours of a dead celebrity cult and had began to assume the dimensions of a redemptive faith'.[2] This was going one step further than simply noting religious parallels. A redemptive faith is one that promises forgiveness of sins and the expiation of guilt. The suggestion was being made that fans were seeking a form of earthly salvation through Elvis.

The psychologist Dr Richard Maddock, who specializes in the study of consumer behaviour and has conducted research at Graceland, has made a similar observation. 'Elvis allowed people to think their impulses were acceptable . . . That's what Jesus did. He took our guilt away,' Twenty years after Elvis's death, Maddock noted how, by attaching themselves to Elvis Presley, many people had discovered a way to rid themselves of guilt.

His whole existence was to take guilt away from people. He started out that way and ended up that way. The first phase, on television in the 1950s, he did things that in those days people only did in private. It was like he was saying OK; you don't have to feel guilty about it. In the second phase of his career, he added something. In his concerts, he not only did the movements and motions, by that time commonly accepted, he also added spiritual songs at the end. In effect he was saying, not only are your impulses OK, now they are blessed.[3]

In Christian teaching Christ, as the Son of God, has the authority to forgive sins. The New Testament tells how he delegated this authority to his Church when he said to St Peter: 'I will give unto thee the keys of the kingdom of heaven: and whatsoever thou shalt bind on earth shall be bound in heaven: and whatsoever thou shalt loose on earth shall be loosed in heaven' (Matthew 16:19). There is no scripture that declares that Elvis has any such authority, yet some Elvis fans have granted Elvis an extraordinary status from which an extraordinary authority might be implied. Not only, they say, was there a supernatural side to him, both in life and after death, but he himself was Jesus-like.

There are parallels between the structure of Elvis tribute concerts and that of the Christian Mass. In both, those attending receive something as well as simply being there to listen. In the Christian context, worshippers are given the body and blood of Christ as symbolized in bread and wine. It was a rite initiated by Jesus at the Last Supper when he broke bread, gave it to his disciples and commanded them, 'do this in remembrance of me'. At an Elvis concert members of the audience reverently receive scarves and a kiss. It is what Elvis used to do and although he did not leave instructions that this practice should continue, it does continue as a remembrance of the King. The photographer Patty Carroll, who met over a hundred Elvis tribute artists in the course of her photography project, says that while the scarf is a souvenir, the kiss is the communion. 'And it is quite a thing if you are in the audience, you have to feel worthy to get the gift.'[4]

The Elvis 'priests' wear 'vestments' to celebrate a kind of Eucharist. A tribute act is an illusion, but it is not the charisma of the individual who is 'Elvis for the night' that creates the illusion alone. He needs the clothes, the props, the lights and the music. The Christian Church teaches that the priest is an ordinary mortal. He is, like his flock, a flawed and sinful human being. But in vestments, at the altar, he becomes, despite his personal faults, the representative of Christ. The Christian vestments are frequently highly decorated, especially in the Catholic tradition. Patterns and motifs symbolize sacred ideas. And so it is with Elvis. Indeed since the Old Testament days of the first Jewish priest, Aaron, the way a priest is vested has been important. 'And thou shalt make holy garments for Aaron thy brother for glory and for beauty. And thou shalt speak unto all that are wise hearted, whom I have filled with the spirit of wisdom, that they may make Aaron's garments to consecrate him, that he may minister unto me in the priest's office' (Exodus 23:28). Some fans have observed it is no ordinary coincidence that Elvis too was given the middle name of Aaron.

Yet it is the theology at the heart of both rituals where the most telling parallel is to be found. The Mass explicitly celebrates Christ's suffering in incarnated form: the belief that God became a man and lived at a known time in history, making a specific place his home. He was then destined to suffer and die, but he ultimately rose triumphantly in glory. The words of the song 'An American Trilogy' take those three key points and make them Elvis's. He was incarnate, a real person, flesh and blood and of a time and place: Dixieland, he sings, is where he was born. He was destined to suffer and he offers words of solace implying that he was destined to die. Then, after saying that his trials will soon be over, he switches to the celebrated and triumphant words of the

Battle Hymn of The Republic: 'Glory, glory hallelujah. His truth is marching on.'

It is this Elvis-focused interpretation of the song that leads some fans to ponder on how 2,000 years earlier there had been another man who was born into a land of poverty, toil and tension. It was his destiny too to suffer and die. But he then triumphed over death. His name was Jesus. In art Elvis has sometimes been shown as the suffering one, akin to the Lamb of God, an atoning sacrifice. One art exhibition featuring the work of the photographers Robert E. Lewis and Lawrence Jasud paired vivid pictures of religious tableaux depicting the passion of Christ with decorated pictures of Elvis laid on his grave or prepared in his memory.[5]

Elvis epitomized the American Dream of working hard to go from poverty to riches, but it was a dream that around the time of Elvis's death was beginning to fall apart for many Americans. In the late 1970s, America, indeed the Western world, was troubled. The values of opportunity and wealth creation that underpinned the American Dream were starting to be challenged. The environmental movement was just beginning to question the consumer values of the age. The idea was taking shape that modern civilization would have to pay and suffer for its materialism and gas-guzzling overindulgence. In ancient times the way to appease a troubled conscience or placate the gods and forestall punishment to come was through sacrifice. It has been argued that the death of Elvis served this purpose.

Yet, for this symbolic magic to work, the sacrifice has to be innocent. The lamb or goat selected to die in Old Testament Jewish practice had itself done no wrong. Christians teach that the crucified Jesus was entirely blameless, and was the sacrificial Lamb of God. Fans however realize that Elvis in life had been no saint. Indeed around the time of his death, a tarnished, discredited flipside of the Elvis they adored became public knowledge. For Elvis to be seen as innocent of his death, despite his excesses in life, the fans had to forgive him. His doctor and friends were instead held responsible for his sad and ignominious end. Some fans even blamed themselves for demanding so much of their hero that he was unable to cope with the pressure.

Some American Christians, scandalized by such talk, believe the very opposite. To them Elvis in life was an unrepentant sinner and in death has become a focus of misguided adoration. In May 2013 the Westboro Baptist Church from Kansas staged a demonstration outside Graceland. The church, better known for its strident anti-homosexuality views, felt called upon to protest against the religious elevation of Elvis. 'They've turned this guy into an idol. They worship and serve him more than they do the living God,' said Shirley Phelps-Roper, a member of the church.[6] Some members quoted from the Bible in support of their stand. 'Thus saith the Lord God; Repent, and turn yourselves from your idols; and turn away your faces from all your abominations' (Ezekiel 14:6). The demonstration was small and was kept apart from a counter-demonstration by a small contingent of police.

Some elements of the online Christian community have not held back in their wholesale condemnation of Elvis Presley. Elvis fans who visit his grave are, in the words of one outspoken critic, David J. Stewart, worshipping the rotting carcass of a lecherous, adulterous pervert and drug addict. Stewart is a controversial figure in the world of American-based religious online evangelism, and has trenchant opinions when it comes to Elvis. He accuses fans of blasphemous idolatry. He describes Elvis's music as a Trojan horse for America's youth, desensitizing them to the evils of hellish rock 'n' roll. The term 'rock 'n' roll', he claims, was originally a slang term with sexual overtones and Elvis was a 'sexually degenerate heathen whoremonger who wasted his life in sin . . . Millions of young believers became corrupted, desensitized to sin by Elvis' hellish music. Elvis spawned a whole generation of adulterers and rebels against God. Elvis was indeed God's enemy.'[7]

It should be made clear that this view is much in the minority, even among conservative Christians. A more commonly held view in Christian circles is that Elvis's music can be used as a tool of evangelization. Many mainstream churches, including Canterbury Cathedral, have held concerts of Elvis music where many of the great gospel songs he had made famous are performed.

Maddy Wilson of the UK-based Elvis Gospel Ministry talks of confirming her Christian faith through listening to Elvis. His recordings of gospel music are certainly among the most emotionally charged renderings ever made of some of the greatest Christian hymns ever written. Elvis was called by God to be a gospel singer and evangelist, Maddy believes.

> He was however unable to escape from the spiritual trap in which he was caught. God in His mercy removed Elvis from this scene of time, but the work he began is not yet finished. We hope to reach the hundreds of thousands of Elvis fans all over the world, with the challenge of the Gospel of Jesus Christ. We are constantly researching into the fruits of Elvis' life and have discovered that many people have given their life to Christ as a direct result of listening to Gospel sung by Elvis, and the Lord has also challenged people as they have been at Elvis' home at Graceland. Our God is a creative God and is capable of using all kinds of, often to us, unusual methods of winning people to Himself.[8]

Maddy believes Elvis can be the means through which people might discover Jesus, emphasizing strongly that to confuse the two is an error. Elvis fans who are also active members of a Christian church insist that any hint of confusion between Elvis and Jesus would never have been countenanced by the King himself. A much-quoted story is told of Elvis's reaction to the suggestion that he had some special, elevated, divine regal status. In one version it is said that he would point upwards to heaven saying, 'there is only one King', to emphasize it was Jesus and not himself.

The religious aspects of following Elvis have been picked up and expanded on by several authors. John Strausbaugh sees an emerging Elvis cult as another indigenous American religion like Mormonism. 'Can faith in Elvis be any stranger than Mormons' faith in Joseph Smith's bizarre visions?' he asks.

> Smith went out into the woods where he received personal visits from God the Father, Jesus and the angel Moroni, who led him to golden tablets on which were written, in a 'Reformed Egyptian' hieroglyphics that was instantly translated for him when he put on a pair of rose-colored spectacles, the Book of Mormon.[9]

Gilbert Rodman's book *Elvis after Elvis* carries a front cover showing Elvis in the Roman Catholic pose of Christ displaying his Sacred Heart. The deification of Elvis is not the intention of the official guardians of the Elvis legacy, he maintains, but they do not stand in the way of the fans who engage in the 'various sanctifying practices'. One example of this is the way Graceland keeps the Christmas lights burning several days after Twelfth Night, the traditional day for taking them down, in order to celebrate Elvis's birthday on 8 January as well as that of Jesus on 25 December.

Not all observers agree with the Elvis religion thesis. Gregory Reece from the University of Alabama titled his book on the subject *Elvis Religion*, but admitted that his conclusions did not match 'the catchy headline'. New religions, he said, need 'charismatic leaders, rituals, sacred objects and sacred places. They need the kinds of things we have looked for at Graceland and among Elvis impersonators, the kinds of things we have looked for and failed to find.'[10]

'I went to Graceland looking for religion,' Reece admits.

> I went looking for pilgrims and worshippers. I went looking for people in prayer and meditation, for people bowing

before shrines and icons and making offerings to Saint Elvis. I did not find what I was looking for . . . I found a gathering of individuals from all over the world who share a common interest and like to get together regularly to share stories and collectables and popcorn and beer. I found happy hour at the Heartbreak Hotel.[11]

Reece saw all the evidence, but somehow felt restrained in acknowledging its religious content. True, there is no church of Elvis with an overt ecclesiastical structure. Fans themselves are reluctant to talk about their religious experiences. 'I know I shouldn't,' one fan confessed after several hours of conversation, 'but I do pray to Elvis.'[12] Reece did acknowledge that there was religious imagery to be seen in Elvis popular culture, but he drew back from interpreting its use as genuinely religious. It was a typically Protestant response. Many people who are or have been members of established churches find faith a serious and solemn business and anything that is fun, they conclude, is unlikely to be sacred as well. Faith, too, in the Protestant tradition, is expressed in words and dogmatic formulae and not rituals and images; it should properly consist of sets of creedal statements and not simply be a matter of how you feel or what you do. Elvis fandom is not (yet) an explicit expression of faith, but it is surely an implicit form of spirituality in that it provides fellowship, ritual and meaning.

The art historian Gary Vikan titled his 2012 study of the Elvis world *From the Holy Land to Graceland*. At first sight, his comparisons between modern Elvis-centred practices and traditional religion might appear to support the case that Elvis fans are not involved in an overtly religious practice. 'There is no Elvis theology, no Elvis hierarchy of clergy, no characteristic Elvis sanctuary design and no Elvis intercession, nor are there Elvis sacraments or Elvis congregations, certainly not in the sense that all of these are understood within the context of the world's great religions.'

Attempts to understand the Elvis phenomenon within the framework of conventional religion are flawed, he argues. Rather one has to look on the boundaries of religion, 'in the much less organized and structured world of charismatics, holy places and pilgrimages that all religions, to some degree, share in common'. Might Elvis worship one day become a fully fledged religion? That, said Vikan, is the wrong question to ask. 'The Elvis/Graceland phenomenon is already comfortably situated within a familiar para-religious world.'[13]

There is some evidence to suggest that there is an evolving Elvis theology. Any form of church, as well as having structures, needs also to have an underpinning creedal identity. Elvis theology is as yet inconsistent and unshaped. While some fans endorse Elvis as having had a quasi-messianic role, some art gives Elvis angelic qualities and some fans value the sacramental aspects of attending tribute concerts: it is all rather muddled. There are no charismatic leaders, as Reece has pointed out, to give Elvisdom direction. Nevertheless, fans do appear to pray and meditate. They bow before shrines and icons and make offerings to Elvis, although often in the privacy of their own homes rather as a public declaration of faith. The religiosity of Elvis is expressed in action and not formulated as doctrine.

Mostly the Elvis churches have been elaborate jokes; at first sight one might suppose that a burlesque dancer who is also an Elvis minister of religion would be party to a huge leg-pull. But like many fans, Minister Anna of the Presleyterian Church in Australia finds having Elvis-related fun does not preclude her from taking a longer-term and more serious view of what she does and celebrates. The First Presleyterian Church is essentially a satire on both organized religion and Elvis worship, she admits. However, the fact that it and other similar Elvis churches exist, she says, is testament in itself to the religious fervour of Elvis fandom. If a carpenter can be a Messiah, why can't a singer? she asks.

The idea of Elvis Presley as messiah, saviour, or divine messenger, is clearly still a new and controversial one. In our predominantly Christian Western society, many believe the very idea to be blasphemous and or ridiculous. History shows that messianic cults existed long before the advent of modern Christianity, and that the Christian church as we know it now, and as it was then, was based on elements of other messianic belief systems that pre-date Christianity.

Today, Jesus is probably the most famous and popular Messiah. This was not always the case however, and in Jesus' own time he was not universally recognized as the saviour of the people. At that time many believed the idea of Jesus as Messiah to be ridiculous. The Essenes, an austere Jewish sect of which it is thought Jesus was a member, thought the idea impossible, just as many today consider the idea of Elvis as Messiah to be ridiculous and impossible. So while Christians may find the claim that Elvis is a Messiah blasphemous, it is not unlikely that those who worshipped Osiris would consider the Christian claim of Jesus as Messiah equally blasphemous. In Jesus' time, his method of worship and his religious ideas were not widely accepted; he was considered morally lax, irresponsible and controversial among religious scholars, including the forebears of the Christian Church he supposedly belonged to. He was altogether too modern. Of course 2,000 or so years later he is not considered modern at all. And so it is with Elvis, the claim that he is a Messiah is discounted due to his perceived moral laxity (according to Christian standards) and the fact that he is 'just' a rock 'n' roll singer.[14]

If Elvis can be understood in messianic terms, what, in Anna's opinion, is the theology behind it? 'If religion is a set of principles and beliefs by which a group of people choose to live,' Anna argues, it is probably too early to distil the vast and varied layers of Elvis worship into a coherent set of principles which could be used to define a belief system based on Elvis. That being said, I think there are some key elements that are common among Elvis worshippers. The Rev Mort Farndu and Dr Edwards of the Presleyterian Church developed a list of commandments (based on dietary items favoured by Elvis) and principles based on the messages of his songs such as 'Don't Be Cruel', 'Don't be a Hound Dog (Catch a Rabbit and be a Friend of His)' and 'Love Me Tender', and appropriated the Christian question 'what would Jesus do', becoming instead 'what would Elvis do?' This is very funny of course, but no organized Elvis religion yet exists where a comprehensive theology or doctrine has been established.

Yet in understanding the 'Elvis religion' it is important, to expand on Vikan's view, not to define religion too narrowly. A religion is not simply a set of beliefs about a deity that is then set out as a creed and policed by a church hierarchy. Religion is a much looser term. It is about what people do, the rituals they perform, the stories they tell, to try and make sense of their own lives and to discover the underpinning purpose, if there is one, of life. It is about the attempts people make to understand those things that defy scientific definition and exploration. It is about discovering that which is mysterious, both within and beyond ourselves as humans. It is about apprehending the spiritual, those ineffable and intangible things which many people instinctively feel to be self-evident truths. It is about the music and images people turn to in order to explore the deeper mysteries of existence.

When Elvis fans are together they have fun. However, it is not aimless fun. Underscoring the enjoyment is purpose. It has been said that once the necessities of physical comfort are found, the primary motivation in life of any human being is the search for purpose and fulfilment. For many fans, Elvis provides both. Elvis fans are not superficial consumers of pop culture, flipping from fashion to fashion and caring for little but the shallow things of life. Many Elvis enthusiasts have wider interests – religious, spiritual, esoteric – and find these interests nourished through Elvis. They share Elvis's fascination with the deeper and inner mysteries of life, not in a scholarly or bookish sense, but instinctively. And the questions they raise in their minds at times of stress, sorrow, awe, love or joy can be explored or focused, they have discovered, through Elvis.

Yet what was, and remains to this day, so special about Elvis Presley? Lisa Marie, his daughter, was once asked the question in a television interview. After some hesitation she collected her thoughts and found the best way she could to describe her father's unique appeal. It was, she said, the way in which 'his spirit' and 'his soul' reached out through his singing and moved people. Today, even her mother, Priscilla, who when living with Elvis had had her doubts about his enthusiasm for esoteric ideas, talks about his spirit. It's the spirit of the singer, and not just his music and history, that keeps the crowds coming to Graceland, she believes. 'Every time I go in there, I feel like Elvis is going to come down the stairs any minute. I have no doubt that he's there, somewhere, his spirit. I think people feel that.' Is it necessary to journey to Graceland to discover the mystical Elvis? Simply the experience of listening to his voice, says Lisa Marie, is a very spiritual one. 'There's an aesthetic plane it hits somewhere,' which 'he penetrated through his voice'.[15] Yet what did Lisa Marie mean? What is an aesthetic plane and how might it be penetrated? Indeed what did she mean by choosing words such as 'spirit' and 'soul', terms which are dismissed as meaningless by contemporary secularists?

She was employing language that would be recognized by most Elvis fans. Indeed they would themselves talk of the soul and the spirit of Elvis. However Lisa Marie's talk of the aesthetic perhaps goes beyond what most Elvis fans would find familiar. It is to embark on an abstract quest for absolute beauty and perfection. In the nineteenth century there were schools of artists dedicated to aesthetic pursuits. They sought knowledge of beauty and asked if nature had qualities of beauty that, if they could only be truly understood, could be copied to produce the finest of fine art.

Later philosophers preferred to see beauty in cultural terms. There were no absolute standards; ideas of beauty came and went in fashions and were decided by society. Thus, for instance, the ideal of female beauty has changed over time and from place to place. In English Victorian society an attractive woman protected her skin from sunlight to keep it perfectly white and beautiful. That woman's great-granddaughter would today be found sunbathing in a bikini to get an all-over tan.

Lisa Marie, in talking of the aesthetic plane, was suggesting that perhaps some standards of beauty do exist irrespective of culture and history. They are to found on another, perhaps higher, plane of existence and Elvis's voice penetrated the barrier separating the earthly from the higher aesthetic plane, where absolute perfection is to be found. Fans could reach out to that perfection through the breach in the barrier created by Elvis. They did this spiritually. It was their souls that were touched by the beauty beyond, not their physical selves. Elvis, seen in these terms, is perceived as a door to transcendence, which is an explicitly religious concept.

It is all very New Age stuff. Elvis and his hairdresser and mentor Larry Geller spent many hours talking of such things. 'Together we studied ancient wisdom and philosophy, religions of both East and West, exoteric and esoteric,' Geller recalled.

> Nothing was off bounds for our inquiring minds. We prac-
> ticed meditation and spiritual healing. We loved to play with
> numbers and words, creating new ways of finding mystical
> meaning in the ordinary. Mysticism spoke directly to Elvis's
> fundamental desire to know what life was about, and thus
> it emerged naturally from the very marrow of his being.[16]

While Elvis was undoubtedly fascinated by such thinking, and his daughter too has an interest in some of the same philosophies, they are not ideas relevant to the day-to-day lives of many ordinary Elvis fans. That is not to say that Elvis fails to penetrate through to the emotions of his fans in a way they recognize. It is just that few will be as familiar as Elvis and Larry with the New Age approach. Nevertheless, the feelings and responses they experience when listening to his voice penetrate them profoundly. And 'penetrate' is an interesting word for Lisa Marie to use in this context, with its sexual overtones.

Looking at what fans do in response to those feelings also helps understand the enduring phenomenon that is Elvis. Many things people do that are essentially religious will not be recognized as such. The study of implicit religion looks for religious-style practice in the patterns of everyday secular life. Level-headed Elvis fans are not members of some Elvis-centred cult. Far from it. By some definitions, a cult requires a leader. The Unification Church has been called a cult because of the dominance of its leader and founder the Rev Sun Myung Moon. Similarly the Scientologists have attracted the cult label because of the leadership and legacy of L. Ron Hubbard. As mentioned earlier, there is no leader of the Elvis world. His family, friends and former colleagues are highly regarded but they hold no sway over what the fans believe and have never attempted to preach an Elvis doctrine. The wholesome, bland Elvis portrayed by guides at Graceland is a neutral image of the King.

Of the several attempts to create a church of Elvis, none have taken control of or held the imagination of his fans in any substantial numbers. Many self-declared churches are solely Internet projects, elaborate jokes or art projects that do little more than poke fun at both Elvis and organized religion. The First Church of Jesus Christ, Elvis, provides a pastiche of Christian scripture with an Elvis theme. 'And Elvis so loved the world that he died, fat and bloated, in a bathroom. He very pointedly did not rise from the

The 24 Hour Church of Elvis – an art installation set up at different times in several shopfronts around the USA where viewers could activate a range of Elvis-related slot machines.

dead three days later, but was nonetheless seen across the world by various and sundry housewives.' The 24 Hour Church of Elvis was an exhibit in a shop window in Portland, Oregon, and the invention of the artist Stevie G. Pierce. Visitors could interact with what they saw through the glass via various coin-operated devices. The 24 Hour Church of Elvis also sold a range of jokey Christmas cards with such captions as 'Christmas comes but once a year, only Elvis is forever'; 'Merry Christmas from Santa and his Elvises'; and 'Silent Night, Holy night, all is calm, all is Elvis'.

Flippant websites are however heavily outnumbered by those celebrating the religious, spiritual or mystical side of Elvis in a more serious, if on occasions kitsch, style, though none style themselves as churches. On one of these sites fans can 'Light a Candle for Elvis'.[17] This can be done virtually by choosing one of six colours at the TLC Shrine, representing reverence, desire, success, peace, memory or joy, and leaving a message. The cyber-candle burns for fourteen days. Another way to light a candle for Elvis, it suggests, is to be tolerant of others, respectful to animals and by spending time listening 'to your inner spiritual being and opening your heart and mind to the evolution of your own soul'.

One popular site claims to have been viewed over sixteen million times. Known as Carolyn's Elvis Site, it is not promoting an Elvis religion in any way, but does endorse an Elvis spirituality. Its main image shows a young Elvis playing a guitar. He is placed within a fantasy landscape featuring the front of Graceland. The image is surrounded by a golden frame set in a starlit sky. Visitors to the site can listen to Elvis's 1961 recording of the song 'Angel'. The site links through to others. Janie's pages show the lyrics of several Elvis songs and offer the choice to go to other pages, including one called 'Jesus Lives'. Click on that and up come images of Jesus and Elvis under the heading 'Elvis Lives'.

If not members of an identifiable cult, a substantial group of Elvis fans do take their devotions close to the realms of explicit religion. At the outer extreme there have been attempts to claim that Elvis was the true Messiah and that the story of Jesus in the Gospels is in reality a prophetic work foretelling the life of Elvis. The confusion, or intertwining, of Jesus and Elvis is far from uncommon in the contemporary Elvis world.

St Elvis

Astudy of the history of religion shows that faith systems do not appear from nowhere. New churches evolve out of old ones, sometimes as a protest, sometimes as the result of new teaching or an inspirational leader emerging. In this way Christianity grew out of Judaism. Mormonism evolved out of Christianity. Sometimes, when an established religion is challenged, it is not an entirely new religion that develops, but a denomination. Denominations do not overturn that which came before, but refocus the existing orthodoxy. They discover their own distinctive ways of expressing the established faith.

The Elvis phenomenon has Western, Christian roots. He was raised in Bible Belt America. The Presley family took Elvis to church when he was young. He sang gospel music. He read his Bible; indeed, the copy given to him by his Uncle Vester, which in 2012 fetched £59,000 at auction, was well thumbed and contained Elvis's own handwritten notes.

Elvis fans from the USA, Europe and the English-speaking world share his Western cultural background, with its historical roots in Christianity. If through Elvis they discover a spiritual dimension to their lives it is inevitable that their insights will be described in language drawn from that background. This does not mean they are setting up an Elvis religion, or even a new Elvis-orientated Christian denomination, though what might happen in the long term remains open to speculation. What can be said at present is that fans have discovered through Elvis a means of expressing their spiritual instincts, something that in the West had once been the sole prerogative of the Christian churches.

A recurring theme found when exploring the spiritual dimension of Elvis fandom is the link made by fans between Elvis and Jesus. Some fans keep pictures of Jesus alongside those of Elvis; both images are of equal size and granted equal status. Artists have frequently blended Jesus iconography with that of Elvis. Sometimes this is done in a spirit of satire, as in the case of a 1995 image by the artist Chris Rywalt. It shows Elvis displaying his Sacred Heart in a style mimicking Catholic iconography. The image has been reproduced in many contexts, in particular by the self-styled First Church of Jesus Christ, Elvis, with the motto: 'For unto you is born this day in the city of Memphis a Presley, which is Elvis the King.'

Some people of faith regard Rywalt's satire as insulting and sacrilegious. Yet good satire also can hint at a hidden truth. 'On the face of it, to compare Elvis Presley with Jesus is absurd,' Rywalt has said. 'Elvis didn't die for humanity, never mind our sins. He was consumed by his own indulgences and his audience's inordinate adoration. Despite everything, his flagrant lifestyle, the gaudiness of his later performances, there was always something vulnerable about the man. Like him, don't we all carry a Sacred Heart within ourselves?'[1]

There is a Christmas card with a message that overturns that of the traditional seasonal greeting. It is also produced in a spirit of satire and is just as offensive to devout Christians as Rywalt's work. It shows Christ in a white jumpsuit paying homage to Elvis, who has his hand raised in blessing. Elvis and Jesus are surrounded by cherubs.

Much sacred Elvis art is however designed to be viewed with genuine reverence. The art of Isabelle Tanner, for instance, is intended to be viewed in all seriousness. She has depicted Elvis in angelic form, transfigured by light. One image appears to be modelled on the Veil of Veronica – the cloth that, in legend, was used to wipe the face of the suffering Christ on his way to Calvary and on which an image of his face was miraculously preserved. She describes her Elvis paintings as 'a creation of a higher inspiration dedicated by Elvis, with his everlasting love and compassion. Living in God Elvis has guided this work proving through it that life is infinite'.[2]

Whether it is the satire or the seriously intended works of art that contain the greater truth is a matter for debate. Sometimes the serious and the satire are difficult to tell apart when it comes to Elvis art. For instance, the intention behind the grotesque and macabre images of Elvis found in Mexico during the annual Day of the Dead is difficult to discern.

The Elvis–Christ connection is now sufficiently embedded in popular culture for a designer clothing brand to have called itself Elvis Jesus. Founded in 2005, it is best known for its eye-catching T-shirts that fuse together religious and rock music imagery. Creator David Mallon's idea was to produce casual clothes, especially T-shirts, on which religious imagery clashed with rock album cover art. Adopting an unorthodox and provocative yet iconic name was a deliberate marketing ploy to appeal to customers with an unconventional outlook on life.

The Elvis–Jesus link goes back to the very early days of Elvis's career, when he gathered around him a select inner circle of friends and employees. One of these, a friend going back to their school days at Humes High School in Memphis, was George Klein. 'I grew up with him and there really was something special about this guy. I don't wish to be sacrilegious, but he's Jesus-like,' he told me in 1997 in an interview for a BBC television documentary.

> He had these powers. He could almost hypnotize you. And he could sway you with his conversation and looks. And his great personality and his amazing talent. I said to the guys

he's got to be something special. And they agreed he was something special. He wasn't just an ordinary human being. You couldn't have what he had and just be normal.[3]

Joe Esposito, who first met Elvis when he was in the army, echoes George Klein's impressions.

As a performer, there simply has never been any equal. Elvis Presley's talent came from another place. Once he 'touched' you, that was it. You were hooked for life. As long as I live, I know I will never see anyone have such a profound effect on people. He could make anyone, and I mean anyone, feel like he was the most important person in the world just by talking with him. He had charisma and charm that is just indescribable. And do you know something? He didn't even have to sing! When Elvis entered a room, even if you didn't see him come in, you could feel the energy of his presence tingle at your nerves because the power of his magnetism was that intense.[4]

The Hollywood screenwriter Alan Weiss has recalled how he watched Elvis on set while he was filming.

The transformation was incredible. We knew instantly that we were in the presence of a phenomenon, electricity bounced off the walls of the sound stage. One felt it as an awesome thing – like an earthquake in progress, only without the implicit threat. To deny his talent would have been as foolish as it was impossible. He was a force, and to fail to recognize it would be the same as sticking a finger into a live socket and denying the existence of electricity.[5]

Sheila Ryan, a girlfriend of Elvis in the 1970s, described qualities in Elvis that no other human being has, had, or will have. Some of them are so hard to describe because the charisma, the qualities that he had were almost not of this world. They were, a lot of times, angelic. He knew things before I knew things. He knew things that I was feeling before I was feeling them. Elvis had that smile and everyone interpreted that smile to be his sexy look. And it wasn't that at all. It was his innocence, his vulnerability. It wasn't at all something that he turned on and off. The man was just not normal.[6]

Mother Dolores Hart, the actress turned Roman Catholic Benedictine nun who starred with Elvis in *Loving You* in 1957, told fans when she attended Elvis Week in 2013 how she would listen to Elvis singing on the film set and 'I couldn't believe the charisma. This man is going to live for ever, that voice is not just for us, that voice is for the people of God.'[7]

Robert Alaniz, the film producer and Presleyana collector, saw Elvis in concert on three occasions. 'He created magic; he was almost surreal, almost like a God. The first time I saw him I could have sworn there was an aura around him as he came on stage. It was almost like the second coming of Jesus Christ. An angel, some sort of God.'[8]

Robert Campbell, a fan who never knew Elvis personally, has recounted the story of his own supernatural encounter with the King. His story contains elements both of the St Paul conversion on the road to Damascus and of contemporary descriptions of near-death experiences. 'I found myself in paradise and very suddenly I saw a blinding, or near blinding white light. And out of the light came a voice like rolling thunder, though the words were very recognizable. The words were as clear as day. The voice coming out of the light said, "Go back and tell them Elvis."' From this Campbell concluded that Elvis did not simply have a special place in world history, but was the ultimate judge and saviour.

He's Emmanuel, the only begotten son God said he would send. Not only would he send him to the tribes of Israel but to the Gentiles also. Emmanuel and Elvis are synonymous. No question the Son of God, the very incarnation of God and he was led to the slaughter like the lamb. The gospels are myths and legends foretelling the coming of Elvis. He has risen and will come again in judgement. That will be Judgement Day, which is very soon.[9]

Campbell's interpretation was based on a vision. The Australian author Christopher Matthews, however, spent ten years in research and produced nearly 1,800 pages of 'proof'. His Elvis version of *The Da Vinci Code* is both eccentric and esoteric and is available in three volumes titled *The Name Code: The God of Elvis* (volumes I and II) and *The Path to Graceland*. Matthews claims that by decoding hidden meaning within the names of Elvis and his family he has found a range of sacred and messianic messages. The Bible, too, Matthews says, is full of code, discernible to those with a knowledge of Hebrew. His studies, he says, have uncovered the hidden knowledge that Jesus was not the Messiah and Elvis Presley is in fact the son of El Baal or God.

Another author has mined the same biblical seam for evidence of Elvis's divine purpose. The promotional material for Cinda Godfrey's book *The Elvis–Jesus Mystery* claims that readers will discover the evidence that Adam, Jesus and Elvis are all the same soul.

Learn why God had to conceal Elvis' true identity–the greatest secret of all ages! See the hundreds of clues Elvis left behind to help us discover the truth! Read Elvis' life story in the Holy Bible! Find out how the Great Pyramid in Egypt is a monument to Elvis! Does the empty sarcophagus in the pyramid's King's Chamber represent the empty grave at Graceland? Read how the great seer Nostradamus and Edgar

Cayce prophesied Elvis' appearance and disappearance! Find out what it means to have Elvis' face in your finger-prints! Learn the real reason Elvis had to fake his death and disappear in 1977 and who wanted Elvis Presley dead! Discover how astronomy, astrology, numerology, scripture and ancient folklore all foretell Elvis' coming into the world at this late hour of human history![10]

Godfrey claimed that her book presented the shocking scriptural evidence that Elvis, and not Jesus, might have been the long-anticipated Messiah.

There is a small coterie of fans who offer prayers to Elvis, commune with him spiritually and set up shrines in his name, as they regard him as a super-being who came from beyond the earth. The term 'Elvii' has been used to describe the truly devout who, by almost any definition, have created a religious practice around their love of the King. It is a secretive faith and it is said that they refer to Elvis simply as 'E' or 'El' (an Old Testament name for God). It is by that sign they recognize each other.

A recording of a telephone conversation allegedly made between Elvis and Wanda June Hill, a friend and, she says, confidante of Elvis, suggests that the singer had some strange ideas of his own to explain his extraordinary life and career. 'I am not of this world,' the Elvis-like voice on the recording says. 'I am a man, a human being now, but what is "me" is not from here. I am from out there. Did you ever hear of Rigel?' Rigel is the brightest star in the constellation of Orion and the seventh brightest in the night sky. 'My home is near there – my other home – where I am from, and I have the Blue Star for my sun. I have eight moons and a mansion beneath the outer shell of my planet. You think I'm making this up, but its true – you'll know that one day.'[11]

Esposito confirms that his friend struggled to make sense of his success and the effect he had on others.

Elvis was just as perplexed by this phenomenon as you or I are today. For the most part, he was a very humble man. But he was keenly aware of his unique gifts and spent most of his life searching the realms of spirituality for clues as to why he was chosen to be "Elvis Presley". Over and over throughout his life he asked himself, Why me?'[12]

His religious upbringing had not prepared him to ask such significant questions. His background was in Southern gospel-music-centred, Bible-based worship, a style of funda-mental Protestant Christianity. Churches of that kind evolved to meet the spiritual needs of those who do not acquire fame or riches. They provide exciting spiritual experiences, by way of compensation, in this world with promises of riches in the next. As an adult, when trying to understand his astonishing rise to fame, Elvis's interest turned to alternative sources of religious answers, New Age and esoteric teachings, under the guidance of his unofficial tutor, his hairdresser Larry Geller.

Elvis called Larry his guru, but the hairdresser never became a true insider despite spending a great deal of time with Elvis. Colonel Parker distrusted him and was perhaps worried that his own hold over Elvis would be diminished the more Elvis came under Geller's spell. He called Geller a magician who peddled illusions. Priscilla too did not appreciate Elvis's obsession with mystical introspection that Geller encouraged. Elvis's Memphis Mafia, the entourage made up of old school friends and body-guards, had no interest in Geller's ideas and resented anyone who interfered with their macho-laddish relationship with Elvis. Geller was sacked by the Colonel shortly after Elvis had had a fall, when he was in no condition to protest. Elvis's collection of books, which he had built up under Geller's guidance, was burned on the Colonel's orders. Geller returned to Graceland much later towards the end of Elvis's life and was shocked to find Elvis in bad psychological and physical shape. It was Geller who prepared

Elvis to be viewed in his open coffin. Later he wrote a book, *If I Can Dream*, about his time at Graceland that provided a fascinating account of the singer's life spinning out of control.

'Elvis was fascinated by Jesus, not just the image of Jesus but who he was,' Geller later recalled. 'He didn't think that Jesus was the only begotten Son of God. He thought that all people had Christ in them and had the same potential.' Elvis's idea of Jesus Christ differed from the Jesus depicted by modern Christianity, Geller maintains.

> Elvis felt that while on earth Christ revealed very deep, profound secrets, but that what we read today of what Jesus supposedly said is a watered-down version. He thought that Jesus experienced everything that all people experienced, that he was the flower of humanity, that he suffered, and yet his suffering was ecstasy. Later in life, whenever he felt that he was truly suffering, Elvis would say, 'this is the way Jesus was . . . He knew the sufferings of humanity. I understand that, and that's why I am who I am. That's why God put me on earth. That's part of my mission.'[13]

Geller has said that Elvis's birth, life and death resonate with biblical themes. The nativity story the fans tell is of Elvis's birth in a small shack in Tupelo, 'a house little bigger than a stable', in the words of one common version. At the moment of his birth a blue light hovered over the place, it is said, inviting comparison with the star of Bethlehem. Wanda June Hill has given this version of what happened when Elvis's father Vernon went outside shortly after Gladys had given birth. The first twin, Jesse, had been stillborn, but Elvis had arrived alive. 'Vernon raised his eyes to Heaven and thanked God for giving them one live child. As he turned back to the house, he saw streaming down from the sky a glowing blue light bathing the humble home where lay his wife and newborn son.' Twenty-five years later, Vernon was to say, 'I knew Elvis had to be a special baby, he had the light of Heaven on him from birth.'[14]

Hill believes that Elvis's entry into the world fits the pattern of 'sacred births' throughout the ages. 'Those who are born to serve the masses in a unique way, beyond the normal role of leadership, have had situations of conception and birth that were far from normal in their circumstances. I do not imply here that Elvis was a "god", but I do see his birth, life and death as paralleling other human beings who were destined as spiritual leaders in various degrees of brilliance.'[15]

Some fans also say that the house shook at the very moment Elvis entered the world. In his song 'Tupelo', the singer-songwriter Nick Cave gives the birth story a blood-and-thunder gothic make-over. The live Elvis and his dead twin arrive into this world as black rain lashes the family shack, hens refuse to lay and children are too scared to sleep.

Larry Geller's birth narrative is a little less dramatic and he describes how he heard the story directly from Vernon. His version adds an extra more mundane detail. At the time Vernon witnessed the blue light, the reason he had gone outside was to have a cigarette. The conception story that Vernon told Geller is more intriguing. 'I remember exactly the moment Elvis was conceived because at that moment when I was with his mother, all of a sudden my mind went blank. I went into this big black vastness and then I came back into my body and I knew something had happened. I just knew something monumental had happened. So when my wife said she was pregnant, I wasn't surprised at all.'[16]

Apocryphal stories are told about Elvis as a child that illustrate Elvis's supposed extraordinary status. They parallel the stories told about Jesus in some of the childhood narratives found in the apocryphal gospels. 'When he was a young child he would go out into the fields alone and by the streams and these beings would talk to him and sometimes they would appear to him as shining ones,' says author and mystic Maia Chrystine Nartoomid. 'They would tell him that he was blessed and sent to earth for a special purpose. He was also shown, in his mind, a man in a white suit standing on a stage with lights all around him. Of course the little boy in Tupelo had no idea what he was seeing. But they were showing him his future.'[17]

Nartoomid believes that Elvis, after death, still communicates with the world and she herself has received messages from him. Her co-author and collaborator Simeon Nartoomid believes that Elvis's soul was 'a master-type soul, a teacher-type soul that came from the outer realms'. He came to earth in a great light to inhabit a human personality 'that was not in its perfected state'.[18] Maia's book *Blue Star Love* shows a picture of Elvis on the cover riding a unicorn through a fantasy science-fiction world. The book also publishes a transcript of the recording said to have been made of the conversation between Wanda June Hill and Elvis in which Elvis admitted to his mysterious origins in another star system. Maia says that according to 'her mystical sources' Elvis deliberately sacrificed his own health in order to fulfil his mission on Earth. He was a spiritual being who had a life purpose far beyond entertaining. She says that he used his God-given talent and his desire to share it with people as a means to spread the greater Light within him around the world. Maia writes of Elvis teaching his daughter how to see angels and of how he prepared himself spiritually before each concert. Elvis was also able, she believes, to move objects with his mind and teleport his voice to distant locations, although such claims are not widely made and were never tested in his lifetime.

Elvis's spiritual mentor Larry Geller emphasizes that Elvis knew who he wasn't. He was not divine. Yet in the stories he has told about him, Geller has encouraged the idea that Elvis had superhuman gifts and insights. 'I once saw Elvis heal a man who was having a heart attack,' Geller wrote in *If I Can Dream*.

Another time Elvis treated Jerry Schilling after he had taken a nasty spill on his motorcycle and was unable to move. 'The next thing I knew,' Jerry said later, 'I woke up the following morning healed.'

Understandably the healing business was kept quiet, even among our group. Though, I witnessed hundreds of concertgoers carrying their sick or crippled children to the stage and crying out, 'Elvis, please touch my baby,' or 'Elvis, just hold her for a minute.' Thousands apparently sensed that he had some ability to heal.[19]

Other associates of Elvis have gone on record to describe Elvis's gifts as a superhuman, and maybe more. Sonny West, who was later seen to be the Judas of the inner circle through publishing a candid account of Elvis the man, said that Elvis 'could touch your life'. 'When you were around him personally, boy, he had a charisma.' The devotion he inspired was such that Rick Stanley, Elvis's stepbrother, said, 'he was my all, my father, mother, teacher, boss, best friend, and there wasn't anything right or wrong that I wouldn't have done for him.'[20]

If this is what those who knew the man say, what of those who only know the mythical Elvis? They arrive by their thousands at Graceland and many, especially the younger fans, leave messages written on the wall outside. Some of these are jokey. Others leave a record of their visit, a name and date and a simple message. 'Thanksgiving Pilgrimage'. Some messages are expressions of love. 'I love you Elvis' is one of the most common, and many fans also play with the words of Elvis songs. 'You are always on my mind.' There are expressions of gratitude – 'Thank you Elvis for making the world a better place' and expressions of faith: 'The King is alive', 'Elvis you are alive in our hearts', 'Elvis is love, true love never dies.'

Some of the messages are directed at Elvis as if he is in some way connected with Earth from beyond death. They might be lighthearted: 'Elvis, tell Michael hi, we miss him too.' Others are more prayerful: 'Remember us Elvis.' A few make the Jesus connection: 'The Lasters love Elvis and Jesus. Jesus loves Elvis and the Lasters.' 'Only two people have moved the world so much. Jesus our Lord and Elvis our King.' Occasionally a couple will record on the wall that they became engaged to be married during a visit to Graceland. 'I popped the question in the Jungle Room,' said one. 'Signing the wall at Graceland was the highlight of my life,' one fan wrote later on Facebook. 'Thank you Elvis for the memories.' 'My family and I signed the wall about 10 years ago,' another fan wrote. 'Just about the time we were done the Heavens opened up and Elvis shed his golden tears upon us.'

At first glance it would seem few of the messages suggest anything more than fan devotion. Yet in and among the hundreds of scrawlings in black marker pen there are some of poignancy and deeper meaning. 'Loving you makes lonely street a lot easier'; 'Every mountain I have had to climb, Elvis carried me over on his back.' This message has echoes of the popular story of the footprints in the sand in which Jesus carried the writer through the difficult times in life.

'He touched me and now I am no longer the same'; 'I heard the call, I made the pilgrimage, I came to Graceland'; 'Mansions in heaven, I see myself walking with the King. The angels are descending to carry me up'; 'I saw the ghost of Elvis. He walked up to the gates of Graceland and I saw him walk right through them'; 'Wishing, hoping and praying to see Elvis on a paradise earth one day'; 'How Great Thou art Elvis'; 'Elvis died for our sins'; 'Elvis is a God.'

Many of the more profound messages are left anonymously. Perhaps, protected by anonymity, as a penitent is protected by the confidentiality of the confessional, the fans feel they can express their true feelings. 'Yes, I have written on the wall. Only Elvis and I knows what was written!!!!' one fan confides on Facebook. Certainly many fans appear to believe Elvis reads the messages they write. 'The wonderful thing is that if he is not seeing them from the sky (very likely he is) he would have read them, one by one, with deep delight. Love you Great man of all of us!'

In the same way that fans take away souvenirs of their visit to Elvis's home, so they feel the obligation to leave something of themselves at Graceland. Many bring elaborate wreaths and tributes to lay on the grave. Every day new gifts arrive: flowers, messages, prayers and pictures. The Meditation Garden is always decorated with colourful and elaborately made gifts. One item, noted by Professor Erika Doss, that was sculpted from tinfoil, gift wrap and plastic flowers, included a pledge of devotion from Ralf, a fifteen-year-old disabled fan from Germany; another combined Elvis images with pages from Kahlil Gibran's poem *The Prophet*, said to be one of Elvis's favourite books. Doss compared the gifts to

ex-votos, or milagros, made of tin and shaped like body parts (hearts, hands, feet), commonly left at the shrines of saints or holy figures. Ex-votos act as petitions or thanks for cures and healing. An ex-voto of a leg might be left at Lourdes, for example, to thank the Blessed Virgin Mary for mending a broken bone. Offerings of Elvis dolls and pictures, which simulate his body or face and are placed in close physical contact with the spot where he is buried, seem to have simi-larly powerful connotations for the fans who leave them at the Meditation Gardens.[21]

The actions of fans have been compared to those of Christian pilgrims visiting the holy sites of their faith. On a wall beneath Jerusalem's Church of the Holy Sepulchre a pilgrim from a bygone age has scratched a picture of a boat and the words 'O Lord, we have come.' It is not dissimilar from the many messages at Graceland simply saying, 'we made it', 'we are here.'

The other special site for fans visiting the land of Elvis is Tupelo, his birthplace. There they find the small white-painted wooden house where he was born. Close by is the church he attended as a child, transported in its entirety from its former site to the Elvis Presley Birthplace Complex. Today, says the tourist website,

> visitors can experience the Assembly of God Pentecostal services of the 1940s through a multimedia presentation. The plain, humble, wood-framed structure will greatly contrast with the lively and intense nature of the sermons and the music. Guests will experience the preacher walking about, the choir filled with the spirit, and the congregation swaying to the rhythm of inspiring praises.[22]

The birthplace complex is not owned by or controlled by EPE. Fans say it has a very different feel, less commercial and more spiritual. There is a museum and there are places to buy souvenirs, but the complex has a more meditative air. The fact that at the centre is the 'humble shack, little bigger than a stable' and not an ostentatious mansion contributes to this. Visitors are not bussed and controlled as they are at Graceland. Around the birthplace they can take the 'Walk of Life', a circular path in which are inscribed the years of Elvis's life from 1935 to 1977. In many respects the path resembles a labyrinth, as found in a Christian context. The 'Walk of Life' allows fans to walk through every year of Elvis's life, 'perhaps giving them an opportunity to stop and reflect on memorable events of Elvis's life, as well as their own.'[23]

Nearby is the Elvis Memorial Chapel, with its distinctive stained-glass window in the abstract design of which both Christian and Elvis iconography can be discerned. It was Elvis's own idea that a place of meditation should be built near to his childhood home. Today the chapel 'offers a time for meditation and a venue for weddings and special services'. Visitors who make the 100-mile journey from Memphis to Tupelo can also tour the city looking for significant Elvis venues. Places of interest include Lawhorn Elementary School, the first school Elvis attended, and

Tupelo Hardware, where Elvis bought his first guitar. Tupelo resonates with Elvis visitors in that it touches two core elements of the Elvis story: the fact that he was born into poverty and the influence over his career of his early musical roots in gospel music. And perhaps there is a third element lurking almost unrecognized: the symbolism of the twin, as noted by Minister Anna – a symbolism that crops up frequently in classical mythology. The little shack that was Elvis's birthplace was also where his twin brother was stillborn. Jesse's tiny body was, according to legend, placed in a shoebox and buried in an unmarked grave. Some fans visit the town's Priceville Cemetery and pause there at an unmarked grave where Jesse is said to be buried, though it has never been proven.

Bill Yenne's book *The Field Guide to Elvis Shrines* is described as the definitive guide to hundreds of places where Elvis lived, played, performed, recorded, made movies, attended church, ate, drank or swivelled his hips. It features every home Elvis ever owned or lived in, from Bel Air to Memphis; every concert hall, auditorium or other site where he performed, in over thirty states in America. It also features walking and driving tours of Memphis, Tupelo, Las Vegas, Hollywood and more, along with engaging and colourful explanations of the historical significance of the sites. 'It's enough to wear out several pairs of blue suede shoes,' said the *New York Times*. With guide in hand, fans can walk many miles in Elvis's shoes. However, many of the places mentioned have no surviving connection with the King. There is no commemorative plaque or souvenir shop. They are simply places Elvis passed through. A true shrine is a dedicated space, an altar or alcove, dedicated to a saint or a God. An Elvis shrine is a special place where pictures of Elvis are set and where the fan can sit and listen to Elvis music. He or she might light a candle.

'He lifts my spirits,' fans often say, and however they might be feeling, they can always find an Elvis record to match the mood. Thousands of fans treasure small items or seemingly valueless objects, which to them are priceless and if kept together become a focus of devotion. These objects might be newspaper clippings, twigs or leaves picked up from the drive at Graceland, things of no monetary value, or they might be elaborate and ornate souvenirs purchased at considerable cost. One fan keeps a life-sized mannequin dressed as Elvis.

Many fans say they cannot go a day without spending Elvis time at their shrine and they listen to little other music apart from his. 'It is as if he is singing personally to me,' one fan said. Elvis time is when they feel free to cry, to think over problems, to share thoughts, emotions and difficulties with Elvis. It is a secretive time; often not even partners know what the fan is really doing when he or she spends time with Elvis. They talk about it rarely, often in hushed tones, feeling awkward and embarrassed to admit what they do. 'You treat him like a god. It's wrong but you do.'[24] It was after many hours of talking about Elvis and her love for him that one fan blurted out those words. It was as if she had made a confession and no longer had to keep up a pretence. Up until that point in our conversation she had kept to the official line. Fans prayed to God for Elvis. Then she admitted it: no, it was to Elvis she was praying.

In summertime fans might set up outdoor temporary shrines with rows of candles casting flickering light on pictures of the King. Typically they will feature a large portrait of Elvis and the candles will be arranged in front of it in the shape of a heart or a TCB lightning bolt, or spell out the name ELVIS. During Elvis Week dozens of such shrines can be seen on the pavements near Graceland. Indoor shrines can be very elaborate, indeed works of art in themselves.

Shrines at fans' homes can also be elaborate. Don Epperley of Roanoke, Virginia, built a mini-hamlet of Elvis landmarks next to his home. Known as Elvis City, or Mini Graceland, it became a popular visitor attraction. Until his health failed Don spent hours every day making new exhibits and refining the old ones in meticulous detail. Some Elvis shrines remain private; others are built both in homage to Elvis and as new focal points for fans. In 2011 a Danish Elvis fan, Henrick Knudsen, opened the most ambitious Elvis museum outside America. Graceland Randers is a replica of Elvis's mansion; indeed, it is twice the size as it includes a restaurant, shop and museum housing 6,000 items of memorabilia. It cost £3 million to build. Henrick Knudsen had run a small Elvis museum for sixteen years that attracted around 25,000 visitors annually. Charging 95 krone (£11) a time, he is hoping to double or treble the number of visitors who will be able to walk around the house and imagine they are in the real Graceland.

The Danish Graceland has attracted consistently good reviews from visitors. 'How can anyone not like this place? It is so beautiful, a crazy yet brilliant idea to build a copy of Graceland, in Randers, of all places,' says one review on the online TripAdvisor site. 'If you are looking for an Elvis experience . . . this MUST be the place outside U.S. And great diner (Highway 51 Diner).' In the Highway 51 Diner they serve an 'EP All Time Favourite' – peanut butter and mashed banana on fried white bread!

As with every aspect of Elvis fandom, there are jokers at work. Sorting the pranksters from the serious fans sometimes presents difficulties. How were visitors expected to respond to Bill Beeny's Elvis is Alive museum, housed in a single-storey shack 45 miles west of St Louis? It included a replica of Elvis's open coffin, complete with a dead Elvis inside. When challenged by visitors who said that his Elvis did not look much like the real one, he would reply, 'But neither did the guy in the Graceland casket.'

Historically pilgrimages have been both religious obligations and holidays to enjoy. Chaucer's *Canterbury Tales* relates the stories pilgrims told to entertain each other as they journeyed on their way to St Thomas's shrine. The stories were not always of a spiritually uplifting or moral kind. Some were bawdy and secular. So it is when fans go to Graceland, especially for Elvis Week. EPE offers a packed programme of entertainment. Most of it is

Elvis-centred, but not all. For Mary Hancock Hinds the emphasis is very much on meeting with old friends. 'It's my Hajj,' she says, 'but I also come to meet my family and eat good food.'[25]

Graceland is likened by the medieval scholar Gary Vikan to a *locus sanctus*, a holy place associated with an important sacred event or holy person. Graceland has a special potency, as Elvis not only lived there, but died there and is buried in the grounds. 'Christians have believed for many centuries', Vikan writes, 'that the sacred power of a saintly body or miraculous event literally charges its physical surroundings with holiness and that to be there on that spot is to partake in that holiness again.'[26] Practices common to a *locus sanctus* include journeying to it, performing of prescribed rituals, leaving votive offerings and taking away souvenirs. At a *locus sanctus* a pilgrim might pray, venerate relics, perform penance or seek healing. If annual traditions become associated with a place, it increases the longevity of that place as a site of devotion, as the holiness is renewed on a regular basis. The design of a sacred site is also important, especially if it allows pilgrims to find a focus of intense devotion. In the Church of the Holy Sepulchre the legendary site of Christ's tomb is such a focus. At Graceland it is the Meditation Garden. It is the place every fan feels he or she must visit when in Memphis on the anniversary of his death. Yet all the year round it attracts visitors, and fans talk of feeling the sacredness most intently when the garden is almost empty. They stand near the statue of Christ with his outstretched arms, on the base of which the word Presley is written, and look down at Elvis's grave as the fountain plays and the eternal flame burns. For an hour at 7.30 every morning fans have free access – the Walk Up.

Every offering left on the grave tells a unique story of a fan and his or her relationship with the dead Elvis. The offerings frequently take the form of elaborate decorative images that have taken days to prepare, placed like large greetings cards or ceremonial wreaths. The pictures of Elvis chosen for these visual tableaux are those of the greatest significance to the fan. Words written to accompany the pictures may be taken from a favourite song. In 1989 an offering left by a fan caught the attention of Vikan. A photograph of Elvis bowing his head as he finished singing a song was at the centre of a triptych; intertwined with pink plastic roses were pictures of Elvis's grave. 'In front of the composition is a hand-written banner with the words, "I come to the Garden alone. While the dew is still on the roses. And the voice I hear, falling on my ear, the Son of God discloses. And he walks with me, and he talks with me, And he tells me I am his own. And the joy we share, as we tarry there, None other has ever known."' The words by C. Austin Miles date back to 1912 and the hymn in which they are found was sung and recorded by Elvis. Vikan describes the words as being critical to the deeper, contextual meaning of the fan's votive offering:

> The effect is to couple Elvis with Jesus and the Meditation Garden with the Garden of Gethsemane, and to insinuate the creator and the viewers of this votive into a dynamic spiritual mélange during the morning Walk Up – that very special, very private time just before sunrise when the most devoted fans literally come to the garden alone, and there meet and talk with both Elvis and Jesus.[27]

Fans commonly talk about Elvis being with them in the garden and say that the spirit of Elvis pervades the place, as if he never left Graceland except in body. It is only a short step from there to seeing and hearing the ghost of Elvis. Elvis is believed to look out at his fans from an upstairs window at Graceland. Some fans have said they have seen him by his own grave; others have glimpsed him on the stairs inside the mansion house. The story of a young Elvis in army uniform being seen hitching a ride to Graceland has been told several times. Tales have also been told of Elvis and his mother Gladys walking together on the lawn.

An intriguingly creepy story was told by the ghost hunter Susan Sheppard about a visit she made to Graceland with her husband and three-year-old daughter. The little girl went missing. 'We finally found Scarlet outside at Elvis's grave and monument. She was playing and talking to herself. When we asked Scarlet why she ran off, she explained a very nice man in a white suit had taken her by the hand and "showed her things" around the house. This man then led her outside to the white monument and fountain and disappeared.'[28] And the ghost of Elvis also makes an appearance in Marc Cohn's song 'Walking in Memphis'. It is not only in Memphis that the Elvis ghost appears; there are places in Las Vegas that Elvis is said to haunt. A spooky Elvis figure in a white rhinestone suit has been seen in the Hilton Hotel, but if apprehended he vanishes. A spectral Elvis is also said to drive a Cadillac around the city before the car disappears into a concrete wall.

Communication with the dead Elvis in some extraordinary or psychic manner extends beyond the ultra-devoted fans. Shortly after Elvis's death, reports were gathered of the singer appearing to people in the form of visions. Some were Elvis fans, but many were not. Ten years after Elvis's death, the psychiatrist Dr Raymond Moody published a study of claims of psychic experiences involving Elvis.[29] In one a police officer finds his runaway son by using information given to him by Elvis in a dream. In another case, parents of a daughter who dies at the age of ten find comfort in believing that Elvis welcomed their daughter into heaven. Moody describes the subjects of these cases as functioning and psychologically normal people, with no special interest in the paranormal, who nevertheless are convinced Elvis chose to communicate with them. He believes that hundreds of people have had similar experiences involving Elvis. He stresses the normality of those he interviewed, while acknowledging that cases exist of people with identifiable mental health problems who become obsessed by Elvis, fixated on some aspect of his life or reputation. They might believe he is controlling their minds;

some are certain, despite complete lack of evidence, they are his children or that they were married to him. One curious case reported by Moody involved a mother who was convinced she had given birth to a reincarnated Elvis. Her son Jeremy, six years old when Dr Moody spoke to him, also confirmed that he was Elvis. He would be a man of 35 now.

It is not the only claim that Elvis has returned in reincarnated human form. A South African singer called Ray Dylan has his followers. He was born on the first anniversary of Elvis's death. He is said to have a resemblance to Elvis and is a talented singer and guitar player. Events in his life are said to resemble those in Elvis's. There are also claims made on behalf of a singer called Adam Lambert, who appeared on *American Idol*. Might he be Elvis returned? If a young performer of the right age, gender, sex appeal and an ability to sing takes to the stage, someone is bound to make the comparison.

Elvis the Messiah

When Elvis is portrayed in a religious context, or is linked directly or by implication with Jesus, it is not the raunchy early rock 'n' roller, but the respectable Elvis of latter years. The Jesus shown is not the radical preacher who condemned the rich and overthrew the moneylenders, but the sentimental 'gentle' Jesus of nineteenth-century art, often shown shimmering with light and seated in a heavenly paradise. It is the relationship between these two figures that is fascinating. Even fans with no command of English are captured by the sound of Elvis's voice. Many fans on hearing it for the first time have compared the moment to a religious experience. Some say it is as if they have been touched by the hand of Christ. They then feel compelled to search out images of Elvis, to see what the face behind the voice looks like. They are never disappointed. Some talk of falling in love the moment they set eyes on an icon of Elvis.

Minister Anna of the Presleytarian Church of Australia talks of Elvis's voice being so uniquely special 'that he was able to connect very strongly with his audience and never more powerfully than in his spiritual singing. I know there are many fans who have felt "touched" by him, and others who have found a deeper spirituality in themselves or developed a connection to Christianity through this aspect of Elvis work, by listening to him sing his own songs of worship.'[1]

Yet even before he recorded his spiritual repertoire, back in the days when he was about to become the dangerous young man who challenged the traditions of popular music and culture, friends detected the 'spiritual qualities'. Joan Buchanan West first met Elvis in 1953. 'Elvis was different in every way. There was a mystical magnetism about him. It was not anything that he did or said, but simply his presence. Now this same magnetism surrounds Graceland, constantly pulling you to it,' Joan said many years later, following Elvis's death.[2] That a place can be believed to preserve the charisma of a person associated with it is one reason why pilgrimage has been and remains a popular activity.

In medieval times pilgrims were encouraged to go on several pilgrimages in a lifetime, if they could afford it. Journeys could be made to Canterbury in Kent, where St Thomas Becket was murdered; Rome, forever associated with St Peter; or Jerusalem, where Jesus himself had walked. Today Elvis fans can also extend their choice of destination. Having seen Graceland, Tupelo and Las Vegas, they might also wish to visit the Holy Lands of Jesus. There they can not only visit the many Christian sacred places, but find at least one significant Elvis place as well. Just off the road from Jerusalem to Tel Aviv there is a larger-than-life statue of the King next to an Elvis-themed inn at Abu Ghosh. It has been noted by fans with interests in such esoteric matters that a line on a map drawn from the Mount of Olives, the place from where Jesus ascended into heaven and to which it is said he will return in glory, to Abu Ghosh passes through the Church of the Holy Sepulchre, the site of the death and Resurrection.

Special Holy Land trips for Elvis fans have been arranged. For $3,000 in 2013 a fan could fly from New York for a ten-day tour in the footsteps of Jesus. They 'have the chance to explore the Gospel side of Elvis with an Israel tour experience unlike any other,' says the brochure. They sail on the Sea of Galilee, float in the Dead Sea and see Jerusalem, both from the Mount of Olives and within the old town. To be baptized in the Jordan River involves an additional charge, but the price includes a robe and a certificate.

There have been other musicians and celebrities who have inspired a religious-like devotion. The sixth of February is the birthday of Bob Marley and a day of special significance to Rastafarians, when thousands of fans gather for an annual celebration of his life and a music festival near his grave by his childhood home in Jamaica. Followers of Jim Morrison leave messages and offerings at the grave of their hero in the cemetery of Père Lachaise in Paris. His fans are reputed to celebrate the darker powers of faith. Past attempts have been made to disturb the grave and the detritus has been found around it of occult practice, Satanic worship, orgies and drug taking. Neither they, nor any of the others whose graves are the focus of fan interest, are given any special Christ-like status, with one possible exception: Michael Jackson.

Digital iconography exists showing Jackson in rapt and heavenly poses. He is shown in clouds and in the arms of Jesus. In one sickly-ironical image he is a haloed Christ calling the little children to him, 'for theirs is the Kingdom of heaven'. Yet these examples of religious devotion to Jackson do not occur with anything like the same frequency as do those involving Elvis. This can perhaps be explained by the fact that Michael Jackson did not have the same interest in gospel music as Elvis did. He had been raised in a very different church tradition. While Elvis went to a church that rang with rhythmic gospel songs every Sunday, Jackson was brought up in less exuberant surroundings as a Jehovah's Witness. At several stages in his life, Michael Jackson expressed an interest in spiritual matters, but there remains an ongoing debate as to what faith he professed, if any, at the time of his death in June 2009. Was he a Christian, had he converted to Islam like his brother Jermaine, did his Jehovah's Witness roots still exert an influence?

Whatever he might have believed himself, fans have not created a theology around him of the kind attached to Elvis. Michael

Elvis statue at Neve Ilan, Israel. Fans visiting the Holy Land can visit the places associated with the Bible and pay homage to 'the King'.

Jackson has no Graceland, no focus of pilgrimage, as yet. The body of legendary stories does not yet match those of Elvis, but time will tell. His fantasy estate of Neverland fell into disrepair after his death. At one stage Michael Jackson's daughter Paris talked of it being made available for the enjoyment of ill children.

It was, however, extensively redeveloped and in 2015 it was put up for sale under its new name of Sycamore Valley Ranch.

The identification of Elvis with Jesus is now well established, but how long might it last? Its longevity may depend as much on Jesus being known about as Elvis. In Britain, as the years go by, the public awareness of Christianity decreases. Church attendance falls and Christian ideas, images and stories form a smaller and smaller part of the body of popular culture. The same can be said of many European countries and even the USA. People who are not brought up with a background of Christian knowledge are less likely to confuse Elvis with Jesus. Or, on the other hand, to paraphrase the writer G. K. Chesterton, when people cease to believe in God, they are open to believe in anything. Maybe, as formal Christianity declines, an improbable Elvis faith will fill some of the vacuum. It is not forty years since Elvis died; time will tell.

There are examples of people who have made flippant or confusing comparisons between Jesus and Elvis and later had regrets and subsequently recanted. A case in point is Louie Ludwig, who published a book in 1995 described as a work of reverent fiction, titled *The Gospel of Elvis: The Testament and Apocrypha of the Greater Themes of 'The King'*. Ludwig, said the book's promoters, 'reveals why Elvis was truly King of his times, while tossing a gentle poke at those who take his Kingdom a bit too seriously'. The book explored the life and times of the King of Rock 'n' Roll in a pastiche of King James Bible English. With its tongue firmly in its cheek, it tells the tale of how a poor boy with few prospects in a land of plenty nevertheless rises to be declared the priest-king of the whole world.

The book was set out in chapters and divided into verses to resemble the scriptures. Printed notes in the margins in a smaller italic font were included to give the pages the appearance of a study Bible. Characters and places found in the narrative were those from the real Elvis story, but renamed. Thus Colonel Parker was known as the Snake and Priscilla was the Virgin. Las Vegas was restyled Babylon. Elvis, of course, was the King. Verse five of Golgotha reads, 'The Virgin came to the King on the cross, begging him to come down and live again with her in the residence. The King kissed her and blessed her, then banished her.' The accompanying note explains this passage as a reference to Elvis and Priscilla's divorce.[3]

Then, unexpectedly, Ludwig denounced his book in a speech given during Elvis Week in 1997. He called on his publishers to withdraw the book, which, he admitted, had started out as a 'punk prank'. He said he no longer wished to be one of the many who tried to make money from Elvis's memory. He called his book 'a bad joke based on a worse lie, which I hereby publicly renounce and repudiate . . . Elvis was no Messiah. He was a first-rate singer doing largely second-rate material, except for the songs he nicked.' He acted 'woodenly in last-rate films' and 'his taste in clothing, cars and home furnishings reflected perfectly his background: a country boy come to the city, trying to look cool and show he had "class".' So why do we deify him? Ludwig asked of Elvis. He was

so naive that he signed over half his earnings to a carnival huckster, so repressed about his Oedipal problems that only a fourteen-year-old girl could represent a woman as worthy as his mom, so much in denial about his addiction that he asked the president of the United States to deputize him to fight drug use in the entertainment business. Have we become so spiritually impoverished that we're ready to crown such a creature of pathos king? Even the King of Kings? At least the original King had the chutzpa to kick over the moneylenders' tables, saying the temple should be a house of prayer and not a den of thieves. I'll let the theologians and sociologists duke out the big questions, and offer only my own cynical, selfish, professional viewpoint.

As a record producer and music publisher, it would be nice to see the market get over Elvis and make some room on the airwaves and record store shelves for a few new artists. Elvis, get a death.[4]

Was the recantation genuine, or a clever stunt to publicize the book? Either way, it was impressive.

The theologian and writer Karen Armstrong once described the Elvis phenomenon in this way. 'People are mythologizing Elvis and trying to explain in universal, archetypical religious language, what he has meant to their inner lives. Just as they did for Jesus and Mohammed. People have somehow found the sacred in Elvis, strange as it might seem.'[5] Some observers have taken a more cynical view. The Elvis phenomenon, even the Elvis–Christ connection, it is argued, has been encouraged and fostered by clever mass marketing. 'Explicit manifestations of "Elvis Christ" do not exactly evolve,' says the journalist John Windsor, 'they are cunningly contrived.'[6]

So who, or where, are the mysterious forces at work elevating Elvis to the level of Jesus? The Elvis Jesus designer clothes company appears to be jumping on a bandwagon rather than designing and constructing one and setting it rolling. The earliest references to Elvis as Jesus-like pre-date the creation of Elvis Presley Enterprises. The company that handles the business affairs of the Presley estate itself, although opportunistic and profit-driven, is restrained by its publicly stated policy that it exists to ensure that whatever is done in Elvis's name is done with good taste. Although it has sanctioned several projects in dubious artistic taste, it has never stepped over a line into territory that would offend or alienate traditional Christian Elvis fans. That would be far too commercially risky.

At one stage fans became concerned that the company might come under the control of the Church of Scientology. Lisa Marie had, like several other American celebrities, shown an interest in the controversial and powerful movement, but in reality there was no evidence of any proposed takeover of the company by the church. It was no more than speculation in the minds of fans.

There is, as far as can be discerned, no shadowy organization or leader manipulating Elvis fans and turning their minds to religion. The remembrance of Elvis in religious terms appears to be a spontaneous and grass-roots phenomenon. Yet the survival and the elevation of the memory of Elvis Presley cannot be understood in terms of religion alone. He was born into the land of free enterprise. His values were those of a child of capitalism. He and his family knew what poverty was like and making money was important to him. Money meant security and status. He lived in a world of advertising and commodification. His own manager Colonel Tom Parker saw him as a product to be marketed and sold for profit. Today, what fans understand about Elvis in spiritual terms is not a concern of Elvis Presley Enterprises, as long as it does not impede the flow of revenue. It might not have been a deliberate marketing strategy, but in reality the spirituality of Elvis has been successfully disciplined and organized by the commercial arm of the Presley estate, and income streams remain strong. EPE does not need to understand the spiritual side of the Elvis phenomenon. It just needs to go with and monitor the flow. No one at Authentic needs to look up from the balance sheet and start asking questions about the innate religious impulse within the human species.

Yet these are fascinating questions. Capitalism and religion might seem strange companions, but to most Americans they coexist with no perceived contradiction. Some American churches go so far as to teach that faithful practice of Christianity leads to prosperity in this life, as well as rewards in the next. Elvis in the modern world is a brand as well as an icon. The sociologist Professor Mark Gottdiener has called the dead Elvis 'the Other Jesus'. 'This is not the same as saying that Elvis is Jesus or led a life analogous to Jesus,' he stressed in a paper given to the University of Mississippi's First International Conference on Elvis Presley in 1995.

> Elvis, as the other Jesus, as Dead Elvis, is a medium of self-expression and liberation through material culture in a way that identification with Jesus is not. This aspect is the powerful force behind the Dead Elvis phenomenon. Attaching oneself to the Dead Elvis is an act of liberation from the constraints of most religions because it enables you to celebrate popular culture, secular ideas, commodity fetishism, eroticism, black–white integration and, most specifically, Southern Culture.[7]

In other words, the appeal of constructing a religion around Elvis is that the devotee is free to improvise in any way he or she wants, unfettered by official teaching, dogma or ancient tradition. The fan is also able to weave his or her Elvis devotions into everyday life, rather than keep those things considered religious in a special protected category. Gottdiener's approach makes several important points, but omits three core aspects of the dead Elvis phenomenon. First is its international appeal: thousands of Elvis fans around the world have no shared interest in Southern culture apart from its associations with Elvis. Second, he overlooks, or discounts, the theology behind the Jesus connection, the spirituality and religiosity of so much that is done in the name of Elvis; the messianic status and the claimed supernatural qualities of the mythic Elvis. Third, he overlooks the role of religion in protecting a sacred memory or idea. Jews, Muslims and Christians are instructed not to take the name of their God in vain. Many Islamic countries have enshrined the protection of the name and reputation of the Prophet in law. Across national borders, Muslims often combine to condemn religious insult – as was the case when a Danish cartoonist produced a drawing that was deemed insulting to the Prophet. Christian countries have frequently had blasphemy laws on the statute books. Similarly, Elvis fans are highly protective of the image of their hero. It is the one thing on which Elvis fans, of whatever kind, agree. Elvis devotees feel that it is their responsibility to protect his name and image.

'Fervently defending his holiness and simultaneously denying his failings . . . they mythologise his story, and use its aspirational elements as inspiration in their own lives,' Minister Anna of the Presleytarian Church of Australia, notes.

What has fascinated me most is the belief held by many fans that they are responsible for 'protecting' Elvis's image and reputation from scandal, ridicule or doubt. This is also true of many religions whose followers fervently crusade against criticism of their doctrine, behaviour or scripture. We have seen that there is disapproval among the Elvis faithful of impersonators who seek to parody Elvis or portray him in an 'unfavourable' light, and this extends also to the worldwide community of Elvis fans. These fans are so devoted to 'the King' that any mention of contentious issues such as food, drug-taking or lustful behaviour on Elvis' part is dismissed as ridiculous and the accusations, in their minds, are tanta- mount to blasphemy. On the Internet many fan clubs and Elvis-related sites use a disclaimer at the beginning such as this one from a message board: 'comments that are a dis- grace to Elvis will be deleted.'[8]

Given that Elvis's life was so well documented and reported by his friends and colleagues and the media, it is impossible to deny that Elvis was at various stages during his life unfaith- ful to his wife and addicted to prescription drugs, and that he had a penchant for guns. Nevertheless there are Elvis crusaders and apologists who prefer not to see the facts. Admittedly these aspects of Elvis's life detract from the good works he did and the generous, spiritual and empathetic man that he was, but they are no less true because of that. There are two camps in the argument over Elvis's image and reputation, both among the fans and in the wider community. This duality is a reflection of the duality evident in Elvis's own life and personality. 'This duality can also be seen in almost all organised religions where conflicting or even disturbing elements of scripture or history are denied or consciously ignored while other more positive elements are celebrated.'[9]

An observation by Minister Anna is perhaps worth noting in this context, as her Presleytarian Church of Australia has been

> attacked in equal measure by Christian zealots who assure me I will burn in Hell for idolising anyone but Jesus, and by Elvis fans for the satirical use of his image (such as The Sacred Heart of Elvis) and my logo that depicts Elvis in an iconographic way on a cross made of a guitar neck, and I shall burn in Hell for defacing his image and besmirching his name. There is essentially no difference in the nature and vigour of these attacks, which can only lead me to conclude that these Elvis fans are as fervent and committed to their doctrine as any religious fundamentalists.[10]

It can be argued that in the years immediately following Elvis's death, Elvis fans found themselves in a situation superficially similar to that of the early Christians. It was approximately 35 years after the events of Jesus' earthly ministry that the first systematic account of his life, work, mission and meaning was written down. By that time many of the key players, the apostles and other close witnesses, were dead. Few of those who remained to pass on the stories were from Jesus' inner circle of friends. Much of what they knew and could retell, they themselves had been told. They had to struggle to make sense of Jesus' teaching and legacy without their teacher being there in physical form to guide them. Similarly Elvis fans, following the death of their hero, have had to work out what Elvis's true message to the world might be, and Elvis is no longer around to ask.

In 2012, when fans marked the 35th anniversary of Elvis's death, they were marking an important chronological watershed. There were still those alive who remembered and were close to Elvis, although they were reducing in number. Also, as the years passed, what they had to tell had become so well rehearsed and so familiar in the retelling that they are no longer recollections of events, but stories about them. Those who have no direct memories of Elvis of their own now rely on these witnesses for their knowledge. At any major Elvis gathering, the most popular events are those where musical colleagues of Elvis or members of his inner entourage answer questions from the fans.

If comparisons can be made, however tentatively, between the early Christians and the early Elvis fans, then perhaps the role of Elvis Presley Enterprises parallels that of the Roman State. Initially the Graceland management were suspicious of anything over which they had no control, but eventually they came to endorse activities, such as tribute artists, that they had previously attempted to suppress. In the fourth century the Emperor Constantine, after years of Roman opposition to and persecution of Christianity, adopted Christianity as the state religion and gave it structure and protection. Within the structure set up by the state, the faith was able to flourish. Had this not happened, Christianity might have died out. Many dozens of other ancient religions did. Branches of Christianity that did not come under the protection of the official Church also fell by the wayside. Similarly, as Elvis fans were discovering their spiritual Elvis, the estate was taking care of the secular business. Without an organization promoting Elvis to the wider world, keeping Graceland open and authorizing the manufacture of merchandise, would there be so many Elvis fans today? Would young fans have discovered the King?

It can be argued that people are religious beings and most people at some time in their lives feel a need to ask the fundamental questions about life and its purpose. People also value ritual in their lives and celebrate rites of passage. Philosophies and religions come and go. Over the course of human history there have been hundreds, if not thousands, of religions, most of which have now faded away. Isis, Mithras, Zeus, Baal and Woden are just a few examples of great and supposedly all-powerful deities of the past who are now all but forgotten. History suggests that for a religious enthusiasm to have a hope of longevity it needs organization. As long as that organization, often a very worldly structure of rules and hierarchies, survives, so will the religion. EPE, as a business, and the other commercial enterprises with interests in Elvis, provide the organization that while not endorsing, encouraging or being the slightest bit interested in the religious aspects of the phenomenon, nevertheless protects the spirituality of Elvis fans and enables it to flourish. While not wanting to stretch the church parallel too far, it could be suggested that the relationship between the worlds of EPE and of serious Elvis devotees is a bit like the relationship between the official Roman Catholic Church and the practitioners of folk Catholicism. Under the umbrella of orthodoxy the folk faithful pursue a quasi-underground religion of their own, never challenging the orthodoxy of the Church, but not fully endorsing it either.

As the history of Christendom has shown, especially through the Middle Ages in Europe, the Church became worldly, interested in secular power and accumulating wealth. Its leaders and its structure became further and further removed from the ethos and spirit of the founder and the practical devotions of the people. Similarly the owners of the Elvis empire are far more interested today in money than the spirit of Elvis, so much so that the image is now auctioned to the highest bidder to exploit. 'Eagerness to control the widespread application of Elvis's image speaks volumes about the abiding popular appeal and profitability of that image,' writes Erika Doss. 'But it also threatens the perpetuation and sustenance of an image made meaningful . . . primarily through the desires, rituals and behaviours of a popular audience, especially Elvis's fans.'[11] Whatever happens on the business scene, the fans continue to create for themselves the mythological Elvis they wish to remember through a unique, ad hoc, process involving a serendipitous synchronization of popular culture and religious tradition. And what has emerged has many of the characteristics of religious observance.

A Piece of Elvis

The nearest a devoted fan can get to the real Elvis is the memorabilia that are available to view or buy. Those that would be classified as first-class relics if they were of a Christian saint are very rare. There are no segments of Elvis's corpse on show to be venerated. The official – and, as far as one can ascertain, correct – information is that Elvis is buried at Graceland. Requests have been made for a disinterment to quash rumours that he faked his death, but this is highly unlikely to be sanctioned. If it did happen there would be those curious to know the state of decomposition, for in some religious traditions it is believed that the earthly remains of special, saintly people are incorruptible and do not decay. The only known first-class relics of Elvis are some hair trimmings, possibly some nail clippings and a wart.

Second-class relics, as traditionally defined within the Roman Catholic Church, are items a saint used or wore. In Elvis's case there are many such items, especially at Graceland, which in some ways is a second-class relic itself. The displays of property on show there, especially clothing and jumpsuits, have impeccable provenance and are much admired. Yet Elvis left other second-class relics behind which are not the property of EPE and many of these, with relevant authentification, have come onto the market. Sometimes an article of clothing might have been divided into small segments, each of which is a second-class relic capable of being revered. Twenty years ago fragments of clothing were on sale as souvenirs at Tupelo, although whether they were genuine is now unprovable. On the borderline between first- and second-class Elvis relics are the hundreds of scarves he handed out over his career, most of which had been bought for the sole purpose of giving away. But each will have been worn by the singer, however briefly, and might still retain specks of his sweat. For this reason many fans who own scarves do not ever wash them.

A third-class relic is anything for which a claim can be made that it is of special interest as well as relevance to Elvis. It might be a rare concert ticket, an early poster or item of merchandise from the first years of Elvis's career. And on the borderline between second- and third-class relics there are the letters Elvis wrote, contracts he signed and autographs.

Major auction houses have often been involved when a major item of memorabilia has come on the market, lending their prestige and reputation and upping the interest. Over the years interest from buyers has been unpredictable. While Elvis Presley's Bible sold for $92,000, a pair of his unwashed underpants did not reach the reserve price of $11,000 when offered at auction in Cheshire in the northwest of England in 2012. Less unsavoury items of clothing do sell, however. In July 2011 an Elvis army fatigue shirt sold for $5,069 and a little later another similar shirt fetched $27,500, more than double the pre-auction estimate. The second one was in better shape and had a 'Presley' name patch sewn in. A jacket Elvis gave Charlie Hodge, who provided a letter of authenticity, fetched $13,125, nearly five times the pre-auction estimate. Elvis Presley's white Knabe grand piano, kept at Graceland between 1957 and 1969, twice failed to sell, but in 2010 the price tag was $1 million.

After a temporary slump in prices around the time of the economic crisis of 2008, sales of Elvis jewellery have recently perked up. A 14-carat gold ring with a seven-diamond cluster, plus a photograph of Elvis wearing it, has sold for $15,000. And a 10-carat yellow gold band, crowned by a star ruby and accented on either side by small diamonds, fetched $9,062. At an auction in Dallas, Texas, in March 2013, there was considerably more interest in a telephone Elvis had used in his Beverly Hills home in the early 1970s. Presumably there had been a number of Memphis Mafia cronies around him at the time, because Elvis had written a warning: 'EP's personal phone, do not use'. There were eleven serious bidders and the lot fetched $16,250.

Even historic items that might never have been seen or handled by the King can attract bidders, as long as they have noteworthy Elvis connections. Copies of the 1953 yearbook from Elvis's senior year at Humes High School, Memphis, show up at auction fairly regularly. One sold in August 2010 fetched $7,170. Another copy recently sold for $4,375, despite being written in by Elvis, as it was in poor condition.

Key to the success of any auction of a significant item from Elvis's past are three factors: price, authenticity and good taste.

Exhibit with Elvis Presley's personal belongings in the Elvis Museum, Las Vegas, Nevada.

Some items fail the test on all counts, and instruments said to have been used during Presley's post-mortem examination were withdrawn from a Chicago auction after their authenticity was questioned.

At one stage Graceland stayed aloof from the day-to-day trade in Elvis relics, but since starting to organize official auctions, it has now largely taken control of the business of authentification and has established Graceland Authenticated as a subsidiary business. Graceland Authenticated examines any items due to be officially auctioned and also offers fans an authentification service that, it claims, sets 'the standard for pop culture authentication with archives that are second to none and a team dedicated to preserving the legend of Elvis Presley.' It does of course come at a cost. A $50 fee is payable when an item is submitted online and a charge of 10 per cent of the value of the item when the artefact is valued and verified, with a $150 minimum charge. Items deemed genuine are given an official letter of authenticity.

Graceland's direct interest in the business of authentification has implications, notes Nathan Raab, an authentification consultant and Forbes contributor. 'It will become very difficult to sell a piece of Elvis history without the "Graceland Authenticated" stamp on it.' However, once an item is pronounced genuine the owner will know there is no doubt. 'Evidence will need to exist in the Graceland archives of the creation or use of the piece to earn the seal of approval.' That means if someone has a contract presumably signed by Elvis, even the paper could be matched against similar contracts in the Elvis archives. Since the King saved everything, a watch given to a friend could presumably be tracked back to a note or receipt. 'The risk here is that some authentic pieces will fail to match this standard. Might Elvis have accidentally thrown away the piece that matches yours? Seems possible and even likely in some cases. Here, the owner of the artefact will simply receive a note from the company explaining that it is unable to authenticate the piece.'[1]

A further implication of Graceland Authenticated's involvement is a tidying up of the Elvis collectibles market. Raab notes: 'all the great collectors, dispersed worldwide, will have a place to hang their hats, and with an institution that appreciates them. Graceland will know them all. Having access to well-heeled people who are interested in the product you are selling is a valuable commodity, and this model would seem to accomplish that. Moreover, Graceland is identifying people who are willing to spend money, perhaps a lot, on its main product: Elvis Presley.'[2] Furthermore, through the company Auction a Circle, Graceland not only identifies genuine Elvis items, but organizes their sale.

When it comes to putting a monetary value on any Elvis relics, the most prized and certainly the most expensive are anything he once owned and handled. These, in the main, are the items Graceland's experts examine and are those that come up for auction at the official sales. There the main international collectors bid up prices marked in the thousands of dollars. Even Elvis's driving licence was sold for $11,000 in 2014.

The next most valuable items are commercially produced merchandise with rarity value: a book, vinyl disc or show ticket of which few were manufactured or survive. Then there are the Elvis souvenirs of historical interest, things associated with Elvis places; and finally, in the pecking order of significance, the contemporary goods that can be bought new online or at Graceland. These continue to be traded without Graceland's involvement. At a collectors' fair in London in 2013 dealers mingled with fans buying and selling items with Elvis connections. The fair was set up in a large basement room. 'It's an Elvis heaven,' said one punter. Modern key rings with an Elvis picture could be picked up for under a pound. Second-hand books fetched slightly more, depending on their rarity and condition. A mint-condition boxed toy pink Cadillac was marked at £60. For £600 a collector could buy a scarf handed out by Elvis at one of his many Las Vegas concerts.

There's a busy market in Elvis records and memorabilia, both at collectors' fairs and for buyers on eBay.

Much of the trade in Elvis items revolves around the music. There are collectors both of veteran first-edition pressings and the latest remixes and compilation albums. Film producer Robert Alaniz is an enthusiastic and highly knowledgeable collector of Presleyana. His business Soundz Good Records specializes in finding, buying and selling Elvis records and memorabilia. He is also an associate editor of the Presleyana record and memorabilia price guide. He became a fan in 1964 after seeing the Elvis film *Roustabout*. It was Elvis's sixteenth movie and was panned by the critics for its banal dialogue and predictable plotline, but young Robert was entranced. In the movie Elvis plays a drifter who lands a job as a roustabout, or handyman, with a down-at-heel carnival. Despite the film's shortcomings and the fact that in 1964 the coolest music on the block came from The Beatles, Alaniz was bowled over by Elvis. He bought every record from the soundtrack, sought out the posters and lobby cards and 'became obsessed with collecting anything I could about Elvis'. When he reached adulthood his interest in Elvis remained strong, though active collecting went 'on the backburner'. Also at the time, 'people were writing Elvis off. There had been a set of bad releases and there was not much for collectors. A lot of people thought Elvis pretty much over.'[3]

It was around the 1980s, he says, when people started collecting Elvis again. By that time both Elvis and Vernon, his father, were dead. Priscilla, not the Colonel, was taking care of business. On the music scene there was a revival of interest in 1950s music, with the emergence of bands such as the Stray Cats.

The music industry began to realize the market potential of repackaging, rather than simply re-releasing, Elvis's earlier work. An early initiative was taken in 1980 by Roger Semon, who was managing RCA's national sales promotion team. *The EP Collection*, which he produced, went on to spearhead the whole business of repackaging Elvis's musical legacy and eventually led to the creation by Sony Music of the Follow That Dream label in 1999. The first release was the CD *Burbank '68*, a behind-the-scenes look at Elvis's famous 1968 television special. Today FTD is a record label that exists exclusively for the dedicated Elvis music collector. In 2013 it offered over a hundred different Elvis CDs, books and LPs, with additional titles released at regular intervals.

Interest in Elvis records skyrocketed in the early 1990s, Alaniz recalls. It was, he says, the golden era of collecting. 'It was possible to find real prizes!' He and his wife Carol held their first Elvis

Presley convention in Memphis in 1992 at the Ramada Inn with the idea of providing a place where Elvis collectors could go to buy, sell and trade Elvis Presley records and memorabilia with dealers from around the country. Over the years the event has gone through various name changes from the Elvis for Everyone Convention to ELVIS CON and Collecting the King. In 2013 it was held as usual in the Peabody Hotel in Memphis during Elvis Week. But over 21 years the world of Elvis collecting has radically altered. 'When eBay arrived,' says Alaniz, 'it changed everything.'[4] Collectors no longer needed to travel to fairs and second-hand shops. The excitement of treasure-hunting and discovering something precious in an unexpected place became a thing of the past. Collectors no longer had the thrill of handling and examining a real object. They went online. Admittedly they had access to the whole world at the click of a mouse, but it was a virtual and not a tangible world. Today rare Elvis recordings are easier to find and the demand has dropped. 'Prices and sales are not going up,' says Alaniz. 'Items must now be in mint condition to attract buyers. Also collectors are no longer seeking out the old records so as to hear rare recordings. All of these can now be heard via the internet or on current CDs.'[5] Elvis retains his fascination, but the world of music collecting has changed.

Music aside, paper collectibles still hold their value. Original posters from the early films are much sought after and hold their value despite the economic recession. Even the cheap souvenirs made by Colonel Parker to sell to Elvis's fans in the early years are valuable if they are in good condition. In his years of buying and selling, Alaniz's most memorable deal was the $10,000 he received for the original contract signed by Elvis to appear live at the International Hotel in Las Vegas in 1969. 'Paper', he says 'is often worth more than socks. Paper has provenance, but who can ever prove that Elvis wore the socks?'[6]

Until Elvis's music was made widely available, often the only way fans had to hear rare recordings and studio sessions that had never been released was through the bootleg market. Alaniz recalls being offered under-the-counter Elvis in the early 1980s. Very little new material was then being officially sold and he concluded that RCA had given up

> on the goose that laid the golden egg. I was walking through a record store, when I struck up a conversation with one of the employees. 'You'd think that RCA would release more Elvis songs that we haven't heard,' I said.
>
> The employee smiled and reached behind the counter for a box. 'Check these out,' he said, smiling. 'What's this?' I asked. 'Bootlegs,' he replied. I had no idea what he was talking about, so he explained that these were records that featured unreleased recordings. 'Why are they behind the counter?' I asked. 'They're illegal,' he answered with a smile.[7]

What was on offer was a range of music that even a dedicated Elvis collector never knew he had recorded. 'A strange thrill came over me when I bought a record and took it home and listened to it. Similar to the same thrill I got as a kid when I tried shoplifting for the first time and got away with it.'[8]

Elvis bootlegging had started several years before Elvis's death, although it was not until 1982 that the toughest legal sanctions were attempted to stamp out the trade in unlicensed recordings. There were raids and court appearances and the authorities did their utmost to undermine, if they could not eradicate, what they regarded as being a dangerous and dishonest underground industry.

Alaniz soon discovered that bootleg music was not always as exciting as that which he had first heard. The technical quality was often poor. When sales slipped, the bootleggers realized they had to up their game. They also found themselves facing competition. *Burbank '68* was an officially sanctioned 'bootleg' release of an Elvis dress rehearsal.

Alaniz no longer buys the bootleg Elvis, but he knows bootlegs continue to sell,

> and there are dealers who still insist on selling them no matter what the risk, and make no mistake . . . the risk is great. I know a few dealers who were at a recent show in Chicago that was busted by the FBI and police. It's not a pretty sight seeing people you know being hauled away in handcuffs and their entire CD inventory being confiscated into a paddy wagon.[9]

Two books have been written on the Elvis bootleg industry. In 1983 Lee Cotten and Howard A. DeWitt produced *Jailhouse Rock: The Bootleg Recordings of Elvis Presley*, in which they catalogued and reviewed the bootleg recordings then available. In 2012 *Bootleg Elvis* by Felix Gubeli and four co-authors became the definitive work after being enthusiastically reviewed by fans. The book, said the Elvis Information Network, brought to life the romanticism that has long been attached to the 'underground' vinyl releases. Of course not all bootlegs were quality products, although to many fans it mattered little that the audio quality was very poor. The allure of these records was that they were illicit, which gave many of them a remarkable mystique that still exists to this day.

Over his 23-year career Elvis was not only the most photographed celebrity of the age, but the most recorded. Fans took photographs whenever they could. More rarely, but still quite often, concerts were unofficially recorded. There were studio out-takes and recordings of rehearsals as well. Joan Deary of RCA discovered a priceless cache of master tapes and records casually stored in Graceland. They included tapes of offstage conversations as well as live performances. Her detailed search of Graceland's closets, drawers and shelves eventually turned up a bonanza that included 29 reels of tape. 'Some were in boxes, some were loose, and some more in pieces that we had to splice together,' she recalls. Afterwards she carried the tapes back to Los Angeles in a tote bag. 'I never let them out of my sight during the flight.' Once home she headed straight for RCA's Hollywood vault. Still she didn't know what she had: 'They could have been nothing.'[10] She sat down to listen to the hours of recordings. Duplicates and unrelated materials were returned to Presley's estate, but this still left a huge quantity of material. Among her discoveries were taped monologues and the earliest known recordings of Elvis singing 'Danny Boy' and 'Earth Angel'. There was also a tape from his triumphant 1956 homecoming concert in Tupelo, but it had apparently been recorded on a battery-driven machine that was on the blink. The speed varied, lurching irregularly from fast to slow and back again.

Although hours of previously forgotten tape have been discovered, there remains a limit to the amount of original Elvis tape that exists. What is not limited is the imagination of the manufacturers of Elvis merchandise. Starting with the official Elvis online shop, there are pages and pages of Elvis-themed items. Sixty pounds will buy you an Elvis '68 Special Light-up Desk Sign; for half the price a gold lamé teddy bear is on offer. A huge range of Elvis T-shirts, sunglasses and boxed CD sets are available. Three FTD book and CD combined packages are the most expensive items, at £83 a time. By contrast an Elvis badge can be had for a mere £3. Almost everything has an Elvis image and fans can choose the era and style they prefer, from leather-jacketed and defiant to white-jumpsuited and gospel-singing. What will not be found via the EPE shop is anything that shows Elvis in a disrespectful light. Elvis is never shown overweight. Only standard souvenirs can be found, such as mugs, phone holders and clothing – none of the jokey, or what EPE would view as tacky, Elvis items are offered to official fans. Elsewhere it is possible to find an Elvis-on-a-lavatory ornament; a reproduction of a newspaper announcing his death; a sad last picture of the bloated hero. Strangely several versions of Elvis Potato Head dolls, sharply criticized by the most loyal fans when they were first marketed, can be bought from the official shop.

In addition to Elvis merchandise, there is Elvis art. The overlap between the two is considerable. For instance, a Bruce Emmett picture of Elvis reproduced on a 'collectible plate' is merchandise. If the same picture were sold printed on canvas it would be categorized as art. And Elvis art comes in many forms – kitsch, folk art, Pop art and even contemporary fine art – as hundreds, if not thousands, of artists have been intrigued by the Elvis image.

Generally, Elvis art has been immune from the major trends in contemporary fine art that have dominated the last fifty years. There are no piles of Elvis bricks available. There is no dead Elvis floating in a tank of formaldehyde, although a recently constructed Elvis hot air balloon looks as if the contemporary artist Jeff Koons could have designed it. Elvis artists largely prefer realism to abstraction. It would be bold to assert that there is no Elvis-inspired contemporary art – the world of art is too large and varied to make such a statement – but there would appear to be few, if any, well-known works. One work that was shown in 2013 combined realism with conceptual art. 'Elvis and the Illusion of Time' showed a portrait of Elvis made from sand, trickling away like sand in an hourglass. It suggests that however great a celebrity might be, everything, over time, dissolves away.

That is not to say that high-profile contemporary artists have never invoked Elvis. For instance, both Deborah Kass with 'My Elvis' and Jeff Koons with 'Hulk Elvis' have used the name of Elvis in the titles of shows. Tracey Emin chose 'Burning Love' as one of her Desert Island Discs as it reminded her of Elvis and, she said, the time she was in Istanbul, not having had sex for a year, looking for a man.

But generally Elvis art is not viewed as high art. Much is dismissed as kitsch, naive, sugary or too populist. Where references to Elvis exist in contemporary fine art it is usually not that artists

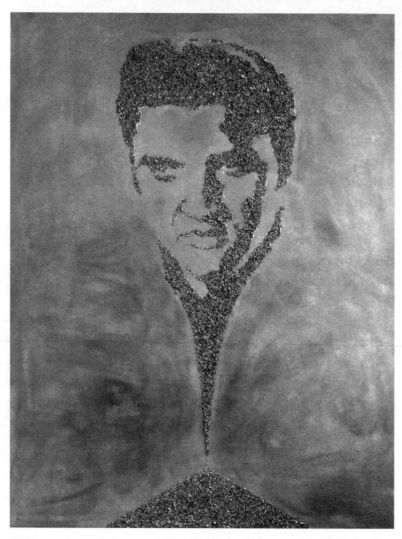

The face of Elvis is an icon regularly adapted by contemporary artists. In the picture 'Elvis and the Illusion of Time' the King is used to imply that all fame eventually trickles away like sand through an hourglass.

are making any personal connection with Elvis; rather they are using Elvis as a convenient image to symbolize aspects of society that are considered trivial, common or beneath serious consideration. Most contemporary art movements have been too elitist or out of touch for Elvis to have been of interest to practitioners.

The only movement in recent art history to have explored the Elvis image on its own terms has been Pop art. The movement began at much the same time that Elvis was making a name for himself. It could be argued that Andy Warhol and Roy Lichtenstein were to the world of visual art what Elvis Presley was to the world of music. Pop art challenged tradition by crossing the divide between fine art and popular culture. It involved adopting images taken from advertisements and placing them in new and unexpected contexts. Pop artists often employed new media and were not limited to brush and canvas. They challenged cultural elitism by taking images that might have been dismissed as commonplace and trite and giving them a significance normally reserved for the products of elitist art. In purely financial terms, it worked. Peter Blake prints of *K is for King* are valued at over £1,000, but in May 2012 Andy Warhol's *Double Elvis* sold for $37 million when it came under the hammer at a Sotheby's contemporary art sale. It is a silver silkscreen image of Elvis Presley depicted as a cowboy, and was the first *Double Elvis* to appear on the market since 1995. Warhol had produced a series of 22 images of Elvis, nine of which are in museum collections. In the picture that sold, Elvis is shown armed and shooting from the hip with a shadowy Elvis figure faintly visible in the background.

There is certainly demand for Elvis art, and evidence of its popularity comes from the fact that a number of highly skilled artists and craftspeople make a living from their Elvis work. Betty Harper is famed for her delicate pencil drawings of Elvis. She had started drawing Elvis before he died, and was in the middle of a work called *American Trilogy* when she heard the news of Elvis's death. A year later the work was shown enlarged on a billboard across the road from Graceland.

Rob de Vries is a Dutch artist who works in pencil, charcoal and oils. His portraits are highly realistic and he says that it was after a visit to Memphis in 2007 that he became fully dedicated to his Elvis art. Besides his many smaller Elvis drawings and paintings,

Rob works on special, large-scale Elvis projects. His 'Elvis 24' project consisted of 24 oil paintings showing Elvis during each year of his 24-year career. His 'Jumpsuits & Stage Wear' project consists of 126 works showing every jumpsuit Elvis wore between 1968 and 1977.

Thomas Kinkade has been described as America's most collected artist. He sells his colourful but rather saccharine landscapes mostly as prints or decorating merchandise. His Elvis work is not of Elvis himself, but Graceland. A popular image shows the famous gates; another depicts a snowy Graceland in an idealistic Christmas-card landscape. Elvis is shown gathering presents in his role as family Santa. 'As he unloads gifts from the famous pink Cadillac, we are captivated by the twinkling tree lights that suggest the magic of the season,' the artist writes. 'Colorful Christmas trees line the drive and the amber sunset suggests a frosty evening ahead. The glow from the porch and windows reminds us that all families, even that of the King of Rock 'n' Roll, will join joyously tonight to celebrate the season. I hope Graceland Christmas will be part of your Christmas celebration for many years to come.'[11]

Naoki Mitsuse produces jokey, cartoony and highly colourful Elvis pictures, which belie the serious origins of his Elvis inspiration. 'I remember reading an article in the morning paper about a local teenage girl who had thrown herself out of a balcony of a tall apartment building, leaving a note saying, "now that Elvis is dead, I have nothing to live for and goodbye." This had a profound impact on me and I realized then, that Elvis was a very powerful man.'[12]

Isabelle Tanner produces ethereal images of Elvis in full colour. Her book *Elvis: A Guide to My Soul* shows Elvis in mystical, angelic poses interspersed with text. Opposite an image of Elvis in a glittering blue outfit cradling a child, she writes: 'God works through all the hearts of his children. The little child I hold in my arms is a wanderer from heaven, announcing the forthcoming birth of humanity's new awareness and higher consciousness; the unfoldment of the New Age.'

Tanner also produced images of Elvis for a series of stamps issued by the Pacific Ocean republic of Palau. Philatelic Elvis art is a genre in its own right. Every country that produces special stamps for collectors has now issued an Elvis design. Some of the most artistically imaginative come from the Republic of Guinea, although the Central African Republic's offering and that from Zaire are not far behind in their colourful reimaginings of the King.

Most collectors' stamps are commercial gimmicks and much Elvis art has a whiff of gimmickry about it. The speed painter Denny Dent has painted Elvis; one artist constructed an Elvis from Cheesy Puffs; and numerous caricaturists have tackled the pout and curled lip – some more successfully than others. There is a gallery of well over a hundred examples to be found on the About Faces website.[13] At one level Elvis's is an easy face to draw, in that several basic and instantly recognized symbols have evolved that allow a few simple lines to say Elvis. Quiff, black hair, sunglasses and sideburns – hey presto, there he is. For the same reason Elvis is a disguise people can adopt easily. The critical rules of likeness are set aside and the few Elvis markers turn anyone, or anything, into an Elvis.

This is why the simple Elvis motifs have been so commonly used in folk and naive art. An unskilled practitioner can nevertheless express their thoughts about Elvis in paint. Some of the folk art is solely Elvis-inspired; other forms combine Elvis with other traditions. The homemade artwork that frequently gets made around the Mexican festival of Day of the Dead, for instance, has been known to use Elvis. His face has been adopted as a mask, or placed on a macabre skeletal figure. This art form specifically pays homage to the dead, but within Mexican folk art generally, references to Elvis are often found which are interwoven with indigenous symbolism in pottery, carvings and paintings.

In North America and Western Europe around Halloween, Elvis costumes are becoming popular alongside the traditional spooks, ghouls and zombies. Thus the dead Elvis lives again at the time of year when since pagan times it has been said that the veil between the world of the living and that of the dead can be breached. The seasonal art of pumpkin carving now has practitioners who can turn a hollowed pumpkin into an Elvis, with his features delineated by the light of a flickering candle.

Folk art that is solely inspired by Elvis is normally produced for a specific purpose. It might be a handcrafted gift into which much time and love has been poured, made to be left as a votive offering at Graceland. It might be a piece designed for an Elvis shrine as a focus of personal meditation. Often such art is childlike and its genuineness trumps its technical deficiencies. All folk art, by definition, is the art of ordinary people who have no pretensions to being artists. It can appear superficial, but it frequently carries deep meaning. It can be cathartic to create, allowing suppressed fears and hopes to come out into the open. Folk art borrows from other forms of expression. It might incorporate mass-produced trinkets or photographs clipped from magazines. It can adopt religious symbolism, and given that Elvis resonates with so many people in a mystical way it is not surprising that much contemporary folk art involves the mythological Elvis.

Two artists from the folk art tradition, both from the state of Georgia, have become particularly well known for their work. The late Howard Finster never met Elvis, but did say that shortly after Elvis died he saw him in ghostly form in his garden. Joni Mabe is the owner of the famous Elvis wart as well as the creator of the *Elvis Prayer Rug*.

One form of Elvis folk art that has been popular is handmade, but at the same time mass-produced. Elvis images painted on black velvet became for a while a much sought-after commodity, available at the flea markets and wayside stalls of unofficial Elvis souvenir vendors. They often came from workshops in Central America where they were hand-painted in bulk. They were particularly targeted by EPE, as their kitsch qualities offended against their declared policy of defending the Elvis brand, and they were also making money. The vendors were successfully harried and 'these paintings are now an endangered species (which may or may not be such a bad thing),'[14] Sean O'Neal wrote in 1996. In 2013 black velvet Elvises were again widely available for a few pounds on eBay.

One of today's most ubiquitous forms of Elvis art is to be found not on black velvet, paper or canvas, but skin. With the rise in popularity of tattoos, Elvis has become a common subject. The truly Elvis-obsessed have had large-scale Elvis works permanently inked onto their bodies. One woman has a portrait covering her entire upper back. Other fans are more modest and have a small-scale TCB lightning bolt on the upper arm or a heart with Elvis written across it. The front cover of John Strausbaugh's *Reflections on the Birth of an Elvis Faith* shows a man's bare arm on which a tattoo of Elvis wearing a crown of thorns is displayed with the words 'He died for our sins'. Even more outrageous, from a Christian perspective, is the elaborate Elvis picture etched onto an arm showing Elvis crucified in Christ-like pose.

Mixing Elvis and religious iconography has become a familiar practice both in tattoo form and in digital art. The earliest example is possibly the image, mentioned earlier, of Elvis displaying the Sacred Heart found on the First Church of Jesus Christ, Elvis website. This is clearly a joke site, but over the years the joke has evolved and gradually lost the sense of the absurd. Today there is Elvis religious art being produced where the spoof element is almost entirely lacking. In some instances it has become a grim, black art form. In one example, attributed to the tattoo artist Darrin White, a skull wearing a crown of thorns is made to resemble Presley. In other instances, however, Elvis is shown dressed in biblical clothes with a halo encircling his head. As he blesses the viewer, no sense of irony is present at all.

The Seattle-based artist Crystal Barbre has taken the Christian tradition of the pietà – a painting of the dead Jesus being held by his mother, Mary – and given it an Elvis makeover. Her version shows a realistic depiction of Gladys cradling the limp corpse of her son. It is painted on black velvet.

Many general references to Elvis in popular culture have little to do with the real man or anything that he did, but are examples of how the mythical Elvis has become embedded in

The Pietà is the traditional depiction of the dead Jesus being held by his mother. Here the American artist Crystal Barbre substitutes Elvis for Jesus and Gladys, his mother, for Mary.

modern language and thought. A well-known example is Kirsty MacColl's hit song, 'There's a Guy Works Down the Chip Shop Swears He's Elvis'.

The dead Elvis is found not only in lyrics, but whole works of fiction. There is John Burnside's *Burning Elvis*, William Buckley's *Elvis in the Morning* and my own *King Clone*. In Daniel Klein's *Blue Suede Clues* Elvis becomes a detective. Only those with strong stomachs should read Gary Panter's *Invasion of the Elvis Zombies*, a graphic novel in which Elvis is eaten by his adoring fans. And of Elvis poetry, of which much has been written, Paul Simpson in *The Rough Guide to Elvis* says some is 'truly awful', although the poets Joyce Carol Oates and Fleda Brown Jackson are credited as the exceptions. The latter's book *The Women Who Loved Elvis All Their Lives* shows a photograph on the cover of a tree on which the words 'Trust Jesus and Elvis' are written. Mary Hancock Hinds, an Elvis bibliographer, observes that while professional poets use Elvis as a device, untrained poets, 'most of whom are fans, write the most remarkable and charming of the Elvis poems' that 'open the door a bit wider to reveal the mystery of our enduring fascination with Elvis'.[15]

Since Elvis himself was an avid reader of comic books, especially the stories of Captain Marvel, it is fitting that Elvis himself has featured widely in comic art. Contemporary adult comics take serious liberties with their subjects, and those with an Elvis theme wrestle with the meaning of Elvis's life and death. Rich Koslowski's 2005 graphic novel *The King!* is about an Elvis impersonator acting as a god with his own religion and church. In *The Elvis Presley Experience*, writers Herb Shapiro and Patrick McCray place Elvis in the afterlife. From floating in eternity he materializes in his heaven-issued therapist's office to work out residual issues by recounting his life.

'Koslowski's King is overweight and white-jumpsuited,' wrote reviewer Carol Borden in 2007.

He's late-stage Vegas Elvis, the most difficult one to embrace. While the story follows each character along the path of traditional American religion – glory, temptation, the fall, and redemption, reading *The King!*, I wonder if the most parodic, overblown and downright unflattering representations are the most sympathetic, even the most respectful and honest. I wonder if somehow it leads to redemption. I'm just not sure if Elvis is redeemed or we are. Still I'm awful fond of Dead Elvis.[16]

Did Elvis Really Die?

What would Elvis make of all this if he were still alive? Well, perhaps he is – some fans are convinced Elvis never died. The rumours started early. In August 1977, as grieving fans arrived at Graceland to pay tribute to Elvis Presley, they heard the whispers, 'The King is not dead.' Almost forty years later, the rumour mill continues to churn. There is a core group of fans who steadfastly maintain that Elvis faked his own death and went into hiding. It is one of the great conspiracy theories of the age that along with the faked moon landing, the secret 9/11 conspiracy, the second gunman involved in the President Kennedy assassination, Princess Diana's murder and the UFO secrets of Roswell, Elvis left the building alive and is not dead.

The body in the casket did not look right, say some, including Elvis's own cousin Gene Smith. 'I just didn't believe it was him,' he said in a television interview. A handwriting expert is said to have studied the writing on Elvis's death certificate and con-cluded it was in the King's own hand, although why Elvis, if he was faking his own death, would have written out his own death certificate is not explained. Perhaps it was one of the clues that Elvis supposedly left behind to reassure his fans that he had not really died. Another clue, it is said, was the deliberate misspelling of his name on his grave. 'ELVIS AARON PRESLEY' is the inscrip-tion in the Meditation Garden, yet in his lifetime, for instance on his army papers and marriage certificate, Elvis always wrote his middle name 'ARON' – although it should be pointed out that on his birth certificate, on show at London's O2 in 2014–15, two As were used. One persistent rumour claims that hours after Elvis's death, a man bought a one-way ticket to Buenos Aires, paying in cash and booking in under the name Jon Burrows, an alias Elvis often used when wishing to travel incognito.

By extraordinary or spooky coincidence, shortly after Elvis's reported death, two American writers, unknown to each other, started work on fictional books with very similar themes. However, when the books were published both Monte Nicholson and Gail Brewer-Giorgio reported that their publishers lost interest and all copies at bookshops were mysteriously bought in bulk and never replenished. Gail's novel told the story of a fictional singer called Orion who faked his death. Such was the reaction to her book that Gail began to wonder if something similar might have happened to Elvis. She started her own investigation and in a second book published a list of alleged oddities and inconsistencies linked to Presley's reported demise.[1]

She elaborated on her theory in a third book,[2] hyping what she had uncovered as 'the shocking evidence'. Why, she asked, was Elvis's life insurance policy never cashed? Why did Vernon, his father, refuse to drape his son's coffin with the American flag? Several of her supposed key points of evidence have since been refuted. The photograph of Elvis watching fans from behind a screen door at Graceland, allegedly after his death, has been explained to be a picture of a Graceland employee. The photographer told the television interviewer Larry King that he never claimed it was Elvis, only that he initially thought the face looked like him.

In the case of another alleged post-1977 photograph of Elvis, the one showing him with Muhammad Ali and Jesse Jackson in 1984, a member of Ali's entourage, Larry Kolb, has come forward to say that the picture is of him, not Elvis. Kolb certainly has a superficial Elvis look to his face. Supporters of the Gail Brewer-Giorgio theory are unconvinced. They suggest that the Graceland estate has been working behind the scenes to discredit the evidence and they hint at dirty tricks. They point to the mysterious death of Jimmy Ellis. He was a modestly successful entertainer and Elvis impersonator who, for a while, performed as 'Orion' and appeared at his gigs as a masked Elvis. Rumours spread that recordings released in his name were so Elvis-like that the King himself must have recorded them. Some fans were convinced that Jimmy Ellis was a front for Elvis, and believed the King himself would sometimes take Jimmy's place and hide behind the mask to perform live at Orion concerts. Jimmy Ellis was a real person, but did he also cooperate with Elvis to provide him with a cover for a second singing career? Unfortunately it is no longer possible to ask Jimmy himself. After opting out of show business to run a shop in Selma, Alabama, he was murdered in 1998.

Every tall story and rumour to date has been summarily dismissed by the Elvis estate. 'Nonsense,' 'not worth commenting on,' is the common response. Aware of the legal nightmare that would ensue should the King decide to reappear, Elvis Presley Enterprises does nothing to encourage them. But the rumour that Elvis is still alive refuses to die and in the Internet age has even been given new impetus. A website dedicated to the subject polled its followers and found that 53 per cent of them did not believe Elvis Presley had died in August 1977. More significantly, independent polls have found that 4 per cent of the population is prepared to believe Elvis faked his death. 'Twice as many people think Elvis Presley is alive than believe Ed Miliband is a natural leader,' quipped a British Conservative MP in 2013, taking a dig at the then Labour Party leader, his political opponent.

The possibility that Elvis might still be alive continues to fascinate and frustrate many Elvis fans. The subject is probably the most discussed 'special interest' topic on the numerous Elvis message boards, with several boards devoted exclusively to the subject. The messages posted number in the hundreds with a similar number of threads, while an Elvis-is-alive 'underground' network has produced several regular newsletters on the subject. There are also competing groups within the is-Elvis-alive? subculture, with one referring to its members as 'Gatheringites'. The name may be a quasi-religious reference to the gathering of the chosen before the Second Coming. An indication of the widespread interest in the subject can be gauged from sales of Gail Brewer-Giorgio's books, which reached the bestseller list in the USA, making her one of the biggest-selling Elvis authors of all time. Public fascination with her theories does not however suggest that the majority of Elvis fans believe that Elvis faked his death.

Nevertheless, so persistent were the rumours that fifteen years after Elvis's reported death, the Presley Commission was formed to undertake an examination into the evidence. It had no official status and after three years of work published a report in 1995. The members of the commission were not entirely impartial investigators and Phil Aitcheson, the commission's director, was a friend of both Gail Brewer-Giorgio and Bill Beeny, the owner of the Elvis is Alive museum. The commission files and 2,915 pages of FBI documents on Elvis Presley were handed over to the museum in Wright City, Missouri, in 2005.

The commission did not produce Elvis, but suggested enough doubt in official accounts to keep the conspiracy theory alive. On the suggestion that Elvis's coffin contained a wax effigy, Phil Aitcheson said intriguingly that the commission was aware of an incident involving a wax figure that was purchased by a prominent member of the family.

An interview was conducted with an eyewitness who was on the premises when this sale took place. What the figure was intended for is unknown, but comments were made at the time of the sale that raised eyebrows. The contention is that the weight of the coffin was caused by the presence of the wax figure and potential cooling equipment, which would cause it to be heavier than an autopsied human cadaver in the same type of casket.[3]

However, it is likely that even if irrefutable evidence were to emerge that Elvis died, there would be some who would dismiss it. A story is told of one Elvis impersonator, Joseph Thomas, who on visiting Graceland found that people began following him around. 'The more I told them I wasn't Elvis,' he said, 'the more they believed I was. They would say, "we know you had to do what you did." I had women stalking me and grown men crying saying, "Elvis, please come back."'[4]

From time to time new and seemingly plausible rumours, erupt on social media. In January 2015 one such was set off by an unsourced story that an eighty-year-old, white-bearded homeless man was found dead under an overpass in San Diego, California. The man was known by his few friends as Jesse Doe. In an effort to identify him a trawl was made by the authorities of the nationwide DNA database and Jesse's DNA was found to be an exact match of Elvis Presley. The story was a hoax, but for a while it was widely believed.

Attempts to have the samples legally verified by an American court have failed twice on legal technicalities, but one lawyer, who took a close interest in the case, said initially that the evidence 'is strong and compelling'.[5] In 2008 Dr Donald Yates of the Arizona-based laboratory DNA Consultants was so convinced by the samples he was given to test that he told a Memphis probate judge that the DNA taken from the person named Jesse was that of Elvis Presley. 'It is from a live person because the DNA is recent,' he said. 'There are a lot of Elvis impersonators, but I don't think you can imitate DNA. It's hard to get your mind around this story.'[6] A set of tests conducted by the Paleo-DNA Laboratory at Lakehead University in Ontario, Canada, also came to the same conclusion. However, shortly after announcing the results the laboratory issued a correction. 'We did some initial tests for Eliza and our calculations did show a relationship, but when an error was discovered in our calculations, another report with corrected values was generated and the results did not show a relationship.' Forensic analyst Stephen Fratpietro explained: 'The correction report was issued about two weeks after the last set of incorrect results was issued. The error was discovered in a routine review of protocols, specifically a database of American DNA frequencies.'[7]

The DNA evidence has been at the centre of a case being brought by Eliza Presley to prove that her father was Vernon Presley, Elvis's father, and that therefore she is Elvis's half-sister. She is the first person to have made any legal headway with a claim relating to Elvis and his family estates. So far her case has foundered on rulings concerning jurisdiction, and not on the evidence.

In addition to the DNA evidence, a forensic graphologist hired by the Missouri attorney general backs the Jesse story. She went on record saying that his writing matched known examples of Elvis's hand. Jesse is the same man who, twelve years ago, was reportedly treated by a Kansas City psychiatrist, Dr Donald Hinton. He too was sure his patient was the legendary King of Rock 'n' Roll living under an assumed name. To date, the truth behind the rumours has never been tested in a court of law. The reason, say the conspiracy theorists, is that the Elvis estate does not want too many awkward questions asked. Eliza Presley, whose case has got closer than any other to a full hearing, believes that the Presley estate hired lawyers to thwart her attempts to prove she is Vernon's daughter, fearing the challenge to Vernon's will could force the real Elvis to emerge from hiding. Should the DNA and other evidence Eliza claims to possess ever have its day in court, four key players would be involved: Eliza Presley, who believes she is Elvis's half-sister; the Kansas City psychiatrist Dr Donald Hinton, the mystery man called Jesse; and an Elvis fan called Linda Hood Sigmon, who says she not only knows the true identity of Jesse, but is in regular contact with him.

Initially Eliza Presley had no interest in proving Elvis was still alive. She had been adopted at birth and was curious to find out who her biological father might be. Her enquiries led her to believe she had connections with the Presley family in Memphis and that she might be an illegitimate daughter of Vernon, which is when she changed her name to Presley. Yet in building up her legal case she says she has uncovered evidence linking her to a claim made twelve years ago by Hinton. He said he was treating a man called Jesse, who was in reality Elvis Presley. He provided a photograph of Jesse, white-haired and arthritic, holding a child. The child, it was claimed, was his grandson, Benjamin, and the photograph, taken in 1997, shows a child with a close resemblance to Lisa Marie Presley's son. Furthermore, the doctor said, Elvis would reveal himself to his fans in 2002.

Following his astonishing revelations, Hinton found himself under tough public scrutiny. He was investigated by his professional body and for a while had his licence to prescribe certain medication removed. It was a difficult time, the doctor later admitted, but he never withdrew his story. He did however lose touch with his patient and had put the whole episode behind him when he was reluctantly drawn into Eliza Presley's case as a potential witness.

In October 2008 a Memphis judge ruled that she could proceed with a claim for a share in Vernon Presley's estate. Eliza Presley's attorney had assured the judge that the DNA evidence was reliable. Eliza says she got hold of a DNA sample from Hinton's patient by lifting it from saliva traces on an envelope. Evidence obtained in this way would not be permissible as court evidence and, as recounted above, doubt has been cast on claims of a match. Eliza Presley's birth mother, however, denied that Vernon was her daughter's father. She admitted that she had known Elvis and used to go to Graceland, but said she had only met Vernon once.

Eliza's journey through the legal process has been monitored by the lawyer Andrew Mayoras, who blogs as The Probate Lawyer. 'Her lawsuit is indeed proceeding; although slower than they'd like it to for a number of reasons. Getting the Estate of Vernon Presley reopened was the first step. That alone was a big accomplishment, because no Presley Estate had ever been reopened, despite the number of people claiming to be related to Elvis. And it now appears that the court case will be coming to a head in the near future.' This Eliza has not confirmed. Although not representing her, Mayoras made contact with Eliza and spoke to her. He later blogged, 'I've found Eliza to be very open and honest with me.' He read the DNA reports and says they were 'nothing short of fascinating'. Yet, he cautioned, 'the public will need to see something more direct and concrete to prove a conspiracy this strong. Relying on blind samples provided by cousins, outside of the court process, is not enough to change the history books.'[8] To settle the matter he said it would require Elvis's only acknowledged daughter, Lisa Marie, to provide a DNA sample. Lisa Marie refused a request for a saliva sample from Fox TV.

'The attorney for Elvis Presley Enterprises said in the past that Lisa Marie won't,' says Andrew Mayoras, 'because once she does it for one person, then she'll have to do it for everyone claiming to be related to Elvis.'[9] Eliza has explored legal ways to compel her to take a single test that could be used in her case and by any subsequent claimant. Lisa Marie now lives in the UK and if she remains on that side of the Atlantic no American civil court can force her to comply. The only other way to test Eliza's claim, says Mayoras, is to exhume Elvis's body.

Eliza Presley claims that in addition to her DNA link with Jesse, she is also linked with members of the Presley family from whom DNA samples have been obtained. In court, however, Eliza's legal team would have to explain how the Paleo-DNA Laboratory's positive findings were subsequently overturned. Asked recently to explain the change of heart, Stephen Fratpietro said, 'our lab doesn't do these kinds of relationship tests very often but for this case we used a rarely-used American DNA database we had on file. The interpretation or way the numbers were presented in this database was in question as they did not follow the way numbers were presented in our other database.'[10] He could not say how often or seldom such errors occurred. Inevitably rumours have circulated that the laboratory was pressured by the Presley estate, but there is no evidence to support this.

Jesse is no longer a patient of Hinton, who still maintains the man he saw was Elvis, though he regrets having spoken so publicly about his contact. Elvis, or Jesse, however retained ongoing contact with a woman called Linda Hood Sigmon, who claims she has known him since 1992. Elvis is alive somewhere in the USA with enough money for his immediate needs, she says, but lives a life devoid of any purpose. In contacts between them he admits to being bored and having problems with depression.

Linda says she has received handwritten letters from Jesse and the writing in those letters and other specimens of writing obtained from Hinton have, it is claimed, been examined by graphologists and compared with letters known to have been written by Elvis in his lifetime. While a professional forensic graphologist engaged by Fox TV to examine Jesse's handwriting, Mary Kelly, could not confirm an indisputable link, a second professional graphologist, Shirley Mae Mason, did go on record saying the writing she studied matched. Her sample came from a letter supposedly written by Jesse in support of Hinton addressed to the Missouri attorney general. 'Sir, I don't know if you believe in my continued existence or not, but if I continue to expose myself like I did in the book, I will be eliminated very easily. Pure and simple as that.'

Handwriting analysis, while used as additional evidence, cannot of itself prove a case. DNA tests however can be viewed as incontrovertible evidence, assuming procedures used to take and store the samples are themselves tamper-proof. If DNA samples are to be used to prove Eliza's paternity, Jesse would have to make himself available to the court, as would Lisa Marie. Will this ever happen? It is unlikely, since too many financial interests are at stake on both sides of the argument. Eliza Presley wants the emotional satisfaction of knowing who her father is, but she also might, as Vernon's daughter, be entitled to a share in his estate. Lisa Marie and the Graceland business are well aware of the legal chaos that would ensue should a court in any way doubt the 'fact' of Elvis's death.

Hinton has explained Elvis's non-appearance in 2002 in terms of financial interests. Simply put, a dead Elvis is worth more than a living Elvis. If a living Elvis emerged from the shadows to confess that he faked his death, might fans be so shocked and angry that sales of Elvis music and souvenirs dry up?

If Elvis had faked his own death, the question to ask is: why? There are several conflicting answers to that question, depending on which group of conspiracy theorists one believes. Some say Elvis simply tired of being Elvis. He wished to return to a simple life, uncluttered by fame, unpursued by fans and without the relentless demands of touring and performing. He wanted to rediscover a life of peace and anonymity. Another theory is that his life was in danger. Following his meeting with President Nixon, it is said, he had become involved in the fight against illegal drugs. Various criminal elements wanted him silenced. By July 1977 the FBI felt it had enough evidence to arrest and convict a worldwide Mafia ring. Arrest warrants were issued on 16 August 1977. Not surprisingly, that was the day Elvis 'died'. Elvis had to be taken out of public, private and Mafia sight to protect him. He is now, goes the theory, a special undercover agent travelling around the globe, which explains why there are many Elvis sightings around the world.

It all sounds very implausible, especially since to have pulled off such a successful and elaborate hoax would have taken organization and money. It would have required a number of key people to be in the know and to remain completely quiet. Secrecy would have been paramount. Could they all have kept the secret for the next 35 years? To have kept it for so long would appear to have been an impossible task, especially as Elvis was 'sighted' so often. His father, Vernon, would have had to know, and eventually Lisa Marie would need to be told the truth.

Elvis's manager, the notorious Colonel Parker, hatched the plot, according to one theory. Ever one for a quick buck, he calculated, correctly, that Elvis was worth more dead than alive. Whatever the reason, it was the Colonel, supposedly, who arranged for a wax effigy to be placed in Elvis's open casket, for a substitute body to be buried in the grave and for all the legal paperwork to be fraudulently completed – or so the Elvis-is-alive lobby believes.

Yet the Colonel's plans must have been executed with a degree of carelessness, for Elvis has supposedly been spotted around North America on many occasions over the years, at gas stations, supermarkets and shopping malls. He was even seen in the crowd at President Barack Obama's inauguration in 2009. Pictures of the mystery man watching the new president were later super-imposed on images of Elvis and facial characteristics were said to be a close match. Kalamazoo in Michigan became a centre of Elvis appearances in the 1980s. In August 1988 a *Detroit News* reporter went to the town looking for him and, she says, had a bizarre encounter with a man she believes was Elvis. He was in an office block, protected by a team of security guards. He never admitted to being Presley and she didn't ask outright, but Kelly Burgess is in no doubt she had a close encounter.

After a spate of Elvis sightings in and around the city of Ottawa, Elvis enthusiasts Earl McRae, Moe Atallah and Ervin Budge estab-lished the Elvis Sighting Society on 1 April 1989, declaring, with their tongues somewhat in their cheeks, that they knew 'that contrary to popular opinion (and petty details like police and coroners' reports) the King was very much alive'.

The conspiracy theories that surround Elvis's death range from the improbable to the absurd. No examination of conspiracy theories would be complete without reference to the Illuminati, that shadowy and sinister organization that is said to control and manipulate all the world's major events, governments and corporations. 'Elvis Presley was . . . programmed by the Illuminati', states one believer and online conspiracy theorist.

> We know that at times he went by code names, one which is publicly known was John Burrows. His group, called the Memphis Mafia, has talked about his ability to go into altered states of consciousness, even to seem dead . . . Elvis' twin brother was dead at his birth, and Elvis knew that this gave him double spiritual power (according to Illuminati beliefs) . . . The Illuminati will often kill a twin, so that the other will get the power of two souls. From what we understand, Elvis Presley's handler/programmer was Col. Tom Parker . . . Elvis is publicly known to have studied yoga, numerology, drugs, and received some new age spiritual training in an academy overlooking Pasadena, CA.[11]

It all makes the idea that Elvis is in hiding and will one day return to surprise his fans appear a little less wacky. But seriously, is Elvis ever going to stage the comeback to trump all comebacks? There have been many false dawns, but should he do so it would be as an octogenarian. A white-haired old gent would shuffle on stage to the sound of Strauss's fanfare. Perhaps it is best that Elvis, alive or dead, rests in peace and the fans wait for the launch of the lifelike performing 'hologram' which is currently being constructed. Or, if one remains in the realm of fantasy, for the Elvis clone to be born.

For cloning to be a possibility medical science has several advances to make, but the raw material, the Elvis DNA, probably exists. One devoted collector of Elvis memorabilia has a collection of Elvis's hair. There is also a small item of human tissue kept in a test tube half filled with formaldehyde, which is said to be the wart removed from Elvis's wrist in around 1957. Hair given for research by Elvis's barber was examined in 2014 and the DNA was sufficiently intact for scientists to postulate new theories about Elvis's medical condition at the time of his death. It was not only his lifestyle that contributed to his early death, the research showed, but a genetically rooted medical predisposition to heart failure.

That Elvis will be cloned is an improbability, certainly in the near future. This has not stopped a spoof organization called ACE, Americans for Cloning Elvis, from starting a petition to get the King replicated. In 2002 a report in Memphis's daily newspaper *Commercial Appeal* quoted Dr Dan Goldowitz, a biotechnology expert at the University of Tennessee, as confirming that Presley's hair trimmings could provide the source of DNA needed for any cloning attempt, but he warned that the procedure would be risky.

> We can do it. The only problem is, there's a tendency for genetic abnormality to occur. We'd get an Elvis, but maybe he would just want to deliver the mail. My biggest worry is he comes out with two heads. Who knows? Or maybe he has only three fingers on his guitar-picking hand. We can't fix that. Or his hips don't swivel, or he doesn't look as good.[12]

If cloning is all in the world of the imagination for now, what of the several other claims that have been made that Elvis's genetic code continues through his children – and not just Lisa Marie?

There is John Smith, a sometime country singer and songwriter from Arizona. 'I've known that Elvis is my daddy since I was 27 years old,' he says. He claims he has DNA evidence to prove his paternity, but requests for copies of this evidence have not been answered. John Smith did finally provide a copy of a birth certificate for the *Phoenix New Times* that showed his birth name to be John Dennis Roach and his birth parents Elvis A. Presley and Zona Marie Roach. 'The document, which could easily have been doctored in a graphic design program, shows Smith's birth date in July 1961, but it was issued in 1985. The Texas Department of Health didn't return phone calls regarding the veracity of the document.'¹³

It is not improbable that Elvis made one of his groupies pregnant, if reports of his early wild lifestyle are to be believed, though that he could have made one of his film co-stars pregnant without the world becoming aware of it is less likely. However, Philip Stanic, a former circus performer from Gary, Indiana, is so convinced that he is the son of Elvis that he changed his name to Elvis Presley Jr. He became an Elvis tribute artist and in 1990 opened an Elvis museum. His mother, he claims, was Angelique Delores Pettyjohn, a young actress who was an extra in the film *Blue Hawaii*. Colonel Parker, says Presley Jr, feared that a marriage to Angelique

as well as his impending fatherhood, would seriously damage the King's reputation thereby destroying his wealth and fame. Great pressure was exerted upon the actress to have an abortion. She did agree to deliver the baby in secret and to allow the child to be adopted immediately following the birth. Colonel Parker, it is said, found a suitable couple to bring up the child.

He found them in a young Yugoslavian couple known as 'The Vargas', performers who were travelling with the Ringling Brothers Circus throughout North America. The young couple very much wanted a child of their own and, at the time, were unable to conceive. Arrangements were made, and immediately following the birth, when Pettyjohn gave up her son, her words to the couple were, 'Take special care of this boy; he belongs to Elvis.' The conditions of the adoption were simple and the young couple adhered to them: first, they were not to reveal, under any circumstances, the child's biological parents until the infant reached his 21st birthday; second, they were not to seek any monetary compensation from the Presley family on behalf of the child.[14]

Elvis Presley Jr might have a half-sister, now known as Desiree Presley. She was not the accidental product of a one-night stand with a groupie. Her mother, Lucy de Barbin, claims she had a 24-year on–off affair with the King of Rock 'n' Roll, and wrote a book about it.[15] She says that Elvis never knew of his love child, and it was only after the singer's death that Lucy mentioned her belief that Elvis was the father of Desiree, her daughter. George Klein and other members of Elvis's inner circle have been dismissive of the claims she makes in her book of her closeness to Elvis, as his confidante and lover. No DNA evidence has been presented to back up the paternity claim, although it has been pointed out that Desiree does have a look of Elvis about her.

Desiree may have a half-sister called Deborah. Deborah Presley claims she is Elvis's firstborn. Her story is that her mother, Barbara Jean Lewis, first met Elvis Presley in 1954, when she was fifteen. They did not have a long affair, but it was long enough for Deborah to be conceived. Shortly afterwards Barbara Jean married and her husband was named as the father on Deborah's birth certificate. It was not until Deborah was 21 and her mother was in the hospital that Deborah asked the question she had been longing to ask. Pointing to a magazine photograph of Elvis, she said, 'Is that my daddy?' Her mother burst into tears, and Deborah's suspicions were confirmed.

Other possible Elvis children include Timothy James Farrell, supposedly the result of a one-night stand in 1954 with nineteen-year-old Rebecca Holland. They met at the Eagle's Nest in Memphis, where Elvis Presley was performing, and spent the night together at the Flamingo Motel on Lamar Avenue. Three months later, Rebecca found out she was pregnant. On 2 April 1955 Timothy James Farrell was born. Rebecca Holland confessed to the story shortly after Elvis Presley's death and repeated it shortly before she died of colon cancer in 2002. Farrell, who works as a truck mechanic in Jackson, Tennessee, is said to look more like Vernon than Elvis, but sounds more like Elvis when he sings.

One of the strangest claims is that of a Swedish woman, Lisa Johansen. She goes further than saying she is one of several illegitimate offspring, claiming to be the legitimate heir to the estate – the real Lisa Marie. Her $130 million lawsuit alleges that when her father died she was exiled to Sweden for her safety. It was feared she might be kidnapped. Lisa Marie Presley, according to Johansen, is an impostor. When she began legal action to investigate possible identity theft and showed up at Graceland she got a stiff letter from the Elvis estate lawyers telling her that her 'malicious false claims and offensive wrongful conduct' would no longer be tolerated and that it could lead to action if the she did not restrain herself.

'So Johansen reacted by filing her own lawsuit . . . in Tennessee federal court against the Presley estate.' She said that the family had been attempting to intimidate her and had been spreading lies about her. 'She says that she went to Graceland by invitation and that the defendants are attempting to harass her away from her claims.'[16] Johansen has a long history of 'outlandish, bizarre and fraudulent conduct', says Graceland's attorney. He wrote of her 'strange obsession with my client's family and her outlandish claims to be the "real" Lisa Marie Presley'. During a 1992 visit to Graceland, it was claimed, Johansen had impersonated Lisa Marie Presley, entered a private room and removed items from the property, fleeing when a security alarm went off.

Others who believe that Elvis fathered them include Joshua Lee Presley and Ernest John Young, also known as Jason Presley, and the twins Jenny and Judy Carroll. 'Our mother has never said yes, but she has never said no either,' they say. But so sure are they that Elvis is their dad that they have said, 'should we have a son we'll call him Elvis'.[17]

Is it all imagination? The fact that no definitive scientific evidence has ever been tested in a court of law suggests it is. However, Elvis was neither faithful to Priscilla when married to her, nor chaste when single. That there might have been little Elvises produced is not impossible. Some of the supposed off-spring do certainly resemble the King. Photographs show Jason Presley in particular to have the Elvis look. But what does that prove? Might it be possible that some of the claimants first noticed a chance resemblance and then started imagining what might have been? Deborah Presley, for instance, never considered Elvis might actually be her father until someone mentioned that she greatly resembled him. What can be said with certainty is that Elvis had one undisputed legitimate heir, Lisa Marie, who is now a very wealthy woman.

The Risen Elvis

Following the death and resurrection of Elvis, some fans are expecting his return in glory. According to one legend, he told his inner circle, 'I'll return in spirit. I have special powers and if there is a way I'll find it.'

Elvis, according to Larry Geller, believed in the White Brotherhood of spiritual masters, including Jesus. He felt connected to them. 'In Elvis's mind, his life was being directed divinely by the brotherhood of masters and illuminated beings, enlightened entities that have existed since time immemorial. And he truly felt that he was chosen to be here now as a modern-day saviour, a Christ.'[1] This idea, absurd as it will sound, did not die with him. It is believed in all sincerity by a section of today's Elvis devotees that Elvis has returned in spirit. He reveals himself in supposedly miraculous photographs and is prone to returning in cloud formations. An Elvis cloud was seen over Graceland shortly after his death, according to one legend. Even as recently as 2011 Elvis was taking advantage of favourable meteorological conditions to reveal himself in a cloud over Spain. The posthumous sightings of Elvis come in several forms: ghosts, dreams, cloud shapes and so on. But he is also said to make himself known in other ways. One category of such revelations comes in the form of poltergeist-type tales. In one reported instance an Elvis record mysteriously melted on 16 August 1977. Another case involved an Elvis picture, a black velvet painting, falling off the wall in a fan's home. There have been reports of Elvis statuettes leaping off shelves and breaking. Two British fans, who had experienced several such strange happenings, were left baffled when an Elvis clock they owned fell over and shattered. Why had this happened? they wondered. Nothing of significance had happened to anyone in Elvis's family at that moment. Priscilla and Lisa Marie were well. Much later they were reassured when they discovered the clock incident had coincided with the death of one of Elvis's favourite horses. They knew it had to mean something!

Elvis was a product of the age of celebrity culture in which mortals are raised to a semi-divine status in that they are worshipped and glorified by millions. When celebrity status collides with natural human religious instincts and the human quest for ultimate answers, in particular when a celebrity dies young, strange things happen in society. The things that have happened in the case of Elvis have been the strangest of all.

Celebrity is a Faustian pact. To be rich and famous, recognized and idolized, has its downside. It is to forgo a private life, to be open to scrutiny and criticism from anyone who cares to have an opinion, to present one's image, work and lifestyle as a public commodity for anyone to embellish or reshape as they please. It is to invite irrational hatred as well as unquestioning adoration.

Elvis became public property in his lifetime, but since his death popular ownership of him has grown to such an extreme extent that even the intimate details of his death in the bathroom at his own home have been the subject of comment, debate and prurient fascination. If during his life Elvis felt overwhelmed by his celebrity status, since his death Elvis and his family have completely lost control. Legal rights to market and license certain aspects of his legacy are traded as a commodity, and in reality Elvis now belongs to anyone who wants to claim their piece.

Elvis has become the yardstick against which all celebrity ambition can be measured. When aspiring wannabe pop stars declare a wish to be famous, they know that Elvis is the ultimate in fame. They realize in their hearts that they will never reach such heights, that just a taste of that fame will suffice. Stardom today is a spectrum stretching from C-list to Elvis. There are many celebrities whose fame spreads no further than their home state or country; Elvis, however, is a name recognized around the world. Elvis is likened to Jesus, who is revered by Christians as the Son of God. Elvis himself now is the focus of a religious fascination. Elvis is the advertising world's dream endorsement. Elvis is an instantly identifiable icon. The voice of Elvis is uniquely recognizable. Elvis is a universally available friend and companion, even to those who never knew and can never know him in person.

Surely no one can ever dare to aspire to such status again. In that sense Elvis defies celebrity culture. There have been stars since whose achievements have soared to equal those of Elvis, but they haven't lasted. There have been those who have become richer than Elvis, but their investments have been counted in dollars and not units of adoration. Every celebrity since Elvis can be measured against him and found wanting. In their day The Beatles matched Elvis in everything he did within the pop industry. Since his death John Lennon has been greatly mourned and George Harrison grieved over, but neither has in death approached the status of Elvis.

Celebrity is not a new concept. Admittedly, modern means of communication amplify and accelerate fame, but essentially it is the same as hero worship of old – and its converse, vilification. There have always been people whose charisma or notoriety has given them recognition way beyond the circle of family and friends. Once a reputation spreads further than the inner circle and is claimed by society at large, it can take on a life of its own. It can be enhanced and embellished or ruined. There is little the individual at the centre can do. Some celebrities achieve their status by virtue of their talent, some through their looks and some by birth. Members of royal families know that their lives are never fully their own to live and control. The child born to rule is embraced as a member of the extended family of everyone in the kingdom and his or her fortune is everyone's concern. In former times the monarch was believed to rule by divine right and to be God's representative on earth. Celebrities are said to have charisma – they have received their talent and fortune as a gift from God. Elvis was not only said to be highly charismatic, he was also the King, putting him on a higher level than all other celebrities.

Throughout history it has also been true that some celebrities and heroes achieve enhanced posthumous fame. If the hero dies young, the chance of achieving posthumous fame increases. If the death itself is significant or meaningful in some way, that too contributes. Elvis died at the right age, but also, arguably, his death was full of meaning. Admittedly there was nothing heroic about the way he met his end – he was no martyr or crusader – but the sad, inglorious nature of his death resonated with meaning. It put some fans in mind of the death of Jesus. The story of his life as related by many ends with the words, 'and he died in ignominy betrayed by his friends'. Conversely the manner of Elvis's death encapsulates a timeless truth: the inevitable realization that all flesh is doomed. Everyone, however exalted in rank or status, is destined to die. Death is no respecter of status. Everything that comes of the earth returns to the earth – the sentiment encapsulated in the words of the Book of Common Prayer burial service, 'ashes to ashes, dust to dust'. All that remains of a person after death is their reputation. Before Elvis died his reputation was inevitably tied in some sense to the living person. It suffered as he grew fat, ill and tired. The death of Elvis released his reputation from all links with the ailing body. Fans could choose which Elvis to admire and mythologize – the young singer, the Vegas star, whichever way they best recalled him.

Although modern technology shapes the way new fans discover Elvis and the way older fans share their ideas, in many ways the Elvis phenomenon demonstrates how human behaviour has essentially changed very little over the centuries. The dead Elvis story, in its various facets as described through the book, is one of myth creation. Mythical figures have been created from the stories of the lives and deeds of real people since time immemorial. People have a primordial disposition to 'desire, to anticipate, to project, to imagine and to hope', writes the theologian Professor Graham Ward in his book *Unbelievable: Why We Believe and Why We Don't*.[2] Elvis feeds desire, imagination and creates hope in his followers' minds. The creation of the mythical Elvis has followed a classic pattern of myth creation, even down to the timing.

History suggests a typical time lag between events happening and the stories about them becoming established myths. This point can be seen by considering the early Christian years, before the New Testament was written, when the authors of the Gospels were still able to hear about the life of Jesus from eyewitnesses. Yet the stories they were told had by that time become set pieces, honed and perfected after many repetitions. And once the witnesses were dead it was these stories, as heard, preserved and written down by the evangelists, that became the sole source of information about the life, ministry and death of Jesus. Christians believe that the resurrected Christ lives on through the unseen presence of the Holy Spirit, but the sole accounts of his limited time on earth are those written down a generation later.

The world of Elvis is at a similar stage. His recordings and films survive and new fans can experience something of the King for themselves. Yet digital formats, tapes and vinyl discs do not tell the full story of the man. That story is what lives on and is recreated through the evolving mythology of Elvis. When Larry Geller tells how he heard at first hand from Vernon about the blue light above the house where Elvis was born and George Klein describes his friend as 'Jesus-like', the legendary Elvis takes shape. Both key witnesses have told their stories on numerous occasions. Fans repeat these stories. Their children hear or read them. Sometimes new embellishments are added. Thus the myth of Elvis is established and the legend lives on.

At the same time, Elvis traditions have grown up. The annual Elvis Week in August and the birthday celebrations in January are the two main events, but away from Memphis other Elvis celebrations have become fixed in local calendars. In Britain there are annual Elvis festivals in Porthcawl and Great Yarmouth. Elvis tribute artist contests are becoming regular events. Fans that meet in their home towns have established their own local patterns of meeting. When they do meet they have their own rituals and traditions to follow.

At the start of his career Elvis's appeal was that he was a groundbreaker. What he did and how he sang did more than challenge old attitudes: it was open cultural rebellion. He appealed to his own age group, those in their teens and early twenties, because he was new and attracted the disapproval of the adult world. It is difficult to imagine after sixty years of rock 'n' roll just how mind-blowingly different he was. Although today rock 'n' roll is such a familiar part of the musical landscape that it has lost its power to shock, there are still people around who recall the first impact. Richard Eyre was thirteen when he first encountered Elvis. 'I heard "Blue Suede Shoes" and was completely capsized by it. I became an Elvis nerd. We, I had never heard anything like it before. Hearing Elvis hit me with the novelty of finding a new planet.'[3]

The old crooners, who had been the pop stars before Elvis, were purveyors of romance. Elvis exuded raw sex appeal. He also had a singing style that created an intimate relationship with the listener. It was not a schmaltzy, phoney intimacy, of the kind Sinatra and Crosby and their kind had specialized in, but an edgy one-to-one passion. The crooners sang of wholesome love; early Elvis dangled forbidden fruit. He enticed his listeners into fantasy relations that promised danger. He was the unsuitable boyfriend par excellence to an entire generation of young women, and to young men of the same age he was the leader of an alluring gang that oozed opprobrium. But the 1950s moved on and early Elvis grew up, as did his followers. The rebel Elvis became a safer, tamer version of his former self. The mature Elvis broadened his appeal. He became a show-business cash cow, able to generate thousands of dollars for all his hangers-on, the record companies, the Vegas casino owners and, above all, his manager. Inevitably his career slipped. Of the eight singles he released in the USA between January 1967 and May 1968, only two reached the top forty. Something remarkable needed to happen, and it did. Colonel Parker managed to fix a television show for Christmas 1968. The famous comeback concert won an astonishing 42 per cent share of viewers in the USA. Elvis pulled off a difficult double; he kept faith with his original fans and won over their parents too.

When he added spiritual music to his repertoire, he brought the same intimacy to gospel music that he had created in his secular recordings. He did it so well that songs first written in praise of God subtly altered direction. He deflected the worship away from the Almighty towards himself. Not that this was intentional, he maintained. He was simply the humble messenger. Yet when he sang 'how great thou art', or 'his truth goes marching on', what did the fans allow themselves to think?

Elvis died at the age of 42, a young man by the standards of the age. Despite the success of his comeback and his revitalized career, he was by then on a second and steeper decline. He was a troubled mind inside a declining body, trapped in a claustrophobic career. Fans reacted to the shocking news of his death in several different ways. Some went into a state of denial. It was a time of emotional turmoil about which they could do nothing. It all seemed so unreal. Elvis was said to be dead, and yet his music and his image were bombarding their senses through the media more than ever.

Some fans felt guilt. They had little idea that their hero and fantasy lover had been in such a bad way. They were still listening to, and in love with, a man in his prime. Might there have been something they could have done? Had they contributed to his death by placing such unrealistic demands on him? Were they in any way responsible for his sorrowful end? They were troubled by unrealistic feelings of guilt. Yet no fan could have done anything as an individual to save Elvis. The feelings of guilt were groundless, but then all emotions they had ever felt towards Elvis had had the same unrealistic quality.

The death of Elvis hit everyone of his age with a realization of their own mortality. If Elvis could die, they too, in the words of 'An American Trilogy', were 'bound to die'. Fans asked themselves, why had such a glorious talent been cut short? What had been the purpose of his life? A host of unanswerable questions demanded attention. Many younger fans, never before having experienced the death of someone so close to their lives, were facing grief and the journey of grief for the first time.

And then, in death and through death, Elvis became the fans' envoy to the existence beyond. Elvis had gone before them into the unknown. Elvis became both transcendent and accessible. He took on the role of intercessor between this world and the next. The personal link he had with each of his fans in life was never broken. That connection survived death, for it had never been a real, physical one, but one based on an ideal. And an ideal can survive the death of the reality.

And in that sense, Elvis rose again.

For the generations too young to have known Elvis in life, and especially those unborn in 1977, Elvis has never existed except in legendary form and as preserved through recorded music, photographs and on film. And the film, tape and digital Elvis retained all his fresh appeal and perfection. Indeed, modern technology enhanced the sound to give it an exciting contemporary feel. New fans discovered his music and in their own way became excited by it. The intimacy and the charisma, captured by the recordings for all time, have never been lost. But who is this Elvis, the new fans ask? We hear him, we see him, but we know we will never meet him, so who was he? And then the stories are told of the poor boy who became a superstar. They hear how he retained the humility of the boy from the wrong side of the tracks, how he never betrayed his origins. They learn that he was blessed with a unique talent; that he discovered rock 'n' roll and transformed popular music for all time. And some fans discover more. They come to believe that Elvis had a supernatural quality; that he was blessed by heaven; that he had a messianic destiny.

And to celebrate Elvis and to experience the living Elvis, fans are offered several choices. They can go to hear a tribute artist. They can visit the places he knew – Graceland and Tupelo. They can see the things he once owned or wore or bought. Some Elvis fans are solitary; their love of Elvis is their secret inner life. However, huge numbers of fans are gregarious and they meet to share their passion. There is a fellowship of fans similar to that of churchgoers who meet each other within the context of their church, but have little else in common. Those who go to Memphis or attend the seaside Elvis festivals in Britain find an immediate bond with strangers that breaks down many social barriers. Elvis groups and clubs provide a network of friendship and support.

'There's no doubt that the Elvis world, both fans who are dedicated strictly to Elvis, and also tribute artists and their families, have received the greatest amount of joy and some of the greatest friendships and romances that have ever been struck up, as well as acts of kindness, in the name of Elvis Presley,' says Robert 'Butch' Polston. 'If you're involved in the Elvis world, and it gets out that you are suffering difficulties, one would be hard pressed to find more giving people both in raising money through charity events, or just performing for a very ill youngster, than the Elvis tribute artists and Elvis fans in general.'[4]

Some fans want to share their enthusiasm with the wider world, and not just by raising money for charity. Fans in Auckland, New Zealand, asked if they could erect an Elvis memorial in a public park. They raised the money and went through the official channels to seek permission. 'We had to make a commitment to care for the Memorial and the site indefinitely,' Susan Brennan-Hodgson recalled, 'and to promise it would be aesthetically pleasing to blend in with the surrounding area. Some of the councillors were not Elvis fans and strongly opposed the whole idea. Fortunately, the Mayor was very supportive, for without his help I doubt we would have received permission.'[5]

The granite memorial showed a silhouette of Elvis dancing on a stage from *Jailhouse Rock*. There was a giant guitar shape as a backdrop, and a gold record was positioned in the guitar to represent his music. Once it was placed in the ground, it was surrounded by a paved circle and set in the circle in front of the memorial were a gold star, a lightning bolt and the letters TCE (Taking Care of Elvis). 'We were all so proud of our magnificent memorial and the fact that our dream had become a reality,' Susan remembers. The memorial was unveiled on Elvis's birthday in 2000 and received a Maori blessing.

Sadly the story does not end there, for the memorial became the target of local vandals and ten years later it was damaged beyond repair. It was uninsured and although the city council did its best to reinstate it, 'the replacement is not a patch on the beauty or quality of the original'. Was the memorial attacked simply because it was vulnerable and in a public space, or was it significant that it was Elvis? Normally Elvis does not provoke hostility. Indifference and mockery perhaps, but hatred? Is it more likely that the memorial fell victim to an act of random vandalism rather than being specifically targeted for what it, and Elvis, represented?

Yet disturbingly, away from the public gaze, there is a sinister, dark and self-destructive side to the Elvis world, a subculture fascinated more with the death than the life of Elvis. It is a place where macabre Elvis art is produced and the artists push against the boundaries of social taste and taboo by using Elvis. 'There is

Jailhouse Rock (1957). Many fans consider Elvis's numerous Hollywood films his least substantial work, although the soundtracks of several provided records that were hits on first release and have since been remixed for the modern market.

even talk of having Elvis's corpse dug up and the stomach ana-lysed for traces of drugs,' wrote Greil Marcus in his seminal work *Dead Elvis*, published in 1991,

> which led me to fantasize. Can you imagine anything more thrilling than getting to stick your hand and forearm

through the hole in Elvis's rotted guts slopping whatever's left of 'em all over each other . . . as you forage fishing for incriminating pill chips . . . and then once off camera now here's where the real kick to end 'em all comes as you pop those little bits of crumbled pills in your own mouth . . . They're all slimy with little bits of the disintegrating insides of Elvis's pelvis. so you've actually gotten to eat the king of rock 'n' roll which would be the living end in terms of souvenirs, fetishism, psycho fandom, the collectors' mentality or even just hero-worship in general.[6]

Marcus went to the outer edges of fandom in a book in which, over twenty years ago, he identified the dead Elvis as a social metaphor. When Elvis died, Marcus suggested, many people found themselves caught up in the adventure of remaking his history, or rather reinventing their own. Elvis Presley was a socially liberating influence in that through his music he reminded people of their own potential for greatness.

The great and lasting appeal of Elvis is not solely his music, there is Elvis himself. It is his humanity, as rediscovered generation by generation through the stories told about him, that resonates. He was godlike to some of his followers, regarded with wonder, love and awe, but he was also a man with acknowledged flaws and faults. That in essence too is the Christian teaching of the incarnation. God, the all-powerful creator and judge, became a human being, able and willing to feel the pain of the human condition. Although it might appear that Jesus and Elvis are fused together into one being by many fans, that is not the case. It is more that Elvis and Jesus represent the same ideal. Thus through his death Elvis links this world and the next. Fans feel he is still with them, for in many ways he still is, through his recordings and films. Yet he is also in that other place to which everyone is destined to go after death. He is ever alive and in an allegorical sense transcends death. Therein, it might be said, lies his resurrection.

The fans who shed so many tears at the gates of Graceland in August 1977 were mourning the end of Elvis, little realizing they were also witnessing a new beginning.

The things Elvis fans do to remember him certainly look very much like religious practices. Might this be because they serve the same purpose? Through Elvis, his fans are exploring their own potential and purpose. Their lives are given meaning by what they do, through their relationship with Elvis and their loyalty to their Elvis friends.

Traditional religion once provided the framework within which people could find meaning and purpose. Religion also provided answers to the mysteries of life. Why are we here? What is our destiny? Today in a secular age other means must be sought and found. For many people it is Elvis who provides them with the means, the tools, to explore the mystical unknown; to delve into their own souls, to discover a potential and purpose within themselves that might otherwise have gone untapped. The Elvis trappings that go with this process look insubstantial. Many outside the Elvis world see them as lightweight and shallow.

Here, the early history of Elvis provides important clues to what is happening. Forget the Vegas Elvis and the gospel Elvis and return to the start of the story, the young white boy from Dixie, learning music from the descendants of the former slaves. The exploited slaves of the New World, deprived of literature, education and Western culture, discovered their own way of retaining their dignity, of keeping their soul-life active, of realizing their potential as beings created, to use the biblical analogy, in the image of God. And they did this through music. Elvis took this music and gifted it to another group of people, a people who were free and affluent in the most part, but spiritually impoverished. The materialist, consumption-driven Western world discovered in and through Elvis something of that world beyond, of what it means to be human. This is what religion is supposed to do – feed the soul – but in a secular society, the soul is frequently left undernourished.

Members of highbrow society have leisure, education, classical music, liturgy, literature and arguably everything they need to explore the deeper mysteries of the human condition without needing to turn to Elvis. Some of them look down on Elvis, seeing only the kitsch and none of the meaning. Similarly, African American music was dismissed by the sophisticated classes of an earlier age. They scoffed at its superficial simplicity without understanding its depth and they also feared the emotions it aroused because they did not understand where they had come from.

The music of Elvis gives joy to many. The myth of Elvis provides many fans with meaning in their lives. Celebrating Elvis brings fellowship. Discovering Elvis brings purpose to many. The commercially driven merchandising, remixes and relaunching of the Elvis sound brings new fans into the Elvis fold. If following Elvis isn't a religion yet, then it is a very effective religion substitute.

What will the Elvis of the future be like? Thanks to the interest of investors and the resources at their disposal to maximize their income from the Elvis brand, it is likely that Elvis will be continually repackaged and remarketed, drawing on the technical capabilities of the age. Elvis will be recreated digitally in a myriad of forms and will be at the cutting edge of commercial innovation. One day it could well be possible to book a life-size, lifelike virtual Elvis for a birthday party, in the same way that today an Elvis lookalike can be hired. Future morphing techniques might even create an illusion of Elvis capable of conversing with the audience and able to take requests for songs. Nevertheless he will remain insubstantial. He might look and sound real, but no one will be able to touch or physically interact with him. A virtual Elvis will not be able to kiss fans or hand out scarves. But who knows what the distant future holds? Might there be some kind of personal device invented to enclose a fan in a virtual Elvis world? Making a headset with 360-degree vision and quadraphonic sound is currently feasible. Might a whole bodysuit be made with sense points to stimulate a whole range of Elvis encounters? The idea may not be entirely in the realm of science fiction. There is one form of technology currently in early development at the University of Sussex in the UK. Research scientists are experimenting with a gadget they call a haptic device, which they claim can create sensations including that of falling rain, a breeze and even a solid object in the hand. 'The user holds his or her palm over the device which emits ultrasound waves that create the requisite feelings. It even has the potential to induce emotions. The challenge is to tailor it for use without it feeling intrusive or creepy. The European Commission has been sufficiently impressed to invest £1 million in the project.'[7] If such technology could simulate contact with a more tangible Elvis, what type of technical, ethical and moral issues would this raise? If fans are able to feel Elvis caressing or kissing them, where might such foreplay lead?

For the time being, tangible Elvises will continue to be available in the form of tribute artists. They have now created a genre of entertainment that exists in its own right and will remain in demand until the virtual Elvises become widely available and affordable, and may even survive to compete with them. All new technological advances in the field of entertainment are very expensive to research and develop. They involve electronic and computer wizardry of the highest order. Whatever presents itself as possible will need to be designed and manufactured by a major multinational enterprise of the size, and with the expert resources, of Apple or Microsoft. That company will only undertake that work if it can see profits ahead. They will need to know that there will be a market for any new gadget they make. There will be no point in developing an all-encompassing entertainment experience around a small-time entertainer with just a small fan base. It will have to be a major star, and none is bigger than Elvis. It will also need to be a star who is already a legally recognized and protected brand backed by substantial investment. This is why it is reasonable to suppose that should such a project be sanctioned, developed and ultimately marketed, Elvis is highly likely to be in the vanguard, thus creating yet another surge in his popularity.

Elvis transcends fashion. He adapts to every new technology. He will undoubtedly be a major force in Western culture for decades to come, changing, evolving and updating such that fans can declare with confidence:

'The King is Dead, Long Live the King!'

References

Introduction

1 Mary Hancock Hinds, correspondence with author.
2 Minister Anna of the Presleytarian Church of Australia, correspondence with author.

1 'The End is Where We Start From'

Chapter title taken from T. S. Eliot, 'Little Gidding', *Four Quartets* (London, 1942).
1 Albert Goldman, *Elvis* (London, 1982), p. 114.
2 Ibid., p. 115.
3 Jon Michael Spencer, 'A Revolutionary Sexual Persona', in *In Search of Elvis*, ed. Vernon Chadwick (Boulder, CO, 1997), p. 113.
4 Ibid.
5 Ibid.
6 Frank Sinatra quoted in *Los Angeles Mirror News*, 28 October 1957.
7 Louie Ludwig addressing the 3rd International Conference on Elvis Presley, Memphis, Elvis Week 1997.
8 Ibid.
9 Stephen R. Tucker, 'Visions of Elvis', in *Elvis: Images and Fancies*, ed. Jac L. Tharpe (London, 1983).
10 Jerry Hopkins, *Elvis: The Final Years* (New York, 1980), p. 222.
11 Ibid., p. 185.
12 Goldman, *Elvis*, p. 48.
13 'The Day Elvis Presley Died', www.worldoftruckdriver.com, 21 July 2015.
14 Goldman, *Elvis*, p. 578.

15 Statement issued by press office at the White House, 17 August
    1977.
16 Press statement from Sinatra's agent, August 1977.
17 Kiki Apostolakos, interview with author, 15 August 1991.
18 BBC Television News, 18 August 1977.

2 'He Has Sounded Forth the Trumpet that Shall Never Call Retreat'

Chapter title taken from 'The Battle Hymn of the Republic'.
1   Gary Vikan, *From the Holy Land to Graceland* (Washington,
    DC, 2012), p. 13.
2   Patsy Hammontree, 'Audience Amplitude: The Cultural
    Phenomenon of Elvis Presley', in *Elvis: Images and Fancies*,
    ed. Jac L. Tharpe (London, 1983), p. 74.
3   David Troedson, 'Elvis Presley and Racism: The Ultimate, Definitive
    Guide', *Elvis Australia*, 18 December 2014.
4   Vernon Reid, 'Elvis is Dead', from *Living Colour* (1990).
5   Interview with Jack Soden by Mike Levin, in *For Elvis Fans Only*,
    13 September 2004.
6   Paul Simpson, *The Rough Guide to Elvis* (London, 2004), p. 284.
7   Ibid., p. 285.
8   Susan MacDougall, 'Hero with a Thousand Faces', paper presented
    to National Elvis Presley Convention, Canberra, November 2004.
9   Maia Nartoomid, at www.elvislightedcandle.org, 1 August 2015.
10 MacDougall, 'Hero With a Thousand Faces'.
11 Ibid.
12 Nartoomid, at www.elvislightedcandle.org.

3 Down to His Last Million Dollars

1   Salley Rayl, 'Did Colonel Parker Take the King for a Ride?', *People*,
    1 December 1980.
2   Sean O'Neal, *Elvis Inc.* (Rocklin, CA, 1996), p. 48.
3   Ibid.
4   Report filed 31 July 1981 at Shelby County Probate Court.
5   Ibid.
6   Alanna Nash, *The Colonel* (New York, 2003).
7   Report, 31 July 1981.
8   O'Neal, *Elvis Inc.*, p. 72.
9   Ibid., p. 73.
10 Ibid., pp. 109–10.
11 Ibid., p. 112.
12 David Wall, 'Policing Elvis', *Entertainment Law*, II/3 (2003),

pp. 35–69 (p. 40).

13 'Disgraceland', open letter written by Sid Shaw, 2003, reproduced
    at www.elvis-express.com, accessed 23 February 2016.
14 Wall, 'Policing Elvis', p. 39.
15 Ibid.
16 Erika Doss, *Elvis Culture: Fans, Faith and Image* (Lawrence,
    KS, 1999), p. 218.
17 Ibid., p. 219,
18 'The King and I', *Managing Intellectual Property* (1 June 2000).
19 Ibid.
20 S. C. Gywnne, 'Love Me Legal Tender', *Time magazine*, 4 August
    1997.
21 Elvis Express Radio report, 26 May 2009, based on news release
    from Elvis Presley Enterprises.
22 Wall, 'Policing Elvis', p. 57.
23 Ibid., p. 68.
24 Ibid., p. 37.

4 Brand Elvis

1   Statement published by Jack Soden.
2   Erika Doss, *Elvis Culture: Fans, Faith and Image* (Lawrence,
    KS, 1999), p. 227.
3   Ibid., p. 228.
4   Ibid., p. 244.
5   Bill Burk interview, 2005, www.elvisinfonet.com, 14 July 2015.
6   Ibid.
7   'Elvis Presley Enterprises to Air First Promotional Ads on TV',
    Memphis Business Journal, 20 April 2005.
8   Ibid.
9   Susan Brennan-Hodgson, correspondence with the author, 29 July
    2013.
10 Open letter published online by Elvis Information Network,
    www.elvisinfonet.com, accessed 24 February 2016.
11 Statement by Jack Soden published ibid.
12 Avaliable at www.elvisinfonet.com.
13 Quoted at www.bloomberg.com, 1 June 2009.
14 Alan Hanson writing on www.elvis-history-blog.com, 28 February
    2013.
15 This version of the Core Media mission statement, since they sold
    Elvis etc., is no longer online as it has been changed.
16 Hanson, www.elvis-history_blog.com.
17 Ibid.
18 Ibid.
19 'The Sale of Marketing Rights to the Elvis Presley Estate is Shaping

Up as a Real Heartbreak Hotel', *New York Post*, 10 June 2013.
20 Alan Hanson writing on www.elvis-history-blog.com, 28 February 2013.
21 News release at *PRNewswire*, 19 November 2013.
22 Quoted from Graceland (EPE) news release, 23 April 2015.
23 'Return to Sender', *Daily Mail*, 2 July 2014.
24 Ed Ulbrich, interview with the author, 23 January 2013.

5 The Followers, the Faithful and the Fanatics

1 Robert 'Butch' Polston, correspondence with the author, 28 July 2013.
2 Jenny Stanton, 'Elvis has Left the Building', *Daily Mail*, 29 May 2015.
3 Adrian Sainz, 'Elvis Presley Fans Hold Vigil in Graceland', *Commercial Appeal*, 15 August 2013.
4 Patsy Hammontree, 'Audience Amplitude: The Cultural Phenomenon of Elvis Presley', in *Elvis: Images and Fancies*, ed. Jac L. Tharpe (London, 1983).
5 Quoted in 'Elvis: The Legacy', *BBC News*, 16 August 2002, accessed 3 March 2016.
6 Quotes are popularly found in various sources.
7 Correspondence with the author.
8 Correspondence with the author.
9 See www.elvis.co.uk, accessed 14 July 2013.
10 As of 1 September 2013.
11 Kiki Apostolakos, interview with the author, 15 August 1996.
12 Jane Kelly interviewed for *Elvis and the Presleytarians*, BBC One, 17 August 1997.
13 Vanessa Bradwell, interviewed for *Elvis and the Presleytarians*.

6 The Billion-dollar Question

1 Nick Keene, 'For the Billionth and the Last Time', available at www.elvis.com.au, accessed 23 March 2016.
2 Interview with Jack Soden, 'A Family Franchise', *Billboard*, 18 September 2004.
3 Ibid.
4 Robert 'Butch' Polston, interview with the author, 23 January 2013.
5 Mary Hancock Hinds, conversation with the author, 30 August 2013.
6 Junkie XL quoted by Elvis Information Network in 2002, www.elvisinfonet.com, accessed 14 June 2013.
7 Jack Soden quoted in Official Graceland Elvis Week online telecast, available at www.youtube.com, accessed 24 February 2016.

8   Elvis Australia, www.elvis.com.au, accessed 24 February 2014.
9   See the Graceland official blog, 12 September 2014.
10 Chester Dawson, 'Coke to Salarymen: Man Up', *Wall Street Journal*, 16 February 2011.

7 You Too Can Be Elvis

1   See www.thenakedscientists.com, accessed 18 July 2015.
2   Robert 'Butch' Polston, interview with the author, 23 January 2013.
3   Dorian Baxter, correspondence with the author, 22 July 2013.
4   'Threat to Stop Elvis Show puts Rocker in a Hard Place', *Chicago Tribune*, 8 July 1987.
5   Sean O'Neal, *Elvis Inc.* (Rocklin, CA, 1996), p. 147.
6   Ibid., p. 147.
7   Ibid., p. 148.
8   Robert 'Butch' Polston, interview with the author, 23 January 2013.
9   Promotional material published by EPE on www.graceland.com, accessed 25 February 2016.
10 Dorian Baxter, correspondence with the author, 22 July 2013.
11 See www.johnbedford.co.uk, accessed 25 February 2016.
12 See www.deanz.com, accessed 30 July 2013.
13 Robert Langford, interview with the author, 18 July 2013.
14 Polston, interview with the author, 2 July 2013.
15 Ibid.
16 Brad Tuttle, '36 Years After Elvis Presley's Death, Could the King's Popularity be Dying?', *Time*, 13 September 2013.
17 Mary Hancock Hinds, conversation with the author, 30 August 2013.
18 Robert Alaniz, interview with the author, 3 June 2013.
19 Robert Langford, interview with the author, 18 July 2013.
20 'Bald Elvis Tribute Act Gets Death Threats', *Metro*, 6 December 2006.
21 Ibid.
22 *Elvis and the Presleytarians*, BBC One, 17 August 1997.
23 Ibid.
24 American Graphics Systems, *I am Elvis: A Guide to Elvis Impersonators* (New York 1991), p. 13.
25 *Elvis and the Presleytarians*.
26 American Graphics Systems, *I am Elvis*, p. 61.
27 John Strausbaugh, *Reflections on the Birth of an Elvis Faith* (New York, 1995), p. 150.
28 Ibid., pp. 150–51.
29 See www.elvisassociation.com, accessed 12 September 2013.
30 *Elvis and the Presleytarians*.
31 Ibid.

32   Gregory L. Reece, *Elvis Religion: The Cult of the King* (London, 2006), p. 43.
33   'Media Celebrity and Social Influence', *Charisma Magazine*, 31 July 2003.
34   Rev Ravi Holy, interview with the author, 2014.
35   Janet Komblum, 'This Elvis Says He's Doing Work of King of Kings', *USA Today*, 6 January 2003.
36   Dorian Baxter, correspondence with author, 22 July 2013.
37   See www.vivalasvegasweddings.com, accessed 2 October 2013.
38   Dave Carlson's website, www.theimageofelvis.com, accessed 25 February 2016.
39   American Graphics Systems, *I am Elvis*, p. 61.

8 Worship the King

1   Kiki Apostolakos, interview with the author, 15 August 1996.
2   Ron Rosenbaum, 'Among the Believers', *New York Times*, 24 September 1995.
3   *Elvis and the Presleytarians*, BBC One, 17 August 1997.
4   Ibid.
5   'Elvis 'N Jesus', South Side Gallery, Oxford, Mississippi, August 1996.
6   See 'Westboro Baptist Protests Elvis at Graceland', www.wreg.com, 17 May 2013.
7   See www.jesus-is-savior.com, accessed 3 June 2013.
8   Elvis Gospel Ministry mission statement.
9   John Strausbaugh, *Reflections on the Birth of an Elvis Faith* (New York, 1995), p. 213.
10   Gregory L. Reece, *Elvis Religion: The Cult of the King* (London, 2006), p. 176.
11   Ibid., p. 21.
12   Author's off-the-record conversation with a fan at Graceland, 1997.
13   Gary Vikan, *From the Holy Land to Graceland* (Washington, DC, 2012), p. 184.
14   Anna Achia (Minister Anna), correspondence with the author, 13 September 2013.
15   *Larry King Live*, CNN, 29 April 2005.
16   Larry Geller, interview with the author for *Elvis and the Presleytarians*, and elaborated in material that was not broadcast.
17   See www.elvislightedcandle.org, accessed 24 November 2015.

9 St Elvis

1   Chris Rywalt's notes on his work can be found at www.sacredheartofjesusbook.com, accessed 25 February 2016.

2   Isabelle Tanner, *Elvis: A Guide to My Soul* (New York, 1993), p. 3.
3   *Elvis and the Presleytarians*, BBC One, 17 August 1997.
4   *The Church of Elvis*, Vision TV, January 2010.
5   Alan Weiss, quoted in 'Elvis Screen Test 1956',
     www,dangerousminds.net, accessed 25 February 2016.
6   Elvis Australia, 'Interview with Sheila Ryan', 1 January 2008,
     www.elvis.co.au, accessed 25 February 2016.
7   Graceland interview with Dolores Hart, online Elvis television
     show, 14 August 2013.
8   Robert Alaniz, interview with author, 3 June 2013.
9   *Elvis and the Presleytarians*.
10 Cinda Godfrey, *The Elvis–Jesus Mystery* (New Philadelphia,
     OH, 1999).
11 *Elvis and the Presleytarians*.
12 Interview with Joe Esposito, www.elvispresleynews.com, accessed
     25 February 2016.
13 Geller, *If I Can Dream*, p. 139.
14 See www.elvislightedcandle.org, accessed 24 November 2015.
15 Ibid.
16 Ibid.
17 *Elvis and the Presleytarians*.
18 Ibid.
19 Larry Geller, *If I Can Dream* (London, 1990), p. 138.
20 Samuel Roy, *Elvis: Prophet of Power* (Brookline, MA, 1985), pp. 76–7.
21 Erika Doss, *Elvis Culture: Fans, Faith and Image* (Lawrence, KS,
     1999), p. 99.
22 See www.elvispresleybirthplace.com, accessed 1 August 2013.
23 Ibid.
24 Author's off-the-record conversation with a fan at Graceland, 1997.
25 Mary Hancock Hinds, conversation with author, 30 August 2013.
26 Gary Vikan, *From the Holy Land to Graceland* (Washington, DC,
     2012), p. 62.
27 Ibid.
28 See www.hauntedamericatours.com, accessed 2 November 2015.
29 Raymond Moody, *Elvis: After Life* (Atlanta, GA, 1987).

10 Elvis the Messiah

1   Minister Anna, correspondence with the author, 13 September 2013.
2   'Tributes to Elvis', www.elvislightedcandle.org, accessed 25 February
     2016.
3   Louie Ludwig, *The Gospel of Elvis: The Testament and Apocrypha
     of the Greater Themes of 'The King'* (Arlington, TX, 1994).
4   Louie Ludwig, report of speech made at National Elvis Conference
     in Memphis during Elvis Week, 1997.

5   *Elvis and the Presleytarians*, BBC One, 17 August 1997.
6   John Windsor, 'Faith and the State of Graceland Enterprises',
    The Independent, 15 August 1992.
7   Mark Gottdiener, 'Dead Elvis as Other Jesus', in *In Search of Elvis:
    Music, Race, Art, Religion*, ed. Vernon Chadwick (Boulder, CO,
    1997), p. 192.
8   Minister Anna, correspondence with the author, 13 September 2013.
9   Ibid.
10 Ibid.
11 Erika Doss, *Elvis Culture: Fans, Faith and Image* (Lawrence,
    KS, 1999), pp. 219–20.

11 A Piece of Elvis

1   Nathan Raab, 'What's Behind Graceland's First-ever Elvis Week
    Auction', *Forbes News*, 6 August 2014.
2   Ibid.
3   Robert Alaniz, interview with the author, 3 June 2013.
4   Ibid.
5   Ibid.
6   Ibid.
7   Ibid.
8   Ibid.
9   Ibid.
10 Elvis Australia, 'Joan Deary and Elvis Presley', 18 April 2012,
    www.elvis.com.au, accessed 25 February 2016.
11 Thomas Kinkade, www.thomaskinkade, accessed 25 February 2016.
12 Naoki Mitsuse, www.goultralightsgo.com, accessed 25 February
    2016.
13 See www.aboutfacesentertainment.com, accessed 24 November
    2015.
14 Sean O'Neal, *Elvis Inc.* (Rocklin, CA, 1996), p. 137.
15 Mary Hancock Hinds, *Infinite Elvis: An Annotated Bibliography*
    (Chicago, IL, 2011), p. 311.
16 See www.theculturalgutter.com, accessed 12 July 2013. The
    site describes itself as 'dedicated to thoughtful writing about
    disreputable art'.

12 Did Elvis Really Die?

1   Gail Brewer-Giorgio, *Is Elvis Alive? The Most Incredible Elvis
    Presley Story Ever Told* (New York, 1988).
2   Gail Brewer-Giorgio, *The Elvis Files: Was His Death Faked?*
    (New York, 1990).

3   Phil Aitcheson, interview with www.elvisinfonet.com, accessed 24 November 2015.
4   Gregory L. Reece, *Elvis Religion: The Cult of the King* (London, 2006), p. 42.
5   Andrew Mayoras, www. probatelawyerblog.com, accessed 14 June 2013.
6   'DNA Lab Owner: Elvis is Not Dead', *Commercial Appeal*, 11 October 2008.
7   Telephone interview with author.
8   Andrew Mayoras, www.probatelawyerblog.com, accessed 14 June 2013.
9   Ibid.
10 Telephone interview with author.
11 See the conspiracy theory website www.educate-yourself.org, accessed 18 July 2015.
12 'Hair Today – Elvis Tomorrow', *Commercial Appeal*, 12 August 2002.
13 Robert L. Pela, 'Is Scottsdale's John Smith the Secret Love Child of Elvis Presley?', *Phoenix New Times*, 4 April 2013.
14 See elvisaaronpresleyjr.com, accessed 24 November 2015.
15 Lucy de Barbin and Dary Matera, *Are You Lonesome Tonight?* (New York, 1987).
16 Eriq Gardner, 'Elvis Estate Sued for $130 Million by King's "Real Daughter"', *Hollywood Reporter*, 29 November 2011.
17 Richard Harrington, 'Elvis: Empty Revelations', *Washington Post*, 8 January 1985.

13 The Risen Elvis

1   Larry Geller, *If I Can Dream* (London, 1990), p. 140.
2   Graham Ward, *Unbelievable: Why We Believe and Why We Don't* (London, 2014), p. 223.
3   'Inheritance Tracks', BBC Radio 4, 2 November 2013.
4   Correspondence with author, 23 January 2013.
5   Susan Brennan-Hodgson, correspondence with the author, 29 July 2013.
6   Greil Marcus, *Dead Elvis* (New York, 1991), pp. 170–71.
7   'First "Movies", then "Talkies" . . . Now Prepare for "Feelies"', *The Week*, 20 February 2016.

Select Bibliography

Brewer-Giorgio, Gail, *The Elvis Files: Was His Death Faked?*
  (New York, 1990)
Chadwick, Vernon, ed., *In Search of Elvis* (Boulder, CO, 1997)
de Barbin, Lucy, and Dary Matera, *Are You Lonesome Tonight?*
  (London, 1988)
Doss, Erika, *Elvis Culture: Fans, Faith and Image* (Lawrence, KS, 1999)
Geller, Larry, *If I Can Dream* (London, 1990)
Goldman, Albert, *Elvis* (London, 1982)
—, *Elvis: The Last 24 Hours* (New York, 1991)
Guralnick, Peter, *Careless Love: The Unmaking of Elvis Presley*
  (London, 1999)
—, *Last Train to Memphis* (London, 1994)
Hammontree, Patsy Guy, *Elvis Presley: A Bio-bibliography*
  (Westport, CT, 1995)
Hancock Hinds, Mary, *Infinite Elvis: An Annotated Bibliography*
  (Chicago, IL, 2001)
Harrison, Ted, *Elvis People: The Cult of the King* (London, 1992)
—, *King Clone* (Shetland, 2010)
Hopkins, Jerry, *Elvis: The Final Years* (New York, 1980)
Ludwig, Louie, *The Gospel of Elvis: The Testament and Apocrypha
  of the Greater Themes of 'The King'* (Arlington, TX, 1994)
Marcus, Greil, *Dead Elvis* (New York, 1991)
Moody, Raymond, *Elvis: After Life* (Atlanta, GA, 1987)
O'Neal, Sean, *Elvis Inc.* (Rocklin, CA, 1996)
Reece, Gregory L., *Elvis Religion: The Cult of the King* (London, 2006)
Rodman, Gilbert B., *Elvis after Elvis* (London, 1996)
Roy, Samuel, *Elvis: Prophet of Power* (Brookline, MA, 1985)
Simpson, Paul, *The Rough Guide to Elvis* (London, 2004)
Strausbaugh, John, *Reflections on the Birth of an Elvis Faith*
  (New York, 1995)

Tharpe, Jac L., ed., *Elvis: Images and Fancies* (London, 1983)

Vikan, Gary, *From the Holy Land to Graceland* (Washington, DC, 2012)

Acknowledgements

My thanks go to the hundreds of Elvis fans I have met over 25 years who, by sharing their love and enthusiasm for the King, have helped me towards an understanding of the extraordinary Elvis phenomenon. Some I met in passing at Graceland, others I talked to at length in their homes and several of these fans have become good friends.

Photo Acknowledgements

The author and publishers wish to express their thanks to the below sources of illustrative material and/or permission to reproduce it.

© courtesy of Crystal Barbre, reproduced by kind permission of the artist: p. 216; photographs by Ted Harrison: pp. 133, 187, 210; iStock: pp. 6, 14, 53, 65, 75, 86, 96, 98, 160, 203; Cpl. Jin Hyun Lee: p. 122; Library of Congress, Prints and Photographs Division, Washington, DC: pp. 35, 246; Library of Congress, Prints and Photographs division, photographs in the Carol M. Highsmith Archive, Washington, DC: pp. 33, 142, 200; Library of Congress Prints and Photographs Division, World Telegram and Sun, photo by Phil Stanziola, Washington, DC: p. 20.

Sam Howzit, the author of the image on p. 56 is reproduced under a Creative Commons Attribution 2.0 Generic license.

Readers are free:

- to share – to copy, distribute and transmit these images alone
- to remix – to adapt these images alone

Under the following conditions:

attribution – readers must attribute any image in the manner specified by the author or licensor (but not in any way that suggests that these parties endorse them or their use of the work).

Index